Boeing 747

Design and Development Since 1969

Guy Norris and Mark Wagner

Motorbooks International
Publishers & Wholesalers

First published in 1997 by Motorbooks International Publishers & Wholesalers, 729 Prospect Avenue, PO Box 1, Osceola, WI 54020-0001 USA

Library of Congress Cataloging-in-Publication Data

Norris, Guy
    Boeing 747 : design & evolution since 1969 / Guy Norris and Mark Wagner.
        p.   cm. -- (Jetliner history)
    Includes index.
    ISBN 0-7603-0280-4 (pbk. : alk. paper)
    1. Boeing 747 (Jet transports)--History. I. Wagner, Mark, 1964- II. Title. III. Series.
    TL686.B65N666   1997
    629.133'349--dc21
                                            97-25441

On the front cover: As launch customer and the main driving force behind the design evolution of the 747, it was only fitting that Pan Am became the first airline in the world to begin operations with the Jumbo Jet, and therefore the first ever to offer wide-body jet services. One of the airline's original aircraft, N749PA, was delivered in April 1970 as *Clipper Intrepid* but was later renamed, in 1980, as *Clipper Dashing Wave*. Unfortunately, like other early -100s not converted for freight use, the aircraft did not survive for very long after Pan Am's collapse; it was broken up for spares in 1992.

Back cover, top: Carbon brakes were part of a massive redesign effort put into the 747-400's undercarriage. Carbon brakes cooled much more quickly than the standard steel brakes, which required up to 2 hours of cooling time. If brake energy per brake exceeded 10 million foot pounds, the brake-temperature indicator in the Classic flight deck entered the amber band. If energy entered the red band and exceeded 30 million foot pounds (for example, due to severe braking or a rejected takeoff), brakes would often catch fire and fuse plugs would melt, deflating tires and leaving the aircraft stranded. If temperatures were still high after takeoff, crews were advised to extend the undercarriage in flight to cool the brakes.

Back cover, bottom: This view of a -400 simulator clearly shows the two duplicated 8-inch-by-8-inch displays in front of each pilot. The left screen, or primary flight display, shows the horizon, attitude, airspeed, altitude, vertical speed, and heading. The right screen, or navigation display, shows a map and superimposed color-weather-radar image. On the main panel between the pilots are two more screens. These are displays for the engine indication and crew alerting system (EICAS), showing engine data, gear and flap positions, fuel status, and other systems status.

On the frontispiece: Even with winglets, wing-tip extensions, and trailing-edge aerodynamic improvements, the basic 747 airfoil had reached its limits with the -400. Boeing knew that further increases in span, either through tip or root plug insertions, would provide limited new opportunities, but real growth lay in an all-new wing design.

On the title page: Two Swissair 747-357s bask in the bright fall sunshine at Zurich. The original SUD design emerged from Boeing's product development group with a 200-inch upper-deck extension, but this was further extended by another 80 inches after wind-tunnel tests showed a longer stretch would give better cruise-drag results.

Edited by Mike Haenggi
Designed by Katie Finney

Printed in Hong Kong through World Print, Ltd.

CONTENTS

ACKNOWLEDGMENTS

Thanks to the countless Boeing employees, past and present, who helped bring this project to life. We are particularly indebted to Joe Sutter, Jack Waddell, and Brien Wygle, who shared memories of the early days. For bringing us up to date, we are grateful to Brian Ames, Mike Bair, Susan Davis, John Hayhurst, Ida Hawkins, Duane Jackson, Jack Jones, Dick Kenny, Mike Lombardi, Tom Lubbesmeyer, Karen Friend, Debbie Nomaguchi, Edward Renouard, Fred Solis, Chris Villiers, Doug Webb, and Ron Woodard. Thanks also to Robert Rosati of Pratt & Whitney, Rick Kennedy of General Electric, Gordon McKinzie of United Airlines, and Gordon Fullerton, NASA astronaut and pilot.

For valuable research and photographic assistance we also wish to thank Capt. Hakata Atushiro, John Bailey, Ed Baker, Tom Begley, John Braden, Austin Brown, Alistair Buchan, Stuart Buchan, Charles Cannon, Tony S. K. Chan, Anthony Concil, Kase Dekker, Bo Draper, Bruce Drum, Pham Duong, Jerry Finch, William Fletcher, Kimberely Foster, Chung Kim-Fung, Mike Greywitt, Capt. Freddie Growler, Robert Grundy, Keith Harman, Dave Hughes, Alan Hurran, Ken Ishikata, Chihiro Ishikawa, Capt. Sadayoshi Ito, Capt. Ian Johnson, Steve Klodt, Kensuke Kotera, Hideaki Kuroki, Jenny P. S. Lei, Capt. Mike Livesey, Andy Marsh, Eric McGahan, Ryuichi Mezaki, Yvonne Napper, Capt. Sueo Ootsuka, Sueo Otsuka, Jim Reynolds, Hiroshi Sakatsume, Naoya Sato, Pat Schoneberger, Capt. Kazuhiko Shindo, Dick Siegel, Bryan Southgate, Aidan Stradling, Tetsuhisa Sugano, Martin Taylor, Hideki Tezuka, Katsuhiko Tokunaga, Hernando Vergara, Tom Winfrey, Anthony Wong, and Katsuhiko Yumino.

We were also encouraged and assisted by the staff of *Flight International* magazine, particularly Allan Winn, Graham Warwick, Forbes Mutch, Andrew Chuter, Max Kingsley-Jones, Kevin O' Toole and Gareth Burgess. Sincere thanks also to Kim Hearn at Quadrant Picture Library, Trevor Norris on the Isle of Man, and to Leo and Sandi Mitchell of the Martha Lake Motel for many months of help and hospitality. Finally, a big thank you to our editor at Motorbooks International, Michael Haenggi.
Guy Norris and Mark Wagner

Guy Norris is the West Coast Editor of *Flight International* magazine.
Mark Wagner is *Flight International's* London-based photographer and a licensed pilot.

INTRODUCTION

The 747 is one of the most significant aircraft ever built. It was the world's first wide-body airliner and heralded the era of affordable mass transport that transformed global society. Since it entered service in 1970, about 1.6 billion people, roughly a quarter of the world's present population, have flown on the 747.

The 747 is instantly recognizable because of its distinctive shape and size. It has appeared in numerous movies and continues to populate the world's airports in ever-increasing numbers, with over 1,050 aircraft flown by over 80 operators. By 1997, the 747 had been in continuous production for 30 years, a record for any wide-body commercial jetliner.

The 747 is the largest civil airliner in existence and, as yet, has no direct competitor. Even Boeing's stretched 777-300, which, starting in 1998, replaced early 747s, is no challenger to the 747-400. Boeing's takeover of McDonnell Douglas leaves Airbus as the only serious contender, with its A3XX project.

At first, the 747 threatened to bankrupt Boeing; but despite its shaky start, it later became the pumping heart behind the company's continuous growth. The notional break-even point was reached about the 400-aircraft mark in the late 1970s. Since then, the 747 has gradually been transformed into a consistent money maker. Adjusted for inflation, the Boeing Commercial Airplane Group (BCAG) has delivered an estimated $130 billion worth of 747s since it first entered service. More than $100 billion of this has been to overseas customers, who by the late 1990s represented more than 90 percent of all sales. The aircraft continues to support a large workforce in both the United States and offshore aerospace industries. Almost 70,000 U.S. jobs are directly tied to the production of the aircraft, more than half of which are at companies other than Boeing. The giant aircraft also accounts for another 10,000 jobs with suppliers around the world.

This book examines the roots of the 747 and describes the forces that shaped it and the background to the many design decisions that created the familiar shape of today's aircraft. It also looks at the complex genealogy of the 747 family tree and details some of the more unusual branches, together with some that never came to fruition. The buildup of the 747-500X and -600X stretch proposals is closely chronicled, and the subsequent decision not to proceed explained. However, this book makes no attempt to list the detailed individual history of every 747 built. There are two main reasons for this. First, production continues at a rapid rate and such a listing would be out of date before the book is even printed. Second, given the availability of dedicated listings for the 747 published elsewhere, it is considered more important to concentrate on the aircraft's full development history.

According to BCAG president Ron Woodard, the 747 is beyond superlatives: "Quite simply, it is the Queen of the Skies. It is the anchor of the world's long-range system, and we believe it will remain so." With production continuing well into the first decade of the twenty-first century, and several upgrades being studied in the wake of the 1997 stretch cancellation, there seems little reason to doubt his words. The 1,100th aircraft (a -400 for Virgin Atlantic Airways), was delivered in January 1997 and, with the order book approaching 1,300, it seems that the Queen of the Skies is set to be around for a long time to come.

CHAPTER ONE

As curious as it may seem, the roots of the 747 go back to the end of April 1945, as World War II in Europe was drawing to a close. The Russians were fighting their way into the ruins of Berlin, when a U.S. exploitation team found what it was looking for in a forest near Braunschweig, a little over 100 miles to the east. Searching through the Reichsmarshal Hermann Goering Aeronautical Research Institute, the team uncovered boxes of wind-tunnel research papers dealing with the new design concept of swept wings.

Team members knew the discovery was a breakthrough, but none of them realized that it would become the equivalent of an aerospace Holy Grail to Boeing. Three of the Seattle-based company's engineers, Bert Kineman, George Martin, and George Schairer, were part of the team, which was led by Theodore von Karman, the renowned aeronautical engineer and physicist. Consequently, Boeing was quickly alerted to the potential leap in design that was possible for future jet-powered aircraft.

BIRTH OF A GIANT

Dwarfed by their creation, the two great visionaries behind the birth of the 747, Boeing Chairman Bill Allen (left) and Pan Am Chairman Juan Trippe, stand together on the eve of the aircraft's introduction into service. *Boeing*

Although the DC-8 had come second to the 707 in the battle for airline orders, it was much easier to stretch than its Boeing competitor, thanks to its taller main undercarriage legs. The difficulty of stretching the 707 was a major contributor to the birth of the 747.

The information helped Boeing take a leading role in the science, some say art, of large-scale swept-wing design that led directly to the highly successful B-47 and B-52 Cold War bombers. The same design teams went on to design the sleek 707, its smaller sisters the 727 and 737, and 20 years after the discovery at Braunschweig, the 747.

The wartime bounty was collected as part of the U.S. Strategic Air Force's classified effort pushed by General Henry Arnold (Hap) to gather advanced and secret German aviation technology under the code name Operation Lusty. Lusty (Luftwaffe Secret Technology) was one of several Allied operations to retrieve valuable German know-how. The Luftwaffe's sudden leap in technology had became painfully obvious to

the Allies in June 1944 when two U.S. Army Air Forces (USAAF) Lockheed P-38 Lightnings and a Royal Air Force (RAF) de Havilland Mosquito had been shot down by a mystery aircraft without a propeller. Another Mosquito survived an encounter and returned to England with photographic evidence of the menacing new jet fighter, the swept-wing Messerschmitt Me 262 Schwalbe (Swallow). About the same time, reports also came in of fleeting glimpses of the smaller, rocket-powered, delta-shaped Me 163 Komet.

Seizing this technology could mean taking the lead in the post-war years. Von Karman's team was therefore one of several independent British, French, Russian, and U.S. military groups that roamed across the war-ravaged country, often only

hours behind the rapidly advancing front line, each intent on being the first to reach the big prizes.

Von Karman's booty was delivered that summer to U.S. shores as part of Operation Seahorse, the U.S. War Department's coordinated effort to deliver "exploited enemy material" safely to the scientists and engineers in the United States. However, the research would have taken Boeing no further but for another vital ingredient—a high-speed wind tunnel. Although other U.S. companies were given simultaneous access to the information, Boeing was able to make the most of the swept-wing research because it had invested $750,000 in its own wind tunnel, which could generate wind speeds of up to 0.975 Mach. This represented a speed of more than 620 miles per hour, far

General Electric's TF39 was the world's first high-bypass-ratio big-fan engine to enter production for the Lockheed C-5A. Developed from the GE 1/6 scale demonstrator engine for the CX-HLS competition, it had its roots in the USAF's Lightweight Gas Generator (LWGG) technology-demonstrator program, which began in the late 1950s. The LWGG program also led to P&W's demonstration STF200 and JTF14 engines, which failed to win the C-5 competition but went on to grow into the JT9D powerplant, enjoying a seven-year monopoly on the 747.

faster than any aircraft could fly at the time. This extension into the futuristic realm of transonic speeds would make all the difference to the family of jet-powered aircraft Boeing was about to develop.

The original swept-wing research stemmed from work begun in 1935 by Professor Adolf Busemann, a German aerodynamicist. The research provided several crucial pointers to Boeing, including the knowledge that swept-back wings could be prone to high-speed instability, and aircraft performance varied considerably with the angle of sweep. Based on the pod-mounted engine layout of the Me 262, the world's first swept-wing jet fighter to enter service, the research also suggested that the designs did not necessarily have to have the engines buried in the fuselage, which

was then the common practice. Some of the early research material also included valuable studies of a more sharply swept wing for a proposed Me 262 variant that was never built. North American used this advanced airfoil angle on the F-86 Sabre, which ironically was one of the only Boeing-owned chase aircraft fast enough to keep pace with the 747 during its early test-flight phase.

Detailed design work on the 8-by-12-foot tunnel was led by Boeing engineer Bill Cook, but the original idea for the high-speed wind tunnel was pushed by test pilot Eddie Allen. Unfortunately, Allen never lived to see the completed tunnel; he was killed in a crash while testing an early B-29 on February 18, 1943, almost a year before the tunnel was finished. An

18,000-horsepower engine drove a 24-foot-diameter fan with 16 blades that formed the core of the tunnel. The true importance of the tunnel can be judged by the number of design iterations that passed through its cavernous interior. In all it tested 34 different B-47 wing designs, 68 B-52 variations, and 53 Boeing 707 designs.

Jet Heritage

Of all its Boeing siblings, the 747 owes most to the 707. The four-engined 707 created the jetliner foundation from which all the Boeing commercial family emerged, as well as the conceptual blueprint for its much larger successor. In a twist of irony, the final inadequacy of the pioneering jetliner was the main reason why the company was forced toward much larger designs.

The 747 could have been very different from today's familiar shape. One finalist in the design competition was a double-decker with similar dimensions to the 707. Seating up to 433 in the largest of three study versions, the aircraft would have had a length of up to 187 feet and a wingspan of 160 feet, much smaller than the design finally adopted. Another significant finalist was the "ant-eater." So called because it appeared to have a droop-snout, the ant-eater was important because it promoted the concept of a wide single deck, as well as the idea of placing the flight deck on a different level than the main passenger accommodation. The design allowed freight to be loaded directly into the main deck without having to swing the nose out of the way. The same basic concept was used 30 years later by Airbus for the A300-600T Beluga transport. *Boeing*

The origins of the 707 went back to the late 1940s and early 1950s when the crews flying the company's sleek B-47 jet bomber were having a hard time flying slow enough to refuel in midair from piston-engined Boeing KC-97 tankers. As the B-47s took on more fuel, their weight increased and they got perilously close to their stall speed. By the end of the refueling sequence, both aircraft would be in a shallow dive in order to stop the B-47 from stalling! There was, therefore, a clear requirement for a faster military tanker/transport powered by the same new-technology jet engines.

Turning the same aircraft into a jet airliner might not have been so obvious had it not been for the spur of foreign competition. The British company de Havilland was pressing ahead with the graceful jet-powered Comet airliner, which it first flew in July 1949. The Russian design bureau Tupolev was also developing the Tu-104 twin-turbojet airliner from the Tu-16 Badger bomber, and in Canada, an enterprising team from Avro Canada was pushing the C.102 Jetliner.

By 1952, all the signs seemed to be pointing to the same conclusion. "Boeing felt that the way to get into the commercial business was to go for a jet-powered transport," said Joe Sutter, who worked on the 707 and later, as director of engineering on the 747 project, became widely known as the "Father of the 747." Sutter continued: "Maynard Pennell, head of preliminary design, Bill Allen [Boeing chairman at the time], and a few other Boeing people went to England, to the Farnborough show, and saw one of the early flights of the Comet. Pennell came home and said, 'We'd better get going!'" Boeing decided to take the plunge and launched into the development of a prototype jet transport, the Boeing 367-80.

Boeing's 367-80, or Dash 80 as it was better known, flew on July 15, 1954. The USAF immediately recognized the potential of the design and ordered 29 of the military tanker version, the KC-135. Pan American World

Airways (Pan Am), the unofficial national flag carrier of the United States at the time, was also sufficiently impressed with the concept and ordered 20 of the commercial version, which was named the 707-120. The jet was the first of what Boeing designated the new 700 series of products. The 300 series were piston-engined products and had included, for example, the Model 367 Stratocruiser. The 500 series was reserved for gas turbines and the 600 for different types of missiles. No one is really sure why the first 700 product suddenly jumped the numbering sequence by seven to become the 707. Most theories suggest it was not only a good way of inviting luck to smile on the project, but it also sounded just right.

Bigger and better versions of the 707 were developed over subsequent years, culminating with the 707-320 Intercontinental, which battled for market share with its constant competitor, the Douglas DC-8. During the 1960s Boeing introduced short- and medium-range stablemates (including the 720, 727, and 737), but the 707 remained the dominant international airliner.

"Along came the 1960s, the economy really began perking up, and more people wanted to fly," said Sutter. Spurred by reliable, money-making jetliners like the 707, DC-8, and a new generation of smaller turboprop and turbojet airliners, the air travel industry was growing at the astonishing rate of 15 percent a year. "All of a sudden Boeing finds out that the 707 is too small," continued Sutter. "Airlines like Pan Am wanted a bigger airplane." It was then that Boeing came in for a disturbing shock. The DC-8, with its taller main landing gear was higher off the ground and could be stretched with ease into the famous Super 60 series seating up to 250. Boeing designers looked at the 707 with its relatively short, stocky gear and tried to do something similar. The first concepts included a 40-foot stretch of the -320B, designated the 707-820. Seating 230 and with a range of 5,000 miles, the aircraft featured a bigger wing and

higher gross weight of up to 400,000 pounds. A smaller, simpler alternative was also studied. This was called the 707-620, which seated about 200.

The smaller stretch failed to impress, and attention was switched to the larger version. A suitable engine, a 22,500-pound-thrust commercial version of the Pratt & Whitney (P&W) JT3D-15 turbofan developed for the Lockheed C-141 Starlifter, provided more options. Boeing looked at increasing the stretch to 46 feet over the -320B, with a version designated the -820/505. It also outlined an even longer version called the -820/506, which was an amazing 56 feet longer than the -320B and could carry up to 279 passengers. The revised 707s offered seat-mile costs 26 percent lower than those of the baseline -320B but, despite the attractive economics, many problems remained. The bigger wing and longer fuselage required fundamental redesign of the main undercarriage and wing carry-through structure. In addition, the tail had to be extended upward as the ventral fin (required for lateral stability) had to be deleted to avoid the danger of tail strikes.

Ultimately Boeing decided that stretching the fuselage any further was simply not a realistic option. "I was in aerodynamics and preliminary design at that time," recalled Sutter, "and Boeing people decided that spending money on the 707 wasn't worth it because it would be a lot of money, and the program would not last very long." Although the stretch 707 had some redeeming features, on paper at least, they were not quite strong enough to convince the planners. "The economics were good," Sutter continued, "but it looked like a halfway job."

Bigger Engines

The last and possibly greatest influence on the emergence of the 747 was the launch of a competition to build a new giant airlifter for the USAF, and in particular, the development of radically higher thrust engines with which to power it.

While airlines worried about moving more passengers, the U.S.

military faced a similar, but significantly more serious problem. The Cold War was at its height in the early 1960s and the USAF's Strategic Air Command was concerned about its lack of airlift capacity. In 1962 it set up Project Forecast to collect data on promising new technology from companies and universities all over the United States to help define future requirements.

A competition was launched in 1962 for an all-new high-capacity airlifter dubbed the CX-HLS, which pitted Boeing head-to-head with its old rivals Douglas and Lockheed. It was not only the airframe manufacturers that would be competing. The proposed heavy lifter was a true monster, capable of ferrying up to 750 troops on transatlantic routes and required huge engines with an unprecedented thrust of about 40,000 pounds per engine, more than double the power of the biggest commercial engines at the time. To meet the demand, the two big U.S. engine makers, General Electric (GE) and P&W, studied new engine concepts involving high-bypass-ratio engines.

A relatively new type of engine called the turbofan had been recently introduced on the 707 when the CX-HLS competition got under way. Unlike the turbojets that powered the first generation of DC-8s and 707s, the turbofan generated much more thrust by passing large volumes of air through a fan at the front of the engine. The fan was driven by the core of the engine, which was basically the same as the original turbojet's core. What was new about the turbofan, however, was that a large amount of the fan-driven air "by-passed" the core and traveled to the exhaust through an annular duct that enclosed the core. The bypass air not only added a lot of thrust, but it also wrapped around the noisy jet blast from the core and smothered it like a cocoon. The effect was revolutionary because, compared to the smoky, ear-shattering turbojet, the turbofan was quieter, cleaner, and more fuel efficient.

Speed versus size. Encouraged by rapid advances in technology during the 1960s, and by high profile technical successes like the space program, the air transport visionaries of the time predicted that supersonic aircraft such as Concorde (above) would soon rule the airways. The lumbering 747, by contrast, was seen as a temporary stopgap until supersonic transports were in mass production and could take over. The picture was soon reversed as successive oil crises, economic recessions, and environmental concerns took over.

The trouble with turbofans, however, was they were still too small for the CX-HLS or anything larger than a 707-300, stretch DC-8, or the British long-range airliner, the Vickers VC-10. Rolls-Royce had come out with the first conventional commercial turbofan, the 17,500-pound-thrust Conway Mk.508, and P&W had followed swiftly with the 18,000-pound-thrust JT3D-3. GE had experience of a different sort of high-bypass-ratio engine, the CJ-805-21, which was developed for Convair's CV-990. The engine was based on the J79 engine that powered the Convair B-58 Hustler, then the world's fastest supersonic bomber. In its first guise the engine was called the CJ-805 and powered the Convair CV-880, a four-engined airliner similar to the earlier DC-8 series but far less successful. General Electric developed it with an innovative "aft-fan" to

produce more thrust, and it became the -805-21 version for the larger CV-990. Unlike the later turbofans, however, the high bypass was achieved with a fan connected to the low-pressure turbine at the back of the engine, rather than the low-pressure compressor up front.

GE realized it had in principle been on the right track with the CJ-805, but it reverted to a more conventional front fan for the CX competition. It also adopted a huge bypass ratio of 8:1 (fan flow to core flow) for its contender, the 41,000-pound-thrust TF-39. P & W rose to the challenge with a new design of its own, the STF200, which was much more advanced than the JT3D turbofan that reigned supreme on the 707. The STF200 was developed as a CX demonstrator and led to the JTF14 that P&W proposed for the C-5A itself. The JT9D engine would be a

direct successor to the JTF14. The era of the high-bypass commercial turbofan was about to dawn.

With the promise of bigger engines, Boeing began studies of bigger passenger aircraft as well as the USAF's big new airlifter. In August 1965, Boeing and McDonnell Douglas lost the CX-HLS contract to Lockheed, which underbid them both. The loss of the $250 million development contract seemed like a shattering blow to Boeing, which had been quietly confident, but as history was to prove, the loss was one of the best things ever to happen to the company.

The USAF's decision coincided with a new phase of aggressive posturing from Pan Am. "Pan Am was a real powerhouse then," said Sutter. "They told everybody else what to do and everyone followed them. They decided they were really going to put pressure on the industry to get a bigger airplane. Juan Trippe, who was their chairman, talked to Boeing's chairman, Bill Allen, and said, 'You either need to propose a bigger airplane or we're going to buy stretch DC-8s, and your 707 line is going to hurt pretty bad.' Almost overnight the Boeing management said, 'Well, we'd better start selling big jets.'"

The day after Boeing knew the USAF heavy-lift battle was lost, Joe Sutter, then chief engineer, Technology, was recalled from vacation and given a new job. "I got about 100 engineers," he said, "and we began making drawings of the kinds of airplanes we could make using these high-bypass-ratio engines. We did not know what size to make the airplane, so we cartooned, if you will, three different sizes—a 250-seater, a 300-seater, and a 350-seater. Then we took the brochure to most of the major airlines like Pan Am, BOAC, Japan Air Lines (JAL), Lufthansa, and

so on, and asked them the question. What size do you want? Pan Am, very definitely, wanted the larger size and practically everybody else voted for the larger size. To be honest, it was a sort of shock because the 707 carried 120 people and suddenly they wanted an airplane two-and-a-half times the size of that."

The results forced Boeing into a reality check. "It was a big change of gauge," added Sutter. "It was going to result in a huge new airplane that was so much larger than anything we had done before that it would take a whole lot of innovative thinking on how to put an airplane like that together." Rumors of Boeing's big-jet intentions circulated at that year's International Air Transport Association (IATA) meeting in Vienna. Although the gossiping executives were astounded at the size of the mythical monster, some were relieved to hear the proposed aircraft was a clean-sheet design, and not a warmed-over military transport design with far too much capacity.

Turning Fantasy Into Fact

In the true traditions of many monumental industrial decisions, the birth of the 747 was achieved with a "gentleman's agreement" and a handshake, rather than a formally signed document. "When we came along with this brochure in the winter of '65, people like Trippe and Allen had a few meetings," said Sutter, "and Trippe pretty much said, 'If you build it, I'll buy it.' And Allen said, 'I'll build it if you buy it.' There was no contract signed or anything, but that pretty much established the program. The firm contract wasn't signed until later because the airplane was still in the preliminary design phase."

More than 200 rough designs were evaluated, many of them using some of the data gathered during the CX competition. These were whittled down to about 50, of which some were high-wing like the winning C-5A, others were mid-wing, and a few were more traditional low-wing designs. Nearly all of them were double-deckers, something that did not sit happily with Sutter. "Everybody was intrigued with double-deckers," he said, "and some of the preliminary designs that Pan Am said okay to were double-deckers, but the group working for me decided that was the wrong way to go. If you had about 1,000 passengers, then a double-decker works, but if you're designing for 500 to 600, passengers you end up with a big wing on a short, stubby airplane. The servicing of the aircraft, the door arrangement, the emergency evacuation situation, and the loading of cargo and baggage all become problems. It's just a clumsy airplane."

Even so, Pan Am was expecting a double-decker and Sutter's design team wrestled with the idea right up until the eve of the formal contract signing. The most basic double fuselage involved laying one slightly larger version of the 707 on top of another. Once again, just as in the early days of the 707, Boeing faced the crucial problem of defining the cabin cross-section, probably the most important decision in any airliner design process. "We knew we wanted to have a swept-wing and just put the engines

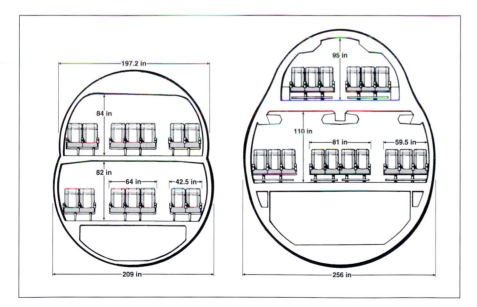

Boeing's original double deck 747-3, -4 and -5 design studies (left) were heavily optimized for passenger carrying, whereas the cross-section finally adopted (right) provided much more cargo capacity on both the main and lower decks. Boeing revived at least part of its 747-3 study more than a decade later when it designed the 767 with an external diameter almost identical in size to the upper deck of the abortive double-decker 747. *Gareth Burgess*

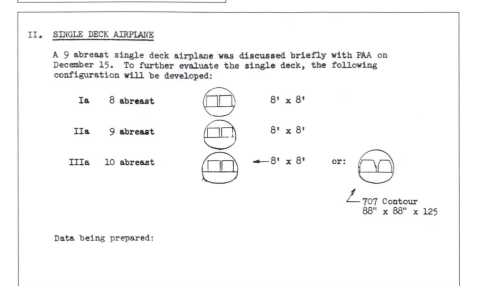

II. **SINGLE DECK AIRPLANE**

A 9 abreast single deck airplane was discussed briefly with PAA on December 15. To further evaluate the single deck, the following configuration will be developed:

Ia   8 abreast   8' x 8'

IIa   9 abreast   8' x 8'

IIIa 10 abreast   ← 8' x 8'   or:

                                          707 Contour
                                          88" x 88" x 125

Data being prepared:

If not the birth certificate, then the DNA of the 747. This hand-drawn sketch is the first known recorded presentation of the 10-abreast, single-deck design to Pan Am. *Boeing*

on that," said Sutter, "so the basic architecture was well defined. The fuselage cross-section was the biggest single decision left to make, and we got help from an unexpected source.

"There was this supersonic transport [SST] lurking in the background," said Sutter. Later designated the Boeing 2707, this 250-seat, Mach 2.7 SST project was a competition against Lockheed, with GE developing the 60,000-pound-thrust engines. Boeing was preparing to build a mock-up, which was finally funded just after the launch of the 747. "Many of the airlines, and the people here at Boeing, thought that the 747 was an airplane with a limited future because the SST was going to take all the business," continued Sutter. "I even had difficulty getting people to work on the 747. People would come up to me and say, 'Keep working on the 747, and when you get done, there might be a place for you on the SST.'" Even if it was not the U.S. SST that would relegate the 747 to cargo duties, then it would be the Anglo-French Concorde. Forecasts presented to the IATA technical conference in 1967 predicted that there would be a market for 1,250

SSTs between 1972 and 1978, of which the British Aircraft Corporation modestly estimated the Concorde would account for "at least 250."

With such strong conviction that the 747 was a temporary "stopgap," at best, Sutter and his team decided to design the aircraft as a cargo carrier from the start. It was one of the best commercial decisions in the history of aviation but, at the time, met with some resistance from the airlines. John Borger, the ebullient Pan Am vice president and chief engineer credited with having one of the largest influences on the final design of the 747, held strong views on just about everything to do with the emerging giant. "John feels the existence of an overrich C-5A background on the 747 project is resulting in several undesirable characteristics, such as too big an airplane and perhaps extensive bias of the design for cargo applications at the expense of passenger use," wrote 747 project engineer Don Finlay to Sutter in a November 1965 memo. Borger told Finlay that some within Pan Am thought, "Boeing body designs tend to be too big and too wide." The famous aviator Charles

Lindbergh, who advised Pan Am, thought a twin-deck design seating six abreast with a single aisle made the most efficient use of floor space.

That same month, Borger told Sutter that Boeing "should tighten up the cross-section." The specter of the C-5 again pervaded all discussions as Sutter noted in a memo to the senior design staff: "He [Borger] began to compare this airplane to the C-5A and said that he thinks we've got two ways we could go; one is to build a competitor to the C-5A, and the other is to build an airplane for the commercial market. His views are that we should do the latter and that we should get close to the C-5A costs but with an airplane designed for the commercial market."

In typical Borger style, the prophetic Pan Am engineer also recognized the future potential of the jumbo even against the daunting threat of the SST. Sutter said, "I asked him how he felt about this airplane operating in the 1975–1980 era when there may be quite a few supersonic airplanes flying. He then said that he felt that the good point of the 747 was low operating costs, and this would be compared against the good point osf the SST which was speed. He implied that if the economics were such that the subsonic could operate at a lower fare, it would have a longer useful life after the SST came into being."

In December 1965, a Pan Am team visited Boeing's Renton design offices to review progress on various designs. By then, both the airline and the manufacturer were beginning to home in on the final shape. Pan Am had completed its mission statement for the 747 over a two-day meeting, November 17–18, and Boeing came up with a short list of final designs to meet the requirement. Pan Am wanted an aircraft capable of carrying about 350 passengers at Mach 0.9 at an initial cruise altitude of 35,000 feet. The passenger version would be capable of flying nonstop from Paris to Los Angeles in 85 percent winter winds with a mixed passenger load

This Boeing publicity shot of the cabin mock-up from the late 1960s illustrates the unprecedented amount of space that was available in the first-class area of the big, new wide-body. Note the spiral staircase to the upper deck and cockpit area and the curtained-off lounge in the nose. Most of the more luxurious and spacious interior configurations disappeared after the 1973 oil crisis, when airlines faced a much harsher economic climate. *Boeing*

of 15 percent first class and 85 percent economy. The required speed also meant that up to an hour could be cut off the timetable flying eastbound from New York to Paris. Pan Am's requirement for the cargo aircraft called for a payload capacity of 160,000 pounds on the New York to London route—an air distance of 2,872 nautical miles at Mach 0.8. Other requirements included a minimum of one stewardess per 30 passengers and even the possible inclusion of "sexed" toilets. The aircraft would also have to be able to carry a spare engine "at minimum weight and drag penalty."

On December 15, 1965, during a Pan Am visit to Renton, the airline was briefly shown a single deck design that seated passengers nine abreast. This was the first time Pan Am saw anything other than a double-decker. When the Pan Am group

returned to Renton on January 4, 1966, four of the seven final configurations were single-deckers. Three were double-deck designs providing seating for six abreast on each deck in one configuration, seven in another, and a third with seating for seven abreast on the top deck and eight across on the main deck.

All the single-deck designs were spread out to accommodate two 8-foot-by-8-foot seagoing containers, at a stroke creating the classic wide-bodied jetliner concept. "Right near the contract signing we conceived this wide single deck," said Sutter. "Of all the decisions we made, the most important was selecting the wide single deck. It gave us an airplane that was efficient and extremely flexible and was one of the main reasons for its success." Furthermore, to enable it to operate as a freighter, it was decided that the main deck should

have a hinged nose section to allow straight-through freight loading. This meant the cockpit had to be moved up and out of the way onto a small upper deck section. Thus was born the distinctive "hump," a classic hallmark of the 747 design.

"The 747 is the only airplane which has passengers sitting ahead of the pilot," added Sutter, "and people said that would cost us too much in weight and drag, but it didn't. All that came from competition with the SST. I think that program did a lot of good for the 747, although at the time it wasn't obvious. They had the engineers, they had the development money, and they had the glamour."

The three main single-deck design options were configured for eight-, nine-, or ten-abreast seating in the passenger version. Crucially, all three could fit 8-foot-by-8-foot containers whereas only the largest of the double deck designs could accommodate these large freight modules. As a standby, Boeing also configured a separate single-decker study with an enlarged "707 contour," or classic Boeing double-bubble cross-section, with room for two 88-by-88-by-125-inch containers side-by-side.

Another factor that helped push the single-deck concept was the final positioning of the wing. Some of the double-deck designs featured a mid and even high wing, rather than the traditional low wing, as on the 707. Borger, as usual, made it quite clear to Boeing exactly what he wanted. The minutes from a particularly stormy meeting with Borger (or J. B. as he was referred to in the minutes) were sent to Sutter. In the meeting, J. B. had said, "You're kidding yourself when you think a medium or high wing is better for evacuation—all it does is make the need for rapid evacuation even more necessary."

Other pointers from Borger included the use of pod-mounted engines on a low wing. "The pod-mounted engines offer the best opportunity for safety—we can do things to the engine to make it less likely to catch fire on a belly landing—few fires on pod-mounted engines," said the notes. Borger

Boeing estimated that more than one-quarter of all 747s ordered over the first six years of the program would be freighters. As part of its preparations for the expected cargo boom, it designed an entire set of special ground handling and loading equipment—at least a few of which made it onto the airport aprons of the 1970s. *Boeing*

also recommended that Boeing, "get the fuel control up from the bottom so it doesn't bust-up on belly slide." The memo was concluded with the note, "J. B. wants a low wing...period."

Other airlines were also being asked for their input. Perhaps one of the most bizarre came from United Air Lines (UAL), which suggested Boeing take advantage of the wide-body interior to come up with novel layouts. In a March 5, 1966, memo, Boeing noted that UAL's John Stern suggested, "We should examine lateral compartmentation, i.e., first class on one side, tourist on the other with divider partition between. He felt interior flexibility was very important and should allow for installation of luxury compartments (six-place) and isolated areas for football teams and their followers, for example. Stern felt that weight then used for safety (exits, escape slides, fire bottles, etc.) could be

used to develop all new concepts such as water or foam systems. He suggested we talk to ship builders."

United also added that, "8-foot-by-8-foot container capability is essential." The airline was, however, worried that achieving the sort of high-Mach-number cruise speed sought by Pan Am might not be technically realistic. Stern illustrated their concern by saying that Convair 990 ride comfort was "no good at high speed. "He suggested we build our technical argument around wind-tunnel data." The Convair 990 had been launched specifically to meet American Airlines' high-speed, all-first-class "Blue Streak" coast-to-coast nonstop service. However, it suffered well-publicized, and financially disastrous problems trying, and failing, to meet the 635-mile-per-hour speed requirement. The whole affair was still fresh in the memory of the airline industry, American having only taken delivery of its first 990 four years earlier.

Trans World Airlines (TWA) was happy about plans for an aircraft able to seat roughly 350 passengers in a mixed-class configuration but was deeply concerned about the prospects for cramming in any more people. In February 1966, senior TWA executives told Boeing, "Four hundred forty-two [passengers] is already too large—the day we fly an airplane this large is a long, long way off. Four hundred to 500 people in one airplane is awfully dreary."

Boeing received support from Northwest Airlines over the basic wide-body concept. After a meeting with the airline's vice president for finance, a memo to Sutter noted, "Mr. Hardesty indicates that many Northwest personnel have an intuitive feel that a single-deck large airplane is the correct way to go."

Go-Ahead

Juan Trippe meanwhile turned on the pressure again as the configuration slowly emerged and Boeing's board of directors finally decided to launch the 747 in March 1966. In an interview with *Flight International* magazine, Malcolm Stamper, the original vice president and general manager in charge of the 747 said: "I remember everyone looking at Bill Allen down the table and it was his call, whether to bet the company on it. The size of the airplane itself was not that much of a technical breakthrough—it was the fundamental scale of the project. I think it was the largest single industrial undertaking in the history of the country."

Bill Allen issued a message "to all members of management," in which he informed them of the go-ahead decision but warned, "The risks of the 747 are several times greater than in any of our previous commercial ventures."

While the risks were high, so were the potential rewards. In its pitch to the board, the 747 team predicted that world traffic growth would average 12 percent per year over the next decade, while cargo growth would mushroom by about 22 percent per year over the same period. The team estimated that, given even conservative growth, up to 346 passenger and cargo versions of the 747 would be needed through 1974. Of the total, some 242 would be needed by U.S. airlines, about 60 of which would be cargo versions. Non-U.S. customers were expected to account for just over 100 with more than a third of these being freighters. Pan Am was expected to be the single largest operator with 50 passenger versions and 14 freighters, and Air France was predicted to be the biggest non-U.S. operator with 15, three of which would be freighters. Ironically, JAL, which became one of the world's largest 747 operators was anticipated to require only eight aircraft in the time period.

The team also estimated that by 1974, when 346 747s would be plying the world airways, the international fleet of Concordes and U.S.-built SSTs would number 146 and be growing at a fast rate. Others also believed the high growth scenario. A report published by a securities underwriters firm in May 1966, only one month after the go-ahead was given, predicted that 24 million departures a year would be required by 707-sized aircraft to keep pace with the growth expected by 1980. It also predicted that by 1975, some 3,000 707-320Bs would be needed to handle the traffic if no wide-body jets were developed.

The announcement was made public on April 13, along with the news that Pan Am had placed an order for 25 aircraft, at $20 million each, for delivery beginning in late 1969. The stakes were high in every sense. "It had a lot of risks in it," said Sutter. "The main risk was the tremendous amount of money required to develop an airplane of that size, with all that new technology. Boeing's investment in research and development, tooling, manpower, and an entirely new manufacturing site at Everett, 30 miles north of Seattle (see Chapter 7), totaled more than $1 billion by the time of the rollout, a sum greater than the company's net worth.

Sutter's team began detailed design work in an old building down by the murky Duwamish River. The building does not exist today—it was knocked down to make room for the Integrated Airplane Systems Laboratory (IASL), where much of the groundwork for the 777, Next Generation 737, and 747-500/600X projects later took place. "Drop hammer testing was being performed in the adjacent building at the time," recalled Sutter. "We were designing the 747 with the ground shaking."

Thirty miles to the north the ground was shaking for other reasons. In June 1966 Boeing took an option on land adjacent to the runway by the rural Paine Field airfield. An army of construction workers started to clear almost 780 acres of forest to make way for the new Everett factory alongside the 9,900-foot runway. The undulating countryside required leveling to make room for what become the world's largest-volume building. Hillsides were blasted, excavated, rolled, leveled, and flattened and valleys were filled in (see Chapter 7).

Cost- and profit-share arrangements were signed with more than a dozen major U.S. aerospace companies that would supply parts. Agreements were also struck with a large number of smaller companies in the United States and around the world covering the supply of systems and equipment. To ease the burden, and share the risk, more than half the total value of the 747 production was handled by companies outside Boeing. In addition, almost every other division of Boeing's sprawling company contributed to the mammoth task. Northrop's Norair Division in Hawthorne, near Los Angeles International Airport, won the biggest share of the structure outside Boeing. It ended up making most of the fuselage from aft of the flight deck to the rear pressure bulkhead by the tail. The company, now part of

Northrop Grumman, supplied more than 40 subassembly panels, the largest measuring about 30 feet by 20 feet. All were shipped to Seattle where Boeing stuck them together into four major fuselage sections. These were then bolted together to form the basic body.

In July 1966, Boeing formally established the Everett branch, later a division of the Commercial Airplane Division (later company). Malcolm T. Stamper was appointed at its head, with responsibility to oversee the design, development, manufacture, delivery, and support of the 747. The organization galvanized into action, and in the bleak mid-winter of 1967, the first 747 manufacturing work was begun, even as the first 200-million-cubic-foot part of the factory was being built around the workforce. The tremendous undertaking, unparalleled in commercial aviation, proceeded at breakneck pace and earned the workers the nickname, "The Incredibles." "It's hard to explain the dedication people up here have for airplanes," Stamper later recalled. "With the 747, it was a romantic thing. We were building the biggest airplane ever."

With the strict timetable it had set itself, Boeing could not afford the luxury of a prototype. Although the first aircraft would never fly in revenue-airline service, it was designed to be totally representative of the production version, and the assembly line was geared to make virtually identical aircraft from day one. By May 1967, most of the major tooling had been set up and the first large pieces of the airframe were taking shape. Three months later, the first eagerly awaited subcontract parts began flooding in to Everett—the "aluminum avalanche" had begun. In September 1967 the sophisticated wing skin/stringer riveting machine was "loaded" for the first time, marking the start of wing construction. The aviation world was witnessing the birth of a giant.

CHAPTER TWO

From the beginning, Boeing knew that its greatest hurdle was to convince the airlines and the traveling public that the new giant was safe, reliable, and efficient. According to Joe Sutter, the huge size of the aircraft meant these factors had an even greater impact on the design than any before it. "There was so much to consider because of the sheer change of gauge," said Sutter. "Let's say the pilots didn't like to fly it, or the passengers didn't like to ride in it. If any of these were the case, then I think the whole program

would not have been a success. So that was on our minds continually. We did everything we could to make an airplane people could be confident in."

The fresh approach ranged from structures, systems, and servicing to cabin design and flying performance. "The thing about the 747 design that's different from other airplanes is the sheer amount of redundancy," explained Sutter. "Here we were, designing a 350-passenger airplane, which was huge at the time, and safety was the biggest single issue.

ANATOMY OF A JUMBO

As the final design was further refined, wind-tunnel testing focused on potentially trouble-some areas such as airflow interaction between the engine nacelles, struts, and wing. The large ventral fin beneath the rear of the fuselage was installed for test purposes only. *Boeing*

Multiple redundancy was a design hallmark of the 747. This is exemplified in the main undercarriage, which was designed with four separate legs for extra safety. This proved its worth within a few months of service entry when a Pan Am aircraft, N747PA, hit runway lights on takeoff from San Francisco in July 1971. The impact drove the right body landing gear up into the cargo compartment, tore two wheels from the other body gear and disabled three of the four hydraulic systems. The badly damaged aircraft landed safely and was later repaired. By 1997 the aircraft had been in storage for several years and was reportedly for sale for $3 million.

So inside the airplane a lot of things were designed to give it the ability to survive incidents. We put in split control surfaces, inboard and outboard ailerons, split spoilers, split elevators, and split rudders. All these systems were powered by four hydraulic systems—an innovation at the time. We even gave it a four-legged main landing gear so that if something happened to part of the gear the pilot could still bring the aircraft home successfully."

Following in the footsteps of the 707, the structure incorporated dual-load paths, or alternative ways for the stress and loads to pass through the airframe. This "fail-safe" approach meant that if a part of the airframe suffered a structural failure, for whatever reason, then flight loads would automatically reroute through different sections of the skin, stringers, and ribs. The aircraft would be able to keep on flying long enough to land safely. A third spar was designed to run out through the wing as far as the outboard engine nacelle. "BOAC had an inci-

dent on a 707 where they lost the outboard wing section because of an engine fire," Sutter added. "On an aircraft the size of the 747, putting a third spar in did not put much extra weight in the airplane. Luckily the feature has never proven to be necessary."

The single-main-deck philosophy addressed the prime concern of emergency passenger evacuation and provided another good reason to stay clear of a full-length double-decker. The rules stated that all passengers must be able to leave the aircraft within 90 seconds without injury, and Boeing felt this was achievable by designing the main deck with 10 exits. To address the potential psychological problems caused by an interior of such huge dimensions, the cabin divisions and interior architecture were carefully designed to create the illusion that the 747 was a series of large rooms rather than a huge tunnel.

"Even the landing gear and flap arrangement was carefully considered from this confidence-creating point of view," explained Sutter. "It's the biggest airplane flying out there, but a lot of pilots will tell you it is also the easiest to land because it just settles in there without scaring the hell out of the passengers—most of the time at least! It was things like that we worked very hard on to make sure there was nothing built into the airplane to cause people to shy away from it."

Once Boeing had concluded the all-important width of the cabin, the rest of the design followed a logical course. As Sutter recalled: "We wanted to design a 350-passenger airplane, and having conceived the wide single deck, we knew that in the tourist section it could go to nine or ten abreast. That pretty much defined the length of the fuselage. The wing we tried to optimize to give the airplane the lifting capabilities, range, and fuel efficiency that we wanted. The span was first determined by the aerodynamic requirements of getting the takeoff weight into the air, getting to a good initial cruise altitude and ending up with a reasonable approach speed so

pilots would have an easy time landing the aircraft.

"There was also the thought that this airplane was going to be a long-range airplane for a lot of its career, so we wanted a fast airplane. Those before it, the good ones at least, had cruised at about 0.8 Mach number, so we settled on one that is capable of about 0.85. This was quite a bit faster and takes you quite a lot closer to the transonic region, so we had to sweep the wings somewhat more than previous airplanes." Pan Am pushed for a sharply raked 40-degree sweep for the highest possible subsonic cruise speed. Boeing, with traditional conservatism, favored the 35-degree sweep adopted for the 707. In the end, a compromise of sorts was reached with a sweepback of 37 degrees and 30 minutes measured at a point a quarter of the way through the chord line (connecting the leading edge with the trailing edge).

In all some 14,000 hours of wind-tunnel testing was performed on the 747, compared to about 6,000 hours on the 727. Much of it was performed in Boeing's own 8-foot-by-12-foot transonic wind tunnel. In addition to helping refine the overall shape, the tunnel was used to define the shape of complex areas such as the large wing-body fairing, empennage, and major externals such as a fifth engine that could be ferried on a revenue flight by attaching it inboard of the port inner engine. Other wind tunnels used included the University of Washington's 8-foot-by-12-foot low-speed facility, which was 75 percent financed by the company, plus the National Aeronautics and Space Administration's (NASA) 16-foot transonic Freon variable-density tunnel at Langley Field, Virginia. The NASA tunnel provided glimpses into the flutter problems that were encountered in the first series of fight tests.

The wing that finally emerged from the tests was highly tapered in cross-section with a sharp leading edge. The ratio of wing thickness to chord was 13.4 percent at the root where it joined the body and steadily decreased to 7.8 percent at the inboard engine strut. From there outboard, the ratio increased again slightly to 8 percent. The entire wing was tilted up to give it a dihedral of 7 degrees and angled into the airflow to produce an incidence angle of 2 degrees. The tail surfaces, including the huge vertical fin, were also swept more sharply than on the 707. Boeing hoped the greater moment arm of the tail would help reduce any drag caused by having to trim the big aircraft. At a late stage in wing design, Boeing decided to introduce almost 4 percent more wash-out to the outboard section after analysis of spanwise wing loadings, wind-tunnel-model tests, and elasticity tests on a wing structural model. For production purposes, the wing tip was straight edged, or sawn-off, despite the slight drag penalty that this incurred.

The four struts carrying the engines, and the pods in which the powerplants were enclosed, were sim-

The sharply swept-wing angle is clearly visible as a BA 747-236 Classic soars overhead on final approach to landing. Note the Krueger flaps on the inboard leading edge, variable-camber flaps on the outboard leading edge, and the fully extended triple-slotted flaps on the trailing edge.

ilarly designed for low drag and high efficiency. The struts were hung under the wing, rather than on and slightly over the leading edge, as on the 707, to conform with flow conditions at cruise and to reduce their effect on the performance of the flaps. Alignment with the same flow patterns, which tended to splay out spanwise, also led to the outboard engines being "toed" inward slightly. The feature, though difficult to spot close up, was visible at high altitude because of the distinctive bulb-shaped contrail that resulted from the slightly splayed exhaust.

The engine positions were similar to those on the 707, at 40 percent and 71 percent along the span. Originally, however, it was intended to put them closer inboard, at 30 percent and 50 percent. This positioning would help lateral control, particularly in the case of an engine failure, but it would also induce unwanted airflow over the double-slotted flaps that would be used to keep landing and takeoffs within 707-like distances. After tests, it appeared that this arrangement, although simpler in principle, would cause too many trim changes with different power settings. In the end more complex, but highly effective triple-slotted flaps were used, and the engines located at 40 and 71 percent along the span to exhaust between, rather than in front of, the flap sections.

The structural engineers were also able to save some wing weight by putting the engines further outboard. The heavy weight of the outboard engines helped "pull down" the wings against their natural tendency to lift. By using bending relief moment, the designers did not therefore need to build in extra strength, and weight, to the wing structure. Another benefit of the revised design was the creation of a gap on the trailing edge between the two main flap sections. The designers filled the gap with a high-speed aileron. This was used for roll control at all speeds when the flaps were tucked away into the wing. When the aircraft was flying at slower speeds with flaps deployed, an outer section of ailerons came into action. Roll control

was augmented by the outermost spoilers when the control wheel was thrown over by more than 9 degrees.

As a result of the wind-tunnel testing, an interesting change was made to the fuselage design. When the upper cockpit was originally planned, Boeing hoped to keep the structural complications to a minimum by attaching it to the fuselage in a blister-like fairing. The remainder of the fuselage would therefore have been easier to build as a basic "cigar" shape with the cockpit mounted in a similar way to the Vickers Viscount. However, the 747 was designed to go virtually twice as fast as the popular British turboprop, and this would have led to severe interference drag at higher cruise speeds. As a result, Boeing adopted the now familiar, fully integrated flight-deck design, which was kept as slim as possible and included some degree of area ruling.

Area ruling was developed as a technique to overcome drag problems experienced with early supersonic fighters of the 1950s traveling at speeds about Mach 1. It was discovered that wave drag increased dramatically with cross-sectional area, particularly at the wing. Aerodynamicists therefore reduced the area of the fuselage in the region of the wing, producing what was nicknamed the coke-bottle fuselage, and slashing the drag. This same technique was used to a much more limited extent to reduce drag around the 747 flight deck.

In addition, the upper deck contouring meant that a part of the forward section, Section 41, would be flat-sided and prone to higher pressurization loads than an equivalent curved surface. Boeing therefore strengthened the area by increasing the gauge of the stringers and frames. Unfortunately, they underestimated the amount of strengthening required, and the results of the design decision later came back to haunt Boeing.

Inside the 747

As "The Incredibles" toiled around the clock to make the first 747, it soon became clear that the giant jetliner bore a close resemblance to its much smaller sister, the 707. However, there were many more changes beneath the skin that made the 747 one of the most cleverly engineered aircraft ever built.

Boeing was forced to make some of these changes when the design of the 747 had reached an advanced stage and metal was about to be cut, in early 1967. The large scale of the aircraft and its huge components meant that weight, cost, and complexity had suddenly threatened to get out of hand and swamp the entire program. An urgent weight-saving initiative called "Lift and Thrift" was introduced and everyone, from the subcontractors right through to the assembly-line workers, was encouraged to find savings.

"Due to the sheer size of the 747, trying to anticipate weight was a big problem," said Sutter. "We fought it tooth and nail and ultimately were forced to make compromises between weight and ruggedness. We designed it with a maximum takeoff weight of 680,000 pounds and very quickly it grew to 710,000 pounds. Part of the reason was the empty weight grew higher, so we needed to increase the takeoff weight to grow the payload. Luckily, the engines and fuel tanks were big enough to cope."

Much of the burden fell on Northrop, which as fuselage builder, had the biggest area of potential weight growth. One of the key targets for Northrop was the manufacture of the stringers that provide the longitudinal support framework beneath the skin of all aircraft. There were an amazing 3 miles of stringers in the fuselage, and Northrop realized it could save a lot of unnecessary weight if it could tailor the manufacture of different stringers to suit the specific load requirements of particular parts of the structure, rather than making them all roughly the same thickness. At the same time, the company had to ensure it could perform this tricky task without incurring the higher costs of expensive manufacturing processes such as chemical milling or complex machining. The solution turned out to be a specially designed stringer-forming plastic wheel. The

wheel could be carefully deformed to produce variably tapered stringers. Other cost- and weight-saving manufacturing initiatives included developing special polyurethane tools for crimp-free forming heavy gauge materials, and fiber-laminated stretch lightweight dies for forming the enormous skin panels.

The basic fuselage cross-section throughout most of its length was actually circular, despite the contrary impression given by the humped nose section and slab- sided over-wing area. The structure was made up, in the conventional way, of circumferencial frames supported by the stringers mentioned earlier. The slab-sided look of the over-wing section was created by the wing-to-body join, and the contoured fairing surrounding the wing root and belly. This was made up of more than a hundred polyvinyl chloride (PVC) filled fiberglass sandwich sections that were sprayed with a bonded coating of aluminum. This huge fairing, measuring 80 feet in length, was the biggest use of plastics applied to an aircraft at that time.

Forward of the wing root, the cross-section became increasingly pear-shaped as the roof of the fuselage was extended to provide the fairing for the raised cockpit and small upper deck. With a view to later stretching the 747, Boeing also designed two convenient production break points. One was located immediately behind the flight deck and forward side entrance, and the other forward of the wing center-section box. To accommodate the freighter version from the start, the sloping bulkhead forming the front face of the nosewheel bay also marked the line for the upward-hinging visor-type nose door.

One of the most unusual aspects of the fuselage design was the large area of open center-section in the belly, needed for the stowage of the four-leg main undercarriage. The large gaping area required a center keel link to connect the lower parts of the rear and forward fuselage.

The huge vertical tail and horizontal stabilizer were major undertakings in their own right, the tailplane

Sophisticated flaps, wheel brakes, and spoilers enabled the 747 to use standard-length runways around the world. With flaps retracted above their initial position, the outboard spoilers to the left on this photograph are electrically locked out. For roll control, flight spoilers operate only when the control wheel is moved beyond 9 degrees. As speed increases, the flight spoilers blow down and decrease in effectiveness relative to the high-speed, inboard, aileron.

having a greater area than the wing of the 727, and the 32-foot, 3-inch-tall fin taking the 747's overall height to more than 63 feet above the ground, or a height roughly equivalent to a six-story building! The base of the fin measured 38 feet, 6 inches in length and tapered to 13 feet, 1 inch at the tip. It produced an area of 830 square feet, about 25 percent bigger than the wing of the first-generation 737.

The fin torsion box was built in a similar way to the wings, constructed around two spars, with ribs and stringers to support a thick sheet-alloy skin. Forged and machined light-alloy body fittings reached up from the fuselage, to which the torsion box was attached with titanium taper-lock bolts. The front section of the fin was a box structure made of light aluminum honeycomb that was permanently fixed to the torsion box. A removable fin leading edge, made of a light-alloy sheet-skin-and-rib assembly, was attached to an auxiliary spar fitted to the front section. A fiberglass tip covered the top of the fin, which housed VOR (VHF omni-directional range) aerials.

The split rudder was made of light-alloy spars and ribs, covered in

This view of the early structural mock-up gives some idea of the vast cabin area available in the 747. The number of main-deck exits was increased to five on each side for the final design to comply with emergency evacuation requirements. Note the space in the floor of the upper deck to provide room for the spiral stairway, and the aft pressure bulkhead at the very tail end of the cabin. *Boeing*

glass-fiber honeycomb skins. The larger top section was mass-balanced with weights attached to spars that protruded ahead of the hinge. The smaller bottom rudder section, measuring 9 feet, 3 inches in height, was simply hinged and controlled with a power control package identical to the unit controlling the upper rudder. The rudder's maximum travel was 24 degrees either side, while trim was limited to 16 degrees.

The horizontal stabilizer was similarly formed around a main torsion box that carried through the fuselage. The huge structure was hinged at the rear and the leading edge connected to a beefy jackscrew. The stabilizer jackscrew could move the entire tailplane to an angle of incidence up to plus 3 degrees or minus 12 degrees. The split elevators attached to the stabilizer were very similar to the rudder in construction and layout; each section was made up of light-alloy spars and ribs covered with fiberglass skins. The larger outer section was also mass-balanced. The elevator could travel up to plus 24 degrees or minus 18 degrees.

Big Wings

Enormous forged and machined main frames joined the wing to the fuselage. These main frames looked more like major parts of an ocean-going ship than an aircraft. Four of these light-alloy main frames were attached to the wing, while a fifth frame at the rear supported the aft center-section landing-gear beam. The front frame took load paths around the circumference of the fuselage, from the forward main spar of the wing, while the second frame took similar loads from the center spar, which extended outward as far as the outboard engine pylons. The third frame was attached to the rear spar, which completed the wing center box running through the fuselage. The fourth frame supported the wing main undercarriage support beam, which was made of titanium. This was the largest single piece of titanium structure in the whole aircraft and was attached to the fuselage center-section frame at one end and pivoted to the wing rear spar at the other. The beam carried the rear bearing of the wing main landing gear retraction

pivot, and was made from this high-strength material because a steel beam of equivalent strength would have been much larger and could therefore not fit in the space available. A total of 8,500 pounds of titanium was used per aircraft and included reinforcing panels around the doors and windscreen.

The wing was structurally continuous from root to tip, unlike that of the 707, which had a production join at the outer pylon. Boeing designed the 747 wing for a target life of 60,000 hours (double previous fatigue-free targets) and placed a third spar in the center of the wing box for increased safety. The front and rear spars formed the walls of the main fuel tanks, which were Thoikol sealed. The skin panels of the wing torsion box were machine milled and tapered, varying in thickness from 1.5 inches at the root to about 0.125 inch at the tip. The lower wing skin and stringers, like the fuselage, were made from 2024 aluminum, while the upper skin, stringers, spars, and ribs were made from 7075 aluminum. The 2000-series alloys were strengthened for high-tension loads with copper and magnesium. The principal alloying element in the 7000 series, which was best suited for compression loads, was zinc.

North American (part of Boeing following the 1996 takeover of Rockwell) made the composite fiberglass/light-alloy leading edge, and Fairchild Hiller produced all the leading- and trailing-edge flaps and controls, which were largely honeycomb skins with light-alloy frames, ribs, and spars. Honeycomb paneling was used to a great extent because it was light yet stiff enough to handle the aerodynamic loads and, together with fiberglass, accounted for more than half the surface area of the wings and empennage. In all, there was proportionately more fiberglass structure used on the 747 than on any previous production aircraft—regardless of size. Fiberglass offered several advantages including corrosion resistance and immunity to fatigue damage from noise resonance.

The flexibility of the fiberglass material also made it uniquely suitable

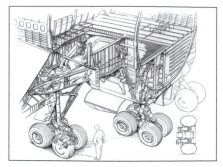

One of the most ingenious aspects of the design was the clever packaging of the main undercarriage, and the complex structure that supported it. This included the pivot-attachment beam for the wing main landing gear, which ran from the rear wing spar (at left) to one of the five fuselage main frames (above man in drawing). Note the massive body bulkhead in the center of the drawing, which formed the main undercarriage beam carry-through structure. Another unusual feature was the large keel member that connected the front and back halves of the fuselage and formed the inboard walls of the unpressurized undercarriage bays. *Flight International/Quadrant Picture Library*

for the variable-camber leading-edge flaps that were folded flat under the wing when not in use, and yet were bent into a smooth aerodynamic contour when extended for low-speed flight. This feature was essential because the "peaky" airfoil shape, chosen by Boeing for the high-speed cruise requirement, had a very sharp wing leading edge that did not leave much room for complex lift devices. Three conventional Krueger flaps were hinged to the leading edge inboard of the inner engine pylon to provide a total of 13 leading-edge devices. All were powered by five pneumatic motors driven by bleed air from the engines at up to 45 psi and operated via torque tubes. The leading-edge flaps could be actuated by backup electric motors if needed.

Six aluminum honeycomb spoiler panels were located on each wing. All were actuated hydraulically. The two larger panels, located inboard of the inner engine, were used mainly to dump lift on the ground during the landing run. The outer group of four spoilers, situated between the engines, were designed for normal in-flight air braking, although the inner spoilers could supplement the outer spoilers in an emergency. The outboard spoilers were also programmed to operate differentially when the flaps were extended, to help decrease lift on the wing on the inside of a turn.

Boeing's extensive experience with complex main-flap design was honed to new levels on the 727 and 737 programs. It was then brought to full use on the 747, which was fitted with a magnificent array of triple-slotted trailing-edge flaps. Together with the leading-edge flaps, the full deployment of the main flaps increased wing area by 21 percent and lift by about 90 percent, enabling the aircraft to make approaches at such stately speeds that the huge 747 appeared to be virtually standing still. The inboard and outboard flap sections were divided to avoid the flow from the inner jet engine and provide a space on the trailing edge for the inboard, high-speed aileron. Each of the flaps were made from aluminum honeycomb skins over light-alloy ribs. The flaps were mounted on steel drive tracks that were shrouded in fiberglass shells. Flap motors, powered primarily by different hydraulic systems and backup electrical systems, turned torque rods that actuated ball-screw jacks to move the flaps down the rails.

As soon as the main flaps were selected to move down, the leading-edge variable-camber flaps automatically deployed. As the main flaps moved through 5 degrees, the inner three Krueger sections also deployed automatically. This sequence was designed to reduce wing loading and prevent excessive asymmetry in the event of a control-system failure. The movement of the flaps also automatically triggered into action the low-speed aileron near the wing tip. The inner aileron was designed for use at all speeds, though Boeing originally hoped flight tests would prove that this control surface could be deleted to save weight and that the outboard aileron could be used for control at all speeds.

Multiple Redundancy

Four separate hydraulic systems, each driven by one engine, formed the heart of the 747's unprecedented level of backup and redundancy. The hydraulics provided actuation for all primary flight controls; all secondary controls (except leading-edge flaps); landing gear retraction, extension, and gear steering; and wheel braking. Systems 1 and 4 could be used for all purposes, while System 2 and System 3 were normally used for flight control only.

Each system was separately pressurized to 3,000 psi by a pump mounted on the engine. Paired in parallel with these shaft-driven pumps were four pneumatically operated pumps that were available mainly when demand exceeded capacity of the shaft-driven pumps, such as when the undercarriage was being retracted on takeoff, or when full lateral control was needed during the landing flare, while the engines were at idle power. System 4 also had a third power source in the form of an alternating-current motor connected to the external power for wheel braking during towing. Each engine also drove a 60-kilovolt-amp, 115/200-volt alternating-current generator to provide electrical power. In addition, two more 90-kilovolt-amp generators were fitted to the 1,100-shaft-horsepower Garrett (now AlliedSignal) GTCP 660-4 auxiliary power unit (APU) in the tail cone. The APU was mainly designed to provide onboard pneumatic power for use on the ground, on takeoff, and climb through 15,000 feet, and as an onboard electrical source for use on the ground. The APU compressor also provided pressurized air for main engine starting, air conditioning, and hydraulic pump drive, freeing the 747 from dependence on ground power at airports. The aircraft also carried direct-current batteries and four 28-volt transformer rectifier units.

With safety as the principal design driver, Boeing ensured that each primary flight control axis received power from all four hydraulic systems. With the exception of the spoilers, each control surface (four elevator sections, twin rudder sections, and inboard and out-

The complex flap and spoiler arrangement is well illustrated in this close-up view in landing configuration. The threaded cylinder running from right to left across the photograph is one of two ball-screw jacks that drive each flap section. Note the control cables and linkages running along the rear spar at top right and the upraised spoilers, with one actuator clearly visible.

The sharp leading edge, particularly in the outer wing, did not leave much room for the stowage of conventional slats, so Boeing developed an ingenious variable-camber flap that formed the underside of the leading edge when stowed. For landing and takeoff, the flap was extended by its linkage mechanism, which bent the panel at the same time, creating a nicely curved aerodynamic surface.

board ailerons) was powered by a dual tandem hydraulic actuator, supplied by two of the four hydraulic systems.

Such high levels of redundancy were needed because the sheer size of the 747 ruled out the possibility of manual reversion. The design also took into account a huge number of potential emergency situations and ensured control in the event of an entire engine dropping off the wing or the loss of an outer wing section, an upper fin section, or of an outboard section of tailplane or elevator. The design meant that the aircraft could be controlled even if all engines failed or two systems were out. It was even capable of landing with only one system remaining.

The control actuators on the surfaces were signaled by redundant, jam-proof cables from the flight deck, with autopilot inputs being fed to the actuators electrically, again via redundant pathways. The pitch trimming movement of the variable-incidence tail was also electrically signaled, but the actual movement was controlled by a large jackscrew actuator driven by two hydraulic motors working in tandem. One of the hydraulic motors was energized by System 2 and the other by Sys-

tem 3, with System 1 acting as a backup to each of them. Two trim motors were signaled from entirely separate but identical electrical circuits from "twinned" switches on the pilot's control wheels. Twinned levers on the cockpit pedestal also provided a duplicated manual control circuit. Further backup was provided by the autopilot circuit.

Although manual control was not an option, Boeing was careful to introduce a realistic "artificial-feel" system on all three control axes. This was basically to prevent the crew from losing touch with the forces acting on the aircraft during maneuvers, which could overstress the airframe. The aileron, or lateral-feel forces, were provided by simple springs that generated a constant resistance of 13 pounds against full control wheel movement at any aircraft speed. Rudder-feel forces were also modulated by a system that varied the amount of rudder deflection for any given amount of rudder-pedal movement according to aircraft speed. At slow speeds, such as takeoff, a full rudder deflection of 24 degrees was provided by only 4 inches of rudder-pedal travel. At normal operating speed (over 350 knots indicated

air speed), the same amount of rudder travel would only produce a 4-degree deflection of the rudder.

Elevator feel forces were controlled by dynamic (speed, or "q") pressure and the position of the tailplane. The available stabilizer trim rate was also modulated so that it was always appropriate to flight conditions. At low speeds up to 185 knots the rate was about 0.5 degree per second, meaning the full 15-degree movement would take 30 seconds. The rate decreased linearly to 0.3 degrees per second at 255 knots and above, meaning that the same deflection would take 45 seconds.

Backups were also found in every other major system, including the extensive fuel system, which held up to 47,210 U.S. gallons in the first 747-100 versions and was later increased to 51,430 U.S. gallons on the -200B. All fuel was stored in four main tanks, two reserve tanks, and a large center wing tank. The distribution of storage areas meant that a separate tank was provided for each engine. Two electric boost pumps supplied fuel from each main tank to the appropriate engine. A cross-feed manifold and valves permitted the delivery of fuel from any tank or tanks to any or all engines. The boost pumps in the center tank overrode the wing-tank pumps until the former was emptied, and Boeing designed in a suction-feed capability in case the boost pumps failed. All valves and pumps were signaled electrically from the fuel system management panel at the flight engineer's station on the flight deck.

Each tank was vented through pipes integral with the wing structure, and vent lines terminated in surge tanks at the wing tips. The fuel was pumped into the tanks through two standard pressure-fueling adapters located beneath each wing leading edge between the engines. Fuel-tank quantity gauges and control switches were located at the port-wing refueling station. Maximum fueling rate was 2,000 U.S. gallons per minute using four adapters, at a maximum pressure of 55 psi. Two pumps were provided in each wing tank for jettisoning fuel overboard, with reserve and outboard main tank fuel being jettisoned through the inboard main tanks.

Perhaps the most externally obvious evidence of multiple redundancy was the 747's main landing gear. Boeing toyed with several options, including an oversized twin-leg layout and a triple-legged arrangement similar to that later adopted by McDonnell Douglas for the DC-10-30/40, before opting for the now-familiar four-post layout. Normal gear extension and retraction was powered by Hydraulic System 4 for the wing gear and by System 1 for the remaining gear. Extension took about 12 seconds and retraction about 14. In an emergency, each main landing strut had its own extension system that electrically unlocked the gear and the wheel-well doors. The gear then fell out and locked in the down position under the influence of gravity, air loads, and springs. The nose gear had provision for manual deployment, as well as by standby electrical means.

The APU on the Classic 747 incorporates an 1,100-shaft-horsepower gas turbine driving an axial-flow compressor and two generators. The unit is carefully monitored for any signs of fire and an extinguisher bottle, mounted on the far side of the fire wall seen to the rear of the APU, is set to automatically inject retardant at the first sign of trouble. The oil filler, starter, and fuel control are seen clustered at the base of the APU, where they are most accessible for ground maintenance.

Boeing hoped to avoid having to put in a weighty (500 pounds) body gear steering system but, after initial taxiing trials, found that it was needed. The electro-hydraulic system was slaved to the nosewheel steering and was operable at nosewheel angles over 20 degrees with Hydraulic System 1 providing the power. An oleo-pneumatic leveling system connected the suspension dampers of the main undercarriage pairs to help keep all four main legs firmly in contact and spread the weight evenly. An oil pipe ran between the shock struts and automatically provided more oil to the suspension damper of the leg, or legs, that were highest off the ground. The legs then instantly extended a few more inches and made contact.

Vacuum-arc re-melted steel, titanium, and forged aluminum were used in the landing gear, and all joints had aluminum-nickel-bronze bushings for extended life, while the axles were fitted with replaceable sleeves. The actu-

With electrically signaled fly-by-wire flight control systems little more than a twinkle in the eye of Boeing design engineers during the 1960s, a more conventional wire-and-pulley-based system was used in the 747.

ators on the landing gear used cast-iron piston rings for increased reliability.

One of the chief features of the 18-wheel gear was that it spread the big aircraft's weight so well that the 747's pavement loading was no greater than that of four-engined jetliners of its day such as the 707 and DC-8. Pan Am's John Borger explained the advantages of the light pavement loading in a Boeing memo from January 1966: "Less than twice the gross weight with twice the wheels will be easy to explain to the airport operator. He [the airport operator] will be hard put to refuse landing rights. I rather like it." In addition, the use of so many legs and wheels meant that 707-sized tires could also be employed. Talking about 707 commonality, Borger added: "707-320B tires and wheels and brakes will be a very good advantage—we don't have to stock additional wheels at all stations and our pool with other airlines will be good."

Flight Deck and Cabin

Perched on top of the fuselage, rather than in front of it, the flight deck kept the pilot's eyes about 29 feet above ground level during taxiing and about 99

This giant jackscrew, controlling the angle of the tailplane, would not look out of place on an oil tanker. Pictured in its fully extended up position, the stabilizer jackscrew is driven by the two independent hydraulic systems mounted on the front of the assembly. Each system has three sources of hydraulic power and separate electric controls. The unit is normally signaled through an electrical circuit from the switches on the control wheel, though a lever-and-cable backup system was provided to override the electric signals.

Boeing developed a bizarre-looking training device nicknamed "Waddell's Wagon," to help crews get used to taxiing the big aircraft from a cockpit 29 feet up in the air. The company also expected that closed-circuit TV would be needed to help the crew taxi but found that the TV system, like "Waddell's Wagon" itself, was unnecessary. *Boeing*

feet forward of the main wheels. The crew also sat 12 feet ahead of the nosewheel, all of which required careful consideration when maneuvering the giant airliner around an airport. A full-scale taxi rig was built to simulate ground handling, and a rather bizarre-looking simulated cockpit was erected on a tower mounted on a truck. The curious training device was nicknamed "Waddell's Wagon" after the project test pilot, Jack Waddell. It was developed to help pilots get used to the height of the cockpit and the offset turning circle. Boeing expected to install a closed-circuit TV system to help the crew, but after trials this was found to be unnecessary. It was to be almost another 30 years before such a system was fitted to a commercial jetliner, the stretched 777-300.

Despite the much greater size of the 747, the flight deck was about the same size as that of the 707. This was mainly due to the area-ruled design of

the cockpit, which minimized drag at high Mach numbers, and meant that the canopy shape was rather "pinched in." As a result, the crew found themselves relatively closer to the glare shield, overhead panels, and windshield (which was curved for lower drag and noise considerations). Although pilots were sometimes taken aback by the small size of the flight deck and the close proximity of the structure, they quickly began to appreciate the design, as it increased the feeling of sitting in, rather than on, the aircraft. It therefore helped raise the accuracy of flight-path control.

In general the instrumentation and displays were state-of-the-art for the late 1960s, but the 747 incorporated some significant firsts. In addition to the normal VOR/DME (distance measuring equipment), ADF (automatic direction finding), and Loran (long-range navigation) receivers, the 747 was the first commercial aircraft to have an inertial navigation system (INS) designed in from the outset and as standard equipment. The INS allowed

point-to-point navigation without any need for ground-based aids and had been recently developed for U.S. nuclear submarines and the Apollo space program. Three independent INSs were fitted, each providing a primary reference for the long-range navigation and for attitude control. The INS consisted of a horizontally stabilized platform, a computer, battery, mode selector, and control and display unit.

Acceleration sensors in the INS provided true heading, pitch and roll, cross-track deviation, track angle error, miles to waypoints and drift. Included in the display were wind velocity, ground speed, and present latitude and longitude. In short, the INS promised to be the answer to the dreams of many a long-range pilot.

Another advance, for Boeing at least, was the automatic flight control system (AFCS), which integrated several functions. These included dual autopilot and flight director systems (AP/FD), a dual-channel yaw damper, and an autothrottle. Boeing called the consolidation of autopilot and flight-director circuitry "a significant innovation in the 747." The combination was achieved because much of the computer capability required for an autopilot was identical to that needed for a flight director. The autopilot function provided fully automatic attitude and heading control and manual control via flight computers or optional control-wheel steering. The flight directors, meanwhile, displayed the required command to the pilot in most autopilot and flight-director modes.

Three identical Sperry (later part of Honeywell) AP/FD computers were fitted at the heart of the system, providing the fail-operational safety margin needed to ensure Category II approach and automatic landing capability in the eventuality of a computer failure. The triple-channel autopilot was certificated to Category IIIA (700-foot runway visual range) by the Federal Aviation Administration (FAA) on February 12, 1971.

The yaw damper, or stability augmentation system, was designed to damp any natural yaw (side-to-side) oscillations and was duplicated so that one channel drove the top rudder section, the other the bottom. This redundancy ensured safety if one system began giving a faulty output, or if one of the rudder sections suffered from structural or mechanical damage. Stability augmentation signals to the rudder were "series-added" to autopilot- or pilot-controlled inputs already being sent to the tail end. Damping deflections did not cause rudder-pedal movement. Each of the channels for the yaw damper system had four sensors providing data to a separate computer. Yaw was sensed by a rate gyro. Automatic turn-coordination outputs to the rudder were computed from a combination of roll rate, side slip, and control-wheel position.

In the initial 747 versions, there was seating for up to 490 passengers. This phenomenal number could be accommodated in an all-economy 10-abreast layout with seats at 32-inch pitch, but all the first operators opted for a smaller capacity in a three-class layout. A typical load was 372 made up of 18 first class, 70 business, and 284 economy. Some chose two-class layouts that would accommodate about 440, with 66 in first and 374 in economy. When the 747 first entered service, the typical two-class seating arrangement provided room for 350 on the main deck, with the upper deck used as a first-class lounge.

The upper deck area was reached by a spiral staircase, and was fitted with three windows on each side and an emergency exit on the starboard side behind the flight deck. These early-build aircraft were certificated to take eight passengers for takeoff and landing in the upper deck. Later aircraft, from line number 147 in June 1971, had 10 windows in each side of the upper deck, which was stretched internally to hold up to 16 for takeoff and landing, and certificated to accommodate up to 25 in flight, when being used as a lounge area.

Air conditioning and pressurization for the cabin was provided by an elaborate system of ducts, heat

Mounted on the forward pressure bulkhead beneath the radome are the weather radar and localizer aerials for the instrument landing system. The 747 was first certificated for Category IIIA landing conditions in February 1971.

exchangers, and air-cycle machines. The area inside the 747 was so huge that when fully pressurized, about one ton of air was added to the weight. Hot air was ducted from the 8th and 15th stages of each engine's high-pressure compressor and pre-cooled before being piped into a cross-feed manifold in the leading edge of the wing. Further hot air was drawn from the APU in the tail. Cold outside air was ducted in via ram-air inlets under the belly at the front of the wing-to-body fairing. It was then mixed with hot air and fed into a heat exchanger and "bootstrap" air-cycle machines before being distributed around the cabin, which was divided into four zones. Each zone had automatic temperature control with a manual override.

Cooling was provided to 80 degrees F, with an ambient of 100 degrees F at any ground altitude up to 10,000 feet. Heating was provided to 75 degrees F at all altitudes and pressurization was maintained at up to 8.9 psi differential. Air was distributed at the rate of up to 20 cubic feet per minute per passenger, with a 20 percent recirculation.

Propulsion

The first civil big-fan engine, the P&W JT9D, was the single most important technical advance on the 747. The enormous engine had been in design and development since 1961, when P&W had begun its fight to power what eventually became the Lockheed C-5A. The competition was won by GE with the TF39, and P&W was briefly without an application for its large turbofan. As events unfolded, however, losing to GE on the C-5A was probably one of the best things that could have happened to P&W, because P&W was able to tailor its powerplant to the more noise-sensitive commercial market and spend a little more time on development of more powerful versions. When Pan Am selected it over GE for the 747, P&W was given a seven-year monopoly on the jumbo.

The engine itself was characterized by an enormous front fan measuring 8 feet in diameter. Some 46 blades made up the fan assembly, which could pump more than 1,000 pounds of air per second at full power at sea level. The blades were supported against one another by shrouds, or clappers, which were located about one-third of the way along the blade from the tip inward. These fitted loosely together and, when the fan was windmilling, produced a tinkling sound as the shrouds made contact. The engine had a bypass ratio of 5:1, which meant that five times more air was passed through the fan than entered the core of the engine. As a result, the fan airflow produced about 77 percent of the takeoff thrust, and more than 60 percent of the cruise thrust.

The JT9D-3 version used on the initial 747s had a maximum takeoff thrust rating of 43,500 pounds, which could be maintained at sea level in temperatures up to 80 degrees F. Due to the high bypass ratio, the engine was capable of a much higher thrust level than earlier engines and higher fuel efficiency. The engine had a specific fuel consumption of 0.34 pound

Pratt & Whitney's JT9D was the single biggest technological advance of the 747, and P&W paid the price of being the pioneer because the engine proved exceptionally troublesome at first. Before long, reliability improved and so did thrust. Over less than a decade, the engine grew in power from the 43,500-pound JT9D-3, to the 54,000-pound JT9D-7R4G2, before it was superseded by the PW4000 family.

individual "cans." This allowed the engine to be proportionately shorter, thereby increasing efficiency.

The engine was designed to run for most of its life at high cruise speeds, and was therefore optimized with a short, thin inlet. This created a problem at takeoff when a blunt-edged inlet is better at allowing air into the engine at low speeds. To solve the conundrum, P&W adopted the same solution used on the 707's JT3D engine and placed inward-opening relief doors around the mouth of the intake. When full power was needed for take-off, these auxiliary air-inlet doors opened to feed sufficient air into the engine. The inlets closed when the thrust requirement was reduced. The slim cowling was also achieved by attaching the engine to the pylon via a single-point front pick-up on top of the fan case, instead of side lugs aft of the fan on the main carcass. Unfortunately, test flying revealed problems with this arrangement which forced a redesign (see Chapter 3). The auxiliary inlets were later omitted to help

reduce takeoff noise, and the inlet contours were redesigned to provide smooth airflow at low speeds.

Thrust reversers were placed in both the fan and turbine airflows. Both were formed out of translating cowls that pulled out a series of vanes as they moved. A series of blocker doors, which were stowed on the inside surface of the sleeve, were also deployed when the thrust reverser was activated. The doors completely blocked the exit area and deflected thrust out through the cascade vanes. Aluminum honeycomb was used for the fan reverser assembly, while the hotter core thrust exhaust reverser was made from heat-tolerant titanium and nickel alloy, Inconel 625. The thrust reverser was actuated by a combination of pneumatic and mechanical devices. The fan reverser was set in motion by a pneumatic motor that drove four ball-screw actuators through an interconnecting and synchronizing flexible shaft. The turbine reverser was actuated by a mechanical unit driven by an engine accessory gearbox, clutch, gear train, and push-pull cables.

of fuel per pound thrust per hour. This was about 20 percent lower than the first-generation turbofans then in use on 707s and DC-8s, and played a huge part in obtaining the 747's 30 percent lower seat-mile cost than the 707.

The whole engine was arranged in two spools, or shafts, one fitting within the other. At the front of the outer, low-pressure spool was the front fan, cantilevered ahead of the front bearing to avoid the need for noise-generating support vanes. Immediately behind the fan stage was a 4-stage low-pressure compressor. At the rear of the engine, the low-pressure spool also supported a 4-stage turbine. The inner, high-pressure spool was made up of an 11-stage compressor and a 2-stage turbine. Innovations included variable stators in the compressor and air-cooled turbine blades, the first time this feature had been used on any P&W commercial engine. The combustion chamber was also made into an annular ring, rather than being made up of

Outside air is scooped up into ram-air intakes beneath the belly of the aircraft and funneled into these large ducts before it is fed into heat exchangers and air-cycle machines. The cold air is mixed with hot air from the engines before being distributed to four main zones in the cabin.

CHAPTER THREE

By the beginning of February 1969, the big aircraft was finally ready for flight. In the last few days leading up to the flight itself, the test crew, led by 747 project pilot Jack Waddell, made progressively faster runs down Everett's Paine Field runway, reaching 160 miles per hour, just short of full takeoff speed. Having checked the operation of brakes, thrust reversers, flight controls, and steering, the crew proclaimed the aircraft ready for flight.

Sunday, February 9, dawned a typical overcast winter day with patches of snow lining the taxiways. After a two-hour delay waiting for conditions to improve, Waddell led his crew—Brien Wygle and Jess Wallick—up into the 747, well aware of the enormous importance of a successful first flight. The test program was already nearly eight weeks behind schedule, and the 747 was due to be certificated and delivered to Pan Am by the end of December, only 10 months away. Waddell recalled the tension:

TESTING
TIMES

Flight testing included demonstrations of the ability to carry a spare engine. The spare powerplant (which was a completely built-up engine except for fan blades and nose cowl) was mounted under the left-hand wing inboard of the number two engine. Fan blades were carried in shipping containers in the bulk-cargo compartment. A nose cowl, fan cowl, and forward strut fairing was provided as part of the spare-engine kit. The kit also contained a plug to cover the exhaust nozzle. Boeing certificated the spare-engine carriage configuration for dispatch in icing conditions and for a maximum speed of 330 knots or 0.85 Mach, whichever was lower. *Boeing*

The era of the wide-body jetliner began at 11:34 A.M. on February 9, 1969, when the developmental 747, RA001, launched into a wintry Washington sky. Boeing marketers, anxious to capitalize on the United States' growing enthusiasm for the Apollo space programs at that time, proclaimed that "The spacious age has begun." *Boeing*

The crew for the first flight was made up of Flight Engineer Jess Wallick, left; Project Pilot Jack Waddell, center; and Copilot Brien Wygle. Wallick and Waddell had been with the program since its inception and had participated in parts of the design, particularly the cockpit. Wygle, who joined the program shortly before the rollout in September 1968, had been chief test pilot on the 737. *Boeing*

"The biggest pressure I felt was the urgency of getting it off, and getting it started. It had been a long period of preparation, and we were anxious to get going."

The engines were started, and the waiting crowd watched as the white, silver, and red aircraft, known to Boeing as RA001 but registered N7470, taxied slowly to the runway. The four P&W JT9D-1s spooled up to maximum thrust, and the now-familiar buzz-saw noise of the big-fan engines grew. The 231-foot-long prototype, weighing only 450,000 pounds for the first flight, quickly gathered speed and, at 11:34 A.M., rotated at about 140 knots, using only 4,500 feet of the wet runway to get airborne. The era of the wide-body had begun and so too had Boeing's urgent task of testing and certificating the 747.

Although not everything went smoothly, the 76-minute flight was a much-needed confidence boost to Boeing. Joe Sutter recalled: "The thing I always remember is the reaction of people around Seattle. People who knew I was the chief engineer on the program would go up to my wife in the grocery store and say, 'What's that husband of yours doing? Does he even know if that thing will fly?' There was a lot of that feeling among the general public, and when it first flew it did actually look like it was flying very slowly because of its huge size. People wondered how it stayed up there. It produced a sort of mystique, and it still does. But most of all, the first flight was very emotional for all of us, and it did what we said it was going to do, and the doubts began disappearing."

Waddell reported over the radio that the aircraft handled easily, despite its huge size. Carrying 60,000 pounds of instrumentation and 1,000 pounds of

The first flight went smoothly until a problem with a misaligned segment of an inboard flap section forced an early return to Everett. *Boeing*

water ballast, the aircraft reached a speed of about 280 miles per hour and an altitude of 15,000 feet. The crew began general handling tests and, at one stage, briefly shut down two of the aircraft's four hydraulic systems to evaluate flying qualities in backup mode. About half an hour after takeoff a "bump" was experienced, accompanied by a loud noise, as the flaps were lowered from 25 to 30 degrees. The pilot in a company F-86 chase plane reported that the inboard end of a center flap vane on the inboard section had come loose. Jess Wallick, as flight engineer, went aft into the cavernous fuselage to peer through a window and confirmed that the flap segment had slipped out of its rail and closed the slot between the vanes. With so much at stake, the crew decided to make a premature return to Paine Field, cutting short the planned flight by an hour.

The flaps were left as they were, and Waddell assessed that the aircraft was in no danger. In case of trouble, the crew were provided with an emergency exit located at the forward cargo compartment. If all control of the aircraft had been lost and the crew elected to abandon the aircraft, they would have run aft from the cockpit to an emergency exit shaft running down from the upper deck to the floor of the cargo compartment, 20 feet down. "We had a pole, like fireman use, running down to the compartment," said Waddell. "We were supposed to slide down and pull a handle, which would have activated a hydraulic ram to drive open the cargo door." A retractable spoiler on the leading edge of the compartment was primed to open at the same time, protecting the crew as they parachuted to safety. "If the aircraft was flapping around, I

don't think we would have made it," he commented.

The crew brought the 747 in for a notably smooth first landing at the end of the 76-minute flight. Brien Wygle, acting as copilot recalled: "At the time, this aircraft was so huge that it drew an enormous crowd of press, notables, and other onlookers. As a result, Jack, Jess, and I were landing into this mob of people, so we were under quite a bit of pressure not to do anything wrong!"

Waddell praised the aircraft's docile handling qualities as soon as they had deplaned. "It is ridiculously easy to fly, it almost lands itself," he said in a post-flight briefing. "Pilots are going to love it. Coming in for a landing it just sits there like a stable platform and the pilot has to keep telling himself to let it alone." Waddell was not surprised that the aircraft handled sweetly as

Engineers toiled around the clock, and in all weathers, to solve problems with the JT9D engines that plagued the test program almost from the very start. The sense of urgency is visible in this picture of the aircraft being readied for engine ground runs within days of its first flight. Note the cage around the intake of the number two engine to prevent the ingestion of FOD (foreign object damage) on the ground. *Boeing*

he had been closely involved in the pre-flight simulations on the "iron bird" test rig and other simulators. He had also helped design the flight-control system and, as well as having flown the B-52, had talked to the chief test pilot of the Lockheed C-5A, which was well into flight testing. "None of us thought its size was a big problem, though we knew that most of the airline pilots expected it to be more of a big deal."

Six days later a second flight was made, during which the flaps were successfully retracted and a fix for the apparent interference problem was tested. The 138-minute-long sortie also included checks of the fuel feed system, the first full cycling of the complex undercarriage in-flight, and an evaluation of general

handling characteristics with flaps at various settings.

On February 17, the 747 made a 23-minute flight to retest handling at the troublesome flap setting of 25 degrees and made checks of the main landing gear shimmy characteristics. The following day marked a mini milestone as two flights were made, totaling 3 hours, 6 minutes in duration. More approach and landing flaps tests were run, and preliminary checks were performed on the nacelle cooling of the JT9D-1s. The sharp-edged nacelles had presented some problems to P&W, and the cooling of tightly packed accessories was a concern. More flap testing was undertaken on February 24, and the following day the 747 flew a 124-minute static pressure and airspeed survey flight

before making a short 28-minute ferry flight to Boeing Field—its new home, off and on, to the present day.

The first phase of flight tests was accomplished in 12 hours, 46 minutes and had included performance at varying centers of gravity from 14 to 30 percent of the mean aerodynamic chord, speeds up to 287 miles per hour, and altitudes of 20,000 feet. However, Boeing acknowledged that speed and height results were "well below its design performance" and recognized that much of the glaring shortfall was due to the inadequate thrust and reliability of the JT9D-1 engines. Pratt & Whitney knew this too but was racing to catch up with the 747's growing obesity. Both companies had their problems and could only solve them by working together.

Propulsion Problems

"We had a huge number of engine failures in the test program," recalled Brien Wygle. "Most of the engine changes were made on the ground [after bore-scope inspections], but we did shut down some in the air, including one within the first four flights. They were overheating, and the flight engineers got into the habit of watching them like hawks." Waddell even remembered one engine that suffered a catastrophic failure as it was being throttled up to full power at the end of the runway at the start of a takeoff run. In all, some 55 engine changes were made during the test program, compared to just one on the 737 program.

Robert Rosati, a P&W deputy program manager on the JT9D, was in the hot seat. He had prime responsibility for getting the engine certificated on the 747. "I got used to being called a variety of unpleasant names by the time we were done," recalled Rosati. "The real problem was the weight growth. We started out with 41,000-pound-thrust engines for a takeoff weight of 690,000 pounds. But as it went along, like all airplane programs,

the gross weight started climbing—in this case to 710,000 pounds. So now we had to get 42,000 pounds of thrust with the same engine and no time to do a growth version. We pushed from 41,000 pounds to 43,500 pounds and then quickly to 45,000 pounds."

Boeing knew that the original engines simply could not produce the speed and 41,000-foot maximum cruise altitude performance that it had promised to Pan Am. More thrust was vital, and the quicker the better. "It was the push to 43,500 pounds that killed us," said Rosati. "That last ounce of turbine temperature was the cause of all our problems at the end of the climb. With a straight jet [turbojet], you don't worry about the end-of-climb thrust, but with a high-bypass-ratio engine that last 400 pounds to 500 pounds of climb thrust is the most important requirement to get you up to 41,000 feet."

Pratt & Whitney's problems were largely due to the fact that it was pushing the edge of known technology. Right from the start the engine had proved to be a "difficult child," as Rosati recalled: "I was working on qualifying the TF30 engine for the A-7, and we had the -9D

group next to us. They could not even start it. It took them a month and a half to get it to run, which made all of us on the TF30 program laugh at the time. We finished qualification tests on the A-7, and it went out to Vietnam, and I was put on the -9D program. I soon learned not to laugh anymore!"

Part of the problem was the jump from the relatively modest bypass ratio of the JT3D (1:1) engine to almost 6:1 for the JT9D, and the similar jump in compression ratio to 25:1, compared to about 15:1 for contemporary jets. "We thought we did not really have much research and development to do," said Rosati. "We believed we just had to go and scale everything up. But when it came down to building something with such a higher bypass ratio, it didn't work like that. We had to junk everything we knew, and go back to Newton's law of physics." The first engine did not operate well when it ran in late 1966. This was so unexpected that P&W engineers suspected problems with the data recording system rather than with the engine itself. "The engine seemed to have a mind of its own, and we finally concluded we had an entirely new beast on our hands," continued Rosati. "We were pioneering, but we didn't know it."

Several innovative features were troublesome yet vital for controlling the JT9D. Variable stators were needed to help modulate the flow through the compressor, and this was the first time they had been used on a U.S. commercial jet engine. Variable stators are adjustable vanes that can move automatically to help alter the compressed airstream to suit the conditions of the engine cycle. The stators on the JT9D were arranged in rings around the compressor and were controlled by movable arms and linkages. "The problem was that they'd work like a charm and then get stuck," said Rosati. The solution was liberal use of lubricating oil. "WD40 saved us; I got to love that stuff," he recalled. Pratt & Whitney also introduced more turbine cooling, which helped the engine cope with higher operating temperatures and therefore produce greater thrust. It also developed

More than a year after completing initial test flights on a B-52E test bed, a JT9D was mounted back on the bomber to evaluate a newly designed inverted-Y-shaped thrust member. P&W and Boeing developed the urgent modification to cure a serious ovalization problem affecting the 747 engine. The fix worked. First engine prototype runs were made in late 1966 and flight tests on the B-52 began in mid-1968. *Boeing*

Desperate days for Boeing and P&W in 1970 as aircraft poured off the Everett assembly line without engines. To meet its delivery schedule, Boeing was producing a 747 every three working days, but P&W found it difficult to keep pace because of the late modifications needed to the engine. In this view of the Everett ramp, only 9 of the 25 complete airframes are fitted with JT9Ds. *Boeing*

a single, annular combustor that wrapped around the waist of the core and burned the fuel-air mixture more completely, reducing smoke emissions. Up until then combustors had been arranged around the engine in a series of discrete "cans."

One of the biggest engine-related problems turned out not to be an issue with the engine itself, but rather the system by which it was mounted on the aircraft. The JT9D was mounted well forward to improve flow interaction between the engine pod and the wing, thus reducing drag, and also reducing the potential for flutter. A single thrust link, to transfer the power of the engine to the airframe, was fitted to the turbine case to save pylon, or strut, structural weight. In previous engines on Boeing jetliners, the thrust link was mounted to the compressor case.

Pratt & Whitney engineers predicted some "bending" of the engine as a result, and calculated a deflection of about 0.020 inch due to thrust moments. However, early testing showed that high-pressure-turbine blades and seals began rubbing at the sides of the circular engine casing, whereas high-pressure-compressor blades rubbed their casings at the bottom of the engine. The compressor rub had been predicted, but the "ovalization" of the turbine casing and the resulting rub in that location was something of a mystery. P&W undertook static load testing of the turbine exhaust casing, and the potential effects of thermal expansion and contraction were also explored.

The rubbing itself was not dangerous to engine operation, but it was disastrous to its efficiency and reliability.

The problem came when the engine was already underpowered, making the urgency of finding a fix even more vital than usual. Putting the problem in the context of the time, Rosati said, "You will kill your grandmother for an improvement of 1 percent in specific fuel consumption!"

In an attempt to cure the performance losses, P&W introduced several internal changes to the engine, including special pin seals in the low-pressure turbine, pre-ovalized abradable seals, and even an offset high-pressure-compressor casing. Static load testing of the whole engine was completed by April 1969, but the problems were still getting worse. By July 1969, up to 0.043 inch of bending had been measured at the combustor chamber case, and 0.050 inch of ovality had become apparent at the turbine. In desperation, P&W started to strengthen the outside of the engine, starting with the exhaust casing and a stiffening ring at the high-pressure-turbine case. This cut ovality by 12 percent at the exhaust and 15 percent at the high-pressure turbine, but the bending continued.

It was then that P&W began looking at the connection to the strut. "The problem was that the engine was so big and heavy it bowed on takeoff," said Rosati. "As the airplane rotates, the wind tries to blow the engine over the wing, so we were rubbing one side out of the compressor shrouds, producing a hole in the bottom side of the engine." Two 45-degree thrust-transfer members were attached to two other points on the exhaust casing. This immediately cut bending by 30 percent, and ovality was reduced to 10 percent of the original movement. Even more successful was a 45-degree frame, shaped like a "Y," which transferred the thrust loads to the intermediate-compressor casing. The final fix was a similar, inverted 60-degree "Y-frame," which prevented all ovalization of the turbine casing and reduced bending movement by 80 percent. At the end of 1969, the redesigned thrust member was test flown on the B-52 test bed

Flight-test engineers prepare a tangle of test-equipment racks for a flight as part of the fast-paced certification effort. Five test aircraft flew 1,449 hours in 1,013 flights, including 539 hours for FAA demonstration, before certification was achieved on December 31, 1969. *Boeing*

used earlier for the original engine tests, and the modification was later cleared for production.

The fix gave P&W some hope that the nightmare would soon be over. Production of 747s was reaching its peak with an incredible one aircraft every three working days (established by mid-March 1970 to become the highest rate achieved on the 747 line), and airframes were stacked all over the Everett ramp without engines. "There was an aluminum avalanche at Boeing with so many aircraft coming off the line that we couldn't supply upgraded engines quick enough," Rosati remembered. "So they were hanging concrete blocks off them, and we were actually delivering engines at a huge rate [up to 40 a month at the peak], with all these stability and temperature problems. They were desperate days, I'll tell you."

In later years, with the problems well behind them, Rosati liked to recall how Joe Sutter had asked him,

as a joke, for a scrapped JT9D engine carcass to be mounted on a plinth outside his Seattle home as a "sort of retirement present." Rosati asked Sutter why he would want an old 747 engine outside his house and was told, "So I can go out every morning with my gun and shoot the damn thing just to make me feel better!"

Airframe Testing

While P&W tackled its engine headaches, Boeing was dealing with the issue of flutter, which began to crop up as testing proceeded at different fuel loadings and higher speeds. Flutter was a greatly feared phenomenon that produced a self-sustaining, and often destructive, vibration of the airframe. Boeing had half expected the big-winged 747 to show this tendency, despite the mounting of the heavy (8,470-pound) engines out as far forward of the flexural axis of the wing as possible. "The main difficulty in the

flight-test program was the lengthy flutter clearance," said Brien Wygle. "We found flutter, or instability, at high cruise speeds of about 0.86 Mach. We didn't get into any real flutter as such, but there was low damping if the wing was upset in any way."

Various fixes were tried and the problems were gradually ironed out. One of the major solutions was an adjustment to the fuel feed system that changed the distribution of weight in the outer wing where the problems were worst. Another fix was the addition of "shot bags" full of 700 pounds of depleted uranium to the number one and four engine struts. With space at a premium, uranium was considered ideal as it was 165 percent denser than lead or other conventional weights, such as sintered tungsten. "We used the weights to dampen out the modes, but we used stiffening on actual production aircraft," said Jack Waddell, who added, "At its worst, the condition was probably better than the B-52, but for a transport airplane that was obviously unacceptable."

Waddell was given the task of evaluating the flutter envelope and finding fixes, using the number one aircraft, a job he described as a "very tedious and long-term series of tests." The aircraft was laid up for 22 days at Boeing Field while flutter-test equipment was installed. This mostly consisted of hydraulically actuated wing-tip-mounted flutter vanes and onboard monitoring systems. The vanes were activated while the 747 was cruising at different speeds, altitudes, and weights. The vibrations, ranging from 1 to 20 cycles a second, were then allowed to diminish naturally. During the second month of testing, while exploring the high-speed-flutter envelope at 30,000 feet, the aircraft flew at Mach 0.98. True airspeed during the run was established at 660 miles per hour, which was later bettered with a top speed of Mach 0.991, achieved in a 20-degree dive.

Flutter testing began in March 1969 and was not completed until the end of August. Boeing's original schedule had called for flutter clearance by

The immense bulk of RA001 dominates the scene as the test fleet prepares for another busy day at Boeing Field in 1969. The 707 prototype, 367-80, was now used as a platform for advanced-sensor-system tests, but its 15-year test career was drawing to a close, and it was retired to Arizona later that year. The short-bodied 737 prototype, N73700 had first flown in April 1967 and, four years after this scene was captured, was sold to NASA, where it began a new career as the Transport Systems Research Vehicle. *Boeing*

March 10. Flutter was not the only part of the ambitious test effort running behind schedule. A total of five aircraft were to be involved in the test program, and all of them were late. The second 747, and the first of the line for eventual delivery to Pan Am, was originally due to fly on January 29. In the event, N747PA *Jet Clipper America* (the "Jet" part of the name was later dropped), rolled out on February 28 but did not fly until April 11. Next to emerge from the giant factory 12 days later was N731PA, which was actually designated test aircraft number four.

This aircraft, later named *Clipper Bostonian*, joined the test program on May 10, about four weeks later than originally planned.

Test aircraft number three, N732PA *Clipper Storm King*, was rolled out on May 16, eight days after aircraft number five, N93101—the first for TWA. *Storm King* actually first flew on July 10, three days before the TWA machine. *Storm King* joined the test fleet behind *Bostonian* because of the extra time taken to fit a 32-foot-long aluminum pole to the nose. This pole was used for gust measurement and to

monitor performance during excessive maneuvering as part of the structure-verification program. Flight data, together with wind-tunnel predictions, were then used to apply realistic loads to the static-test airframe. Aircraft number three was originally due to fly on April 30 and number five on May 22.

Aircraft one was assigned to performance, aerodynamic, stability, control, propulsion system, avionics, and structural testing. The second aircraft was given the job of testing propulsion, fuel, electro-mechanical, and

An over-rotation system is armed as soon as the main gear touches down. If the body angle is at 10.5 degrees, or a few degrees more than this Iberia -256B, the stick shaker will trigger. The tail will be scraped if a fuselage-to-ground angle of 11 degrees is achieved with the main wheels still in contact with the ground.

The two bogies on the body-mounted main gear can be steered and will operate automatically during medium to sharp turns. The body-gear steering is controlled by the position of the nose-wheel, and a switch is provided in the pilot's overhead panel to deactivate the system for take-off and landing. Taxi trials during the certification program proved that body steering was a favored option, despite a slight weight penalty. Tests proved that with body steering operating and 70 degrees of nose-gear steering, the minimum pavement width needed for a 180-degree turn was 153 feet.

avionics systems. Aircraft three was principally dedicated to flight-load survey testing, while number four was assigned to functional and reliability testing, as well as some electro-mechanical system evaluations. The fifth aircraft was also assigned to test aerodynamics, stability, and control.

Clipper Bostonian was taken out of the hectic test program and became the first 747 to venture overseas when it flew to the Paris Air Show just three weeks after its first flight. "It was a big risk because the engines were not reliable," said Wygle, "but times were getting tough, and Boeing wanted it to be there. The crew flew it carefully and got away with it!" The crew for the first intercontinental flight included senior engineering test pilots Donald Knutson and Jess Wallick, with chief experimental flight engineer P. J. DeRoberts completing the line-up.

At the Paris Air Show, the 747 took pride-of-place alongside Concorde number one, and the two attracted huge crowds. Knutson said the 747 "handled superbly, and all systems functioned right out of the book. We could turn around and go home tonight. But I can't find any of the crew who are in favor of that." The 747 covered the 5,160-mile trip from Seattle to Paris in 9 hours, 18 minutes.

Back in Seattle, flight testing continued to demonstrate the 747's benign flying qualities, including favorable stalling characteristics, inherent stability, and good high-speed handling, with no apparent tendency for "Mach tuck," an unpleasant phenomena that had affected many of the first-generation jets and could wreak havoc on an aircraft at high speed. One Pan Am 707-120, cruising high over the Atlantic in the 1950s en route from Paris to New York, had barely escaped total destruction after suffering a tuck-under. Without warning, the aircraft had suddenly flicked into a dive toward the ocean. Hurtling down, it reached Mach 0.95 before the crew managed to haul back on the control columns and force it back into straight and level flight at an altitude of only 6,000 feet. The airframe

Boeing's newly elected president, T. A. Wilson (seated, wearing jacket) accompanied Waddell and his test crew for some of the potentially dangerous Vmu trials at Moses Lake, Washington. A test team member shows Wilson V2 (takeoff safety speed) speed calculations. *Boeing*

One of the most dramatic phases of the flight-test program involved deliberately scraping the tail along the runway to evaluate the lowest speed at which the aircraft would "unstick," or fly off the ground. To prevent structural damage, a laminated oak skid was attached to the sloping underside of the aft fuselage. Speeds (known as Vmu—velocity minimum unstick) as low as 126 knots were recorded with low takeoff weights. *Boeing*

was estimated to have sustained loads of 5-g during the recovery, leaving the wings permanently bent upward by 2 inches. Mach trim devices originally planned to assist with flight control were therefore deleted from the 747 before certification.

Stall characteristics were discovered to be "absolutely conventional" according to Waddell. "You'd begin to pick up buffet at about 10 percent above minimum speed, pull the stick back into your lap and the nose would go down." At the stall there was a clean, straight nose drop. Recovery was straightforward, with full flying speed normally achieved within 5,000 feet, and the aircraft remaining laterally level throughout. Wygle added that "stall characteristics were superb from the beginning. Flaps-down stalls were very benign."

Flaps-up stalling was an entirely different story. "The thing we found with the flaps-up stall was that the buffeting began much earlier than predicted," Wygle recalled. "In fact, there was a massive buffet band of about 50 knots which was huge and severe. You had a lot of warning, but it meant that our slow speeds with flaps up did have to be raised." The low-speed, flaps-up condition would have given the aircraft

the ability to hold in the pattern for longer periods in a lower drag, more fuel-efficient configuration. Stall speed at a light weight of about 400,000 pounds, with 30 degrees of flap in landing configuration, was a remarkably low 92 knots. Even at the early maximum landing weight of 564,000 pounds, the stall speed was a stately 110 knots with 30 degrees of flap. At zero flap, stall speeds ranged from 138 knots at 400,000 pounds weight, to 193 knots at the maximum takeoff weight of 710,000 pounds.

Although longitudinal stability was found to be generally good by U.S. authorities, the UK's Air Registration Board (now part of the Civil Aviation Authority [CAA]) believed that a stick nudger was needed. With an aft center of gravity, it was found that the stick forces fell to zero as the aircraft approached the flaps-up stall. The nudger was similar to a system also fitted to U.K.-certified 707-320B/Cs, and applied between 11 pounds and 16

pounds of nose-down force when the stick shaker, which Boeing had already fitted, began to operate. The nudger remained effective until the stick shake canceled.

The stick shaker was also designed to trigger if the crew pulled back too eagerly on the control column at takeoff or during the landing flare. The big sloping underside of the 747's aft fuselage formed an angle of 11 degrees with the main gear-to-ground contact point, and the over-rotation system would trigger a warning to the crew, via the stick shaker, if the aircraft was in danger of nearing this angle. The approach or takeoff angle, therefore, had to be judged carefully, the normal body angle being between 5 and 7 degrees for the flare on landing, and between 8 and 10 degrees for rotation. For a few seconds during takeoff, the crew was sitting roughly 50 feet up in the air while the passengers in the tail section were between 2.5 and 3 feet from the runway surface.

During takeoff, as the nose gear lifted off the ground, the system was armed and would give stick shakes at 3 degrees per second at a 9.7-degree body angle, 5 degrees per second at an 8.5 degree body angle and 6 degrees per second at a 7-degree body angle. On landing, as soon as the main gear made contact, it would be armed and ready to trigger a stick shake if the angle was 10.5 degrees and a tail-scrape imminent.

Boeing paid a lot of attention to evaluating handling characteristics on and near the ground. It was particularly aware that airline crews, normally used to 707s, DC-8s, CV-880/990s, and VC-10s, would need to make radical adjustments for the leap in size to the 747. On approach, for example, standard practice was to visually aim for a spot on the runway roughly 1,000 feet from the threshold. In a 707, with an approach slope of 2.5 degrees, this aiming point meant that the main gear passed over the end of the runway at about 25 feet. If these factors remained the same for the 747, the wheels would clear the runway edge by only 2.5 feet! Crews of 747s were therefore advised to make their aiming point between 1,600 and 2,000 feet because at least one flight-test accident proved the dangers of misjudging the approach.

The actual landing also required modified technique, even though the very stable 747 had proved one of the easiest jetliners to put down. Crews were advised to make a small flare movement on the elevator when the radio altitude was 50 feet, and to slowly close the throttles at 30 feet, while holding the stick back slightly against any nose-down pitch motion. By about 10 feet, with power at idle, the 747 was normally flying into a giant cushion of ground effect caused by its enormous wings, flaps, and sheer bulk. This cushioning effect was pronounced and helped reduce the landing impact on the main wheels to give a very soft landing.

With main wheels in contact, the spoilers extended automatically and the crew lowered the nose, selected

Boeing's worst 747 flight test incident underlined the vital need to train crews to correctly judge approach angles from their high flight-deck level. The aircraft, *Clipper Storm King*, sustained damage to the number three and four engines and the right wing main gear, which was ripped out of its fittings when the 747 clipped a dirt bank at the end of the runway. N732PA was repaired and delivered to Pan Am eight months after the accident, which occurred on December 13, 1969. *Boeing*

reverse thrust, and applied gentle braking. Crews were cautioned not to be fooled by the apparent slow speed during the rollout, an illusion created by the high cockpit level. The INS provided an accurate speed, and pilots were advised to let speed drop to 25 knots for a fast turn-off taxiway, or to about 12 knots for a sharp turn. Because the body gear turned in the opposite direction to the nose gear to help maneuver on the ground, Boeing test crews also discovered that on slippery surfaces the nosewheel would skid if steered sharply, and the 747 would track sideward in the wrong direction. Nevertheless, ground maneuvering was found to be much easier than previously imagined, and the ground steering simulator, Waddell's Wagon, turned out to be "more of a public-relations exercise in the end," Waddell admitted.

Flight-Test Incidents

By its very nature, flight-testing produces many moments of drama, and the 747 tests were no exception. Highlights on the 747 program included stalling, engine-out takeoffs, and minimum-unstick trials in which the tail was deliberately scraped along the runway to assess the minimum speed at which the aircraft would take

off. However, some events were definitely not scheduled and, in some cases, were clear examples of crews simply not being used to the operations of such a huge aircraft.

On July 21, 1969, for example, test aircraft number two (N747PA), was taxiing out of its parking stall at Boeing Field for a routine engineering test flight. As it left the stall, the right automatic braking system malfunctioned and more power was used to move out. The jet blast blew aero stands, toolboxes, a boarding ramp, and even a wheel-mounted shed down the ramp straight into test aircraft four (N731PA), causing $5,000 of damage (1969 dollars) and injuring four employees. The aircraft was rocked over to its left by the blast sufficiently to cause an aero stand to jam up against the leading edge. Oil smears showed the right-hand wing oleo had extended by about 2 inches.

The sheer power of the JT9Ds in such close proximity had been largely ignored and afterward bigger blast fences became a common sight at all Boeing test sites and, later still, at international airports around the world. Even at idle power, early JT9Ds produced jet velocities of up to 100 miles per hour at about 80 feet behind

The third airframe was condemned to a short life of torture testing as the static-test aircraft from early 1969 onward. A huge array of hydraulically actuated weights and pulleys systematically induced higher and higher loads on the airframe. By early 1970, Boeing began the final test to destruction, which literally bent the aircraft until something gave. On the first attempt on January 5, 1970, a failure of the aft body section at 107 percent of the ultimate design load terminated tests before the wing itself broke. The wings had deflected 23 feet upward at the point the fuselage gave way. The damaged fuselage section was removed, and the body was rebraced for the final test, which occurred in mid-February. *Boeing*

the engine. When the engines were throttled up, velocities reached 300 miles per hour for up to 100 feet behind the jet and were still measurable at more than 100 miles per hour at up to 260 feet behind the tail.

One of the 747 test fleet also suffered an anti-skid system failure during a rejected takeoff test at Roswell, New Mexico, as a result of a brief electrical power interruption. The test was made with electrical power from the APU alone, and during braking all the main-gear tires blew, causing some damage to the undercarriage. The aircraft was repaired and later returned to Seattle.

The most serious incident occurred on December 13, 1969, just two weeks before FAA certification, when test aircraft three (N732PA) crash-landed at Renton. The aircraft was being ferried light from Boeing Field after the completion of its part of the test program, and was to have all its instrumentation removed and its cabin refurbished before delivery to Pan Am. The gross weight for the landing was estimated to be 390,000 pounds, and at this weight in still air, the distance from a 50-foot altitude to a complete stop was predicted to be 3,150 feet, without reversers. The calculation was important because the Renton runway was short, only 5,380 feet, but Boeing was confident that the 747 could stop safely in the available distance, even on a wet runway.

Intermittent rain had been falling during the day, making the Renton runway wet, and a strong, gusty crosswind was blowing as the 747 approached. Seconds before landing, it became obvious to onlookers that the 747 was too low and was almost going to hit the surface of Lake Washington, which adjoins the airfield. Missing the

Final wing failure occurred when the wing was bent upward an incredible 29 feet. Boeing was delighted with the result, which showed failure at 116.7 percent of the ultimate design load, or 174 percent of the maximum load expected in normal operations. The extra structural margin meant that the basic airframe was capable of weight growth without the need for major beef up. *Boeing*

water by a few feet, the right-hand body gear and wing gear struck a dirt bank about 20 feet short of the runway threshold, and 30 inches below the runway level. The impact tore the right-wing landing gear out of its trunnion support fittings and deflected it rearward. Despite the impact, the gear remained attached by actuators and linkages. The side strut also failed, and the right wing settled, allowing the number three and four engines to scrape along the runway. Directional control was maintained, and the aircraft was brought to a stop on the runway centerline after traveling 3,500 feet. There were no injuries to the three crew or eight passengers, one of whom was Joe Sutter.

The headline in the Seattle *Post-Intelligencer* the next day read "747 'Stubs Toe' in Weird Landing." Damage was sustained to the landing gear and wheel well, right-wing trailing-edge flaps, number three and four engine cowlings, and the number four

engine itself, which had thrust reverser and compressor blade damage. The cause was attributed to pilot error, making it the captain's final landing as a Boeing test pilot, but it again emphasized the need for careful assessment of the correct approach height and glideslope. *Clipper Storm King* was repaired and eventually delivered to Pan Am in July 1970. Later renamed *Clipper Ocean Telegraph*, it went on to serve the airline until 1986 when it was withdrawn from use and stored in the desert. Three years later, it was converted to a special freighter and began a second life as a 747-121SCD cargo aircraft.

Six weeks later another 747 used for tests was involved in a mishap. A production-standard Pan Am aircraft was being used to help test the effects of crosswinds on engine performance, a significant problem to the operation of early JT9Ds. The specific tests were being conducted on the JT9D-3 engines with deactivated barometric pressure switches, and a Vance International Douglas DC-7 was brought in as a giant wind machine. As the DC-7 taxied into position to one side of the 747, its vertical fin and rudder struck the right outboard elevator of the 747, causing damage to both aircraft. The 747, N739PA, was repaired and delivered to Pan Am a few days later on February 15, 1970. It served the airline continuously until December 21, 1988, when it was destroyed in midair by a bomb over Lockerbie, Scotland.

Just as the static tests were ending inside the Everett complex, the large-scale fatigue tests were beginning on an outside rig. Fatigue analysis involved testing the aircraft through continuous cycles to simulate a lifetime of operations. During tests, the whole airframe was continuously pressurized and depressurized, and moving parts were cycled in and out. Detailed analysis was focused on 72 locations on the body gear, 29 on the nose gear, 97 on the wing, 62 on the wing gear, 5 on the fin, 14 on the horizontal stabilizer, 37 on the control surfaces, and 178 on various parts of the fuselage. *Boeing*

Static and Fatigue

While the more high-profile task of flight testing went ahead, another set of equally vital developmental tests was quietly going on in the background. Three sets of testing were undertaken to provide a solid foundation for the entire 747 program—wind tunnels, systems, and structures. Wind-tunnel testing had begun with basic flutter investigations of the first wing shapes in late 1965 and continued, on and off, right through to the present day with various models and modifications.

Systems tests began in mid-1966 with the taxi simulator and later were largely focused on the Class II and Class III mock-ups. The latter was virtually a real aircraft with more than 33,000 wire segments (running for more than 136 miles), as well as 2,000 sections of tubing. The Class III mock-up was completed in January 1968, validating the design and installation of thousands of parts and systems. In later years on the 777 and subsequent programs, this function was taken over by three-dimensional computer-aided-design systems, which made mock-ups redundant. Systems tests were also performed on the flight-control test rig, or "iron bird," and on an emergency-evacuation mock-up. This included a demonstration of the extra-wide Type A doors, the first ever used on any commercial aircraft.

Structures testing began in early 1967 with evaluation of discreet parts of the airframe, such as the main-wing torsion box and landing gear beam, and culminated in tests of two complete airframes. The third and sixth structurally complete 747s never flew but became the static- and fatigue-test airframes, respectively. Static, or "torture," testing began in early 1969 with the airframe being pulled, twisted, and stretched to see if anything "gave." Finally, in February 1970, the starboard wing was deflected upward 29 feet and snapped when stresses reached 116.7 percent of ultimate design load. The failure occurred when the wing was taking the equivalent load of more than 3.75-g, or roughly 174 percent of the maximum load expected in normal operation for the initial -100 model. The results of the static test were good news for Boeing, which was then able to offer the 747 at the much higher takeoff weight of 738,000 pounds without any major structural changes.

The fatigue airframe, located in an outdoor rig, began simulated flight cycles at the beginning of 1970. To Boeing's dismay, the first inspection, completed in November at 18,000 hours, revealed principal fatigue failures in the flap track and the huge keel-beam center web. Cracks were also found emanating from the attachment holes of a pipe that passed through the closure, or side of body rib, which formed the attachment point between the wing and the fuselage, as well as the bulkhead between the center and wing fuel tanks. While the discoveries were disappointing, they were made early enough for fixes to be incorporated on the production line for aircraft delivered in May 1971, and some earlier. Earlier aircraft were eventually returned for modification before reaching 9,000 hours of operation.

No significant failures were found during 20,000 hours of subsequent testing, which continued through the rest of 1970 and 1971. The 747 was built with a warranty for 30,000 flight hours, or about 10 years of commercial service, but was designed for a useful service life of double that time. Twenty years later, in 1990, Boeing conducted more pressure tests on a pair of 747 fuselages to set up structural-inspection guidelines for airlines wishing to extend the operational life of their 747s beyond 20,000 long-range flights.

Ready for Service

Although formal FAA certification had not yet been authorized, the first 747 to be delivered to Pan Am, N733PA, *Clipper Young America*, was handed over on December 12, 1969. A week later it was followed by N734PA, *Clipper Flying Cloud*, which joined its sister ship with a provisional certificate to help with initial crew training.

To the relief of some at Boeing, who feared the Renton accident might delay approval, the long-awaited type certificate was granted on December 31, 1969. The award came some three-and-a-half years after the company had announced its intention to develop the 747, and less than a year after its first flight. The five-aircraft test fleet had flown 1,449 hours in 1,013 flights, including 539 hours for FAA demonstration. Certification was approved for a maximum takeoff weight of 710,000 pounds and a maximum landing weight of 564,000 pounds. Tests had included diving to Mach 0.991, takeoffs at 718,000 pounds, landings at 705,000 pounds, and flights at altitudes up to 45,000 feet.

The record-breaking certification effort had been achieved against the odds, but without compromising safety. The pace of the program left many gasping for breath. Joe Sutter recalled that "the 747 was about the fastest airplane Boeing ever developed, and frankly I wouldn't want to go through it again because we could have used another year easily to finish our testing."

Sutter reflected: "There has been some criticism that this airplane program was pushed too hard, but I think the historians ought to look at what was going on at that time. The sixties were going gang-busters economically, and that's why Pan Am and Boeing decided to do the airplane. I think the leaders of both decided it was an opportunity that could be lost. If Boeing had waited a year longer to do the airplane, the 747 may not have happened. Right early in the seventies, the world was hit by a hell of a recession, and when we were first delivering the 747 the airlines could not completely utilize it. She was too big for the low markets. But if anybody had waited for another year, the program would have been dead in the water. It was an opportunity that happens once in a lifetime to make that change of gauge. Juan Trippe and Bill Allen deserve a lot of credit for being visionaries."

CHAPTER FOUR

The 747's service life began rather painfully in the early hours of January 22, 1970, when Pan Am Flight 2 finally left New York, bound for London. The flight had been due to leave several hours earlier, on January 21, with 336 passengers, but problems had cropped up with a faulty door-closing mechanism, the cargo loading, and, almost inevitably, one of the engines. *Clipper Young America*, the first 747 actually delivered to Pan Am, taxied out for takeoff but returned to the terminal with an overheating number four engine.

Clipper Victor, which had been delivered less than 48 hours before, was substituted, and passengers who had not found other transport by then reboarded at about 1:30 A.M. local time, more than 6 hours late. Some were determined to be on the flight, having reserved seats two years earlier at a price of $375 for a first-class one-way ticket.

The historic flight finally got away at 1:50 A.M., as recalled by Steve Eastman, a Boeing general supervisor who had also flown on the first commercial

United Air Lines was the first to operate 747s over the Pacific and had nine in operation by the end of 1970. Its first aircraft, named *William M. Allen* in honor of the Boeing chairman, is pictured on a shakedown flight before delivery in June 1970. The aircraft was still plying the airways 27 years later as a freighter for Polar Air Cargo. *Boeing*

As launch customer and the main driving force behind the design evolution of the 747, Pan Am fittingly became the first airline in the world to begin operations with the jumbo jet, and therefore the first ever to offer wide-body jet services. One of the airline's original aircraft, N749PA, was delivered in April 1970 as *Clipper Intrepid* but was later renamed, in 1980, *Clipper Dashing Wave*. Unfortunately, like other early -100s not converted for freight use, the aircraft did not survive for very long after Pan Am's collapse; it was broken up for spares in 1992.

707 flight 12 years earlier. Writing in *Boeing News* he said, "...a festive mood prevailed among the passengers as we had all had ample opportunity by this time to become well acquainted on the ground and our recent adventures gave us much in common.

"By 2:10 A.M. we were at 18,000 feet and passing over Nantucket while the most efficient stewards and stewardesses (18 in all) busied themselves to see to passenger comfort. They set up a beautiful and tasty buffet and a well-stocked bar which we attacked with relish at 2:30 A.M. During the next three hours most of us walked "halfway across the Atlantic," strolling through the airplane, exploring the luxurious first-class space, the elegant upper deck, and peeking into the busy flight deck area where the business of flying the airplane was being conducted.

"In an incredibly short 6 hours and 16 minutes after takeoff we landed to the cheers of passengers. We were greeted by an enthusiastic crowd of Britons who turned out to be the most courteous and helpful people we have encountered to date."

The engine overheating problem on the original airplane was traced to an insensitive barometric fuel-control system. In most conditions, the system worked reasonably well, but in a crosswind at about ground idle (58 percent high-pressure spool rpm), it failed to keep pace with airflow variations. Normally, the unit controlled fuel flow to the burners according to pitot pressure at the intake face, thus maintaining the correct fuel-air ratio. As the system misread the conditions, it produced an excessively rich mixture, which caused turbine overheating problems.

The engine was also proving difficult to start. It was normally kicked into life by an electric motor that turned the high-pressure spool until light-up speed was reached. But it was soon discovered that if start-up was attempted in a tailwind, the airflow could rotate the low-pressure spool and fan in the opposite direction to the high-pressure spool. This drastically reduced air through the compressor, increased the fuel-air ratio, and produced a high exhaust-gas temperature. For a long time, the only way around the problem was to start with the nose into the wind.

The deformation of the casings on early engines was also largely responsible for a 5 percent rise in specific fuel consumption and failure to maintain a guaranteed 43,500 pounds of thrust at an ambient temperature of 80 degrees F. The initial aircraft were, therefore, low on performance and operated at restricted weights in higher temperatures.

Early operations were also hampered by the FAA's insistence that vertical and horizontal separation from other aircraft should be dramatically increased. It required a 10-mile separation between the 747 and following aircraft on final approach, instead of the 3-mile minimum normally applied, equating to at least a four-minute interval. It also imposed a 2,000-foot vertical separation between the 747 and other aircraft departing on similar outbound routes and in the holding stack prior to landing. The FAA's overreaction was based on the results of wake-vortex tests on the C-5A, but after similar tests were conducted on the 747, the requirement was relaxed within three months.

Despite the problems, Pan Am gradually began to reap the long-awaited benefits of the big jet in service. In the first year it received 25 aircraft and operated them from New York to Amsterdam, Barcelona, Brussels, Frankfurt, Lisbon, Paris, and Rome. Others flew from Chicago to London and Frankfurt, and from Washington and Boston to London. Polar routes were operated from Los Angeles and San Francisco to London and Paris. The 747 was also used to fly from Los Angeles and San Francisco to Honolulu, Tokyo, and Hong Kong, as well as from New York to San Juan, Puerto Rico.

Within six months of the 747's entry into service, the airline was getting used to dealing with the vast numbers of passengers then embarking on every flight. Boarding time for an average load of 272 passengers took up to 19 minutes, though a short time of 10 minutes had been achieved. Full loads took up to 23 minutes to complete boarding, with the average loading rate of between 8 and 12 passengers per door per minute, with two double doors in use. Unloading times were always shorter, usually because people were familiar with the layout by the end of the journey, but also because most passengers could not wait to get off. Average unloading time for 252 passengers was 8 minutes, though the record was 4.

Passenger evacuation is always a major safety issue on any aircraft but was particularly so on one as huge as the 747. Evacuation was tested at Pan Am's training base at Roswell, New Mexico, on January 15, 1970. The test called for evacuation of 362 passengers and 19 crew members from 5 of the 11 emergency doors in 90 seconds. Unfortunately, the tests did not go well. The first attempt was cut short when the emergency lighting system developed a fault. Two emergency chutes failed on

Some aircraft just keep going. United's N4719U makes a splendid picture as it departs Los Angeles International for yet another revenue-making service. Named *Friendship Japan* in 1983, this early 747-122 had been a consistent moneymaker for the airline since it was first delivered in June 1971. By February 1997, however, age caught up with it and the 747 was placed in storage.

another attempt. Finally, the target was beaten by 3 seconds, but the FAA was not too happy with the tests, in which an airline employee broke a leg.

Other issues on the early flights included the in-flight entertainment system, which turned out to be the biggest single cause of passenger complaints. The sound and movie "multiplex" entertainment units were complicated and "either worked or didn't work," said Pan Am at the time. Another concern was the availability of toilets, particularly toward the end of a flight. "Women like to redo their makeup just before touchdown, and each person can block a cubicle for as long as 15 minutes," said Pan Am in June 1970. "We may have to put in special makeup cubicles, but it would mean losing seats."

That same month, Continental Airlines introduced the 747 on its Los Angeles to Honolulu route. In October, Boeing measured the Continental service to quantify turnaround times for the big jet. With the clock ticking, the

unloading began of 343 passengers at a rate of 23 passengers per door per minute. Sixteen forward baggage containers were taken out in 14.5 minutes, and 10 containers and a pallet in the aft compartment came out in just over 12 minutes. Galleys took 22 minutes to service with three trucks and six people, while the toilets were serviced in 29 minutes, the longest single part of the entire turnaround. Three lavatory drains, located on the belly, were drained, flushed, and filled with a chemical pre-charge during the operation. Fueling took 16 minutes, during which 27,000 U.S. gallons were added at 1,700 gallons per minute. Water was loaded in 11 minutes, while the forward and aft cargo compartments each took 16.5 minutes to load. The bulk cargo area took 15 minutes to fill. Boarding of 343 passengers took 11 minutes, with 16 passengers per door per minute. Total elapsed time, including 2.5 minutes for engine starting, was 44.5 minutes.

Other early operators starting 747 services in 1970 included JAL, which

began flying between Tokyo, Hong Kong, and Los Angeles in June. The following month saw Northwest Orient commence 747 services between New York, Chicago, Seattle, and Tokyo. Northwest's wide-body service was later expanded to include its route from Minneapolis to San Francisco, Hong Kong, and Tokyo, and then to Taipei and Hong Kong by September. Northwest operated 10 747s by the end of the first year in service.

United Air Lines became the first to operate the 747 over the Pacific with its San Francisco to Honolulu flights. It flew nine 747s by the end of the first year. National began 747 services in October 1970 with a Miami to New York and Miami to Los Angeles service. Delta also began operations with the aircraft from Atlanta to Dallas and Los Angeles. By December, Iberia was operating its first 747 from Madrid to New York. The Iberia aircraft was the 2,001st jet transport delivered by Boeing when it was handed over to the Spanish carrier on November 16, 1970. Later that winter,

The actuation system of the -200B's trailing-edge flaps and the flap sections themselves were strengthened to handle the higher operating loads of the heavier aircraft.

KLM broke P&W's monopoly on powering the commercial 747 by becoming the first airline to specify GE CF6 turbofans for its new aircraft. The KLM aircraft used the -50E version of the CF6, which was part of the -50 family launched by GE in January 1969. To achieve greater thrust levels than the original CF6-6 versions, the -50 added two extra stages behind the existing single-stage low-pressure compressor. The flow through the core was also increased, which reduced the bypass ratio from 5.9:1 to 4.4:1. To improve flow matching between the two rotors, the engine incorporated variable-bypass doors between the low- and high-pressure compressors.

Eastern leased three Pan Am 747s for services from New York to San Juan, and from Chicago and New York to Miami.

On January 15, 1971, less than a year after the start of 747 services, Braniff introduced the 100th 747, on the Dallas–Fort Worth to Honolulu route. The aircraft was the first of Braniff's famous "Big Orange" 747s and, with an average use of 14 hours per day, became the first to log 3,500 flying hours. By the first anniversary of 747 operations, the fleet had carried 6 million passengers, flown 72 million miles, and 15.5 billion passenger miles. Arrivals and departures averaged 2,900 per week. The 747 was truly making its mark on the air-transport world.

Growing Family

Even as the first 747 was coming together in 1968, Boeing's planners began creating a "747B" version to meet the inevitable airline demand for heavier versions of the giant jetliner. "The airlines wanted more range right away," said Joe Sutter, who viewed the speedy creation of heavier derivatives as vital to the longevity of the program. By offering higher weights, Boeing also knew it could help protect against any performance shortfall in the first models.

Its initial plan was broken into two phases. Phase A was a growth version of the basic 710,000-pound aircraft to 733,000 pounds. Phase B was a more ambitious growth to 795,000 pounds, which included increasing the span by 24 feet to 219 feet, 8 inches and re-engineering the outboard wing structure to move the number one and four engines further outboard. Boeing believed the big-wing 747 would bring instant benefits in terms of creating a perfect North Atlantic freighter and a good passenger aircraft for polar routes. It would also have greater initial cruise altitude,

The 747 became the first aircraft to be offered with all three of the big-fan engines from May 1977 when the Rolls-Royce RB.211-524 was certificated on the initial aircraft for BA. The engine version pictured here is the improved -524D4, which was rated at 53,000 pounds for the 747, compared with the engine's initial thrust rating of 50,000 pounds. Later variants named the G and H were developed with a version of the wide chord fan used on the 757's -535E4 engine. These produced thrust levels up to 60,600 pounds for the 747-400.

shorter takeoff run, and reduced takeoff noise for any given range.

The plan called for the first Phase B passenger aircraft to be available from June 1971, with the first big-wing freighter following by February 1972. But all of it hinged on the readiness of the more powerful JT9D-7 engine with water injection. It soon became clear to Boeing that, with the nagging engine problems on the baseline aircraft, it would have to abandon the original plan. Boeing reorganized a growth plan and was forced to announce it was "unable to offer Phase B due to technical difficulties and cost/price relationships." As a result, Boeing adopted a simpler plan to grow the 747 to 775,000 pounds. This aircraft was then renamed the 747B and remained externally identical to earlier models.

The static tests completed in February 1970 proved that Phase A was still possible, and the weight could in fact be extended by slightly more than originally planned to 735,000 pounds. The new gross weight provided for a 15,000-pound payload increase or a 400-mile greater range. One of the most significant changes was to revise the side of body wing ribs, which had proved inadequate during static tests, and were strengthened to take the heavier weights. Another change was made to the tires, which were switched to 30 ply and could run at 225 miles per hour, allowing higher speed takeoff runs in hot and high conditions.

Already in the 747's short life, the major pacing item was proving to be the availability of more powerful engines. The prototype flew with the 42,000-pound-thrust JT9D-1, but all initial production aircraft had been fitted with the slightly more powerful 43,500-pound-thrust JT9D-3A engines. The -3A engine's power was inadequate for heavier versions, particularly when trying to get to a 41,000-foot cruise altitude. In response to urgent demands from Boeing, P&W came up with a cheap and quick answer in the form of the -3AW version, which used water injection to boost takeoff thrust to 45,000 pounds.

"It was not really a happy solution, but it worked," commented P&W's Bob Rosati. Water injection was a tried and tested method developed by P&W during World War II to increase the power of piston engines and had been successfully applied in many first-generation turbojets. Infusion of water increased mass flow through the powerplant, cooled turbines to lower operating temperatures, and produced more thrust.

Pan Am returned all of its early aircraft to Boeing to take advantage of the higher weight potential and higher-thrust engines. From November 1970 onward the aircraft came to Everett for refurbishing to a new standard that Pan Am called -100A. The additional engine power enabled maximum takeoff weight to be pushed slightly higher again, this time to 755,000 pounds. This translated into 460 nautical miles of additional range, or a 15 percent higher payload. The landing gear, flaps, fuel system, doors, and in-flight entertainment system were all upgraded during the modification. Other -100s were also provided with the upgrades, which included three new engine options: the 45,500-pound-thrust JT9D-7, the 46,950-pound-thrust JT9D -7A, or the 47,900-pound-thrust JT9D -7W.

Production of the 747-100 series tailed off with the advent of the 747-200, but a last batch of structurally strengthened -100s, known as -100Bs, were offered from 1978. The aircraft had stronger landing gear for operation at weights up to 750,000 pounds, and could be powered by any of the three big-fan engines available at the time. In August 1979, Iran Air took delivery of the first -100B, line number 381, powered by 48,000-pound-thrust P&W JT9D-7Fs. The only other customer was Saudia, which took eight 51,000-pound-thrust Rolls-Royce RB.211-524C powered -100Bs between 1981 and 1988.

The first 747-200B, as the "747B" had by then become known, was the 88th 747 on the production line and rolled out of the Everett factory on

Singapore International Airlines became one of Boeing's and P&W's best customers. From 1973 onward, its growth became intimately linked to the 747, which became its workhorse. Beginning in 1972, SIA ordered the first of 20 747-200s, and in 1981 SIA ordered the higher-capacity 747-300, eventually ordering 14. The -400 was SIA's jumbo of choice, however, and by 1997 the carrier had 53 on order. Singapore was one of the world's largest 747 operators, having ordered a total of 87.

September 30, 1970. It was structurally strengthened with thicker wing skin and stronger wing stringers, spars, landing-gear beam, flaps, and a stronger rib-and-wing-panel splice. The fuselage incorporated strengthened gear supports, a stronger keel beam, and beefed up Section 44 bulkheads, skins, stringers, and some door frames. The major components of the landing gear were also individually strengthened and were fitted with 49x17-inch, 30-ply main and nose tires, as well as increased brake capacity. Changes to the empennage included a strengthened horizontal-stabilizer torque box and center section. The trailing-edge-flap actuation system and leading-edge flaps were also improved.

The 747-200B's maximum takeoff weight was increased to 775,000 pounds, and its fuel load went up to 51,430 U.S. gallons. Initial versions of the -200B were powered by the JT9D-3AW (water injection) engine with the water running from tanks at the wing

leading-edge root. Later aircraft were powered by the 45,500-pound-thrust JT9D-7.

After some basic handling trials following the 747-200B's first flight on October 11, 1970, the big jet flew down to Edwards Air Force Base (AFB) in California's Mojave desert, where it began the aeronautical equivalent of a body-building course. The aircraft was loaded with more and more weight for successive flights. Finally, on November 12, 1970, it took off at a maximum takeoff weight of 820,700 pounds. Not only did this break all previous 747 lifting records, but it was 10 tons heavier than the previous unofficial record takeoff weight set by a USAF Lockheed C-5A Galaxy. The weight was a milestone achievement for the 747 and gave Boeing tremendous confidence in the long-term potential of its big new jet.

Airlines were quick to see the advantages of the 747-200B and began to place orders, sometimes at the expense of orders for the -100 series.

Overall orders increased, however, justifying the program's substantial $81.6 million development costs. Although the first -200B airframe was destined for Northwest, the first customer to accept delivery was Dutch airline KLM, which flew the initial -200B to Amsterdam's Schiphol Airport on January 16, 1971, just three weeks after FAA certification. By February the KLM jet was in service.

Extra weight capacity meant extra passengers and payload, so the 747-200B was soon modified to take advantage of its brawn. Some of this growth was accommodated on the upper deck, and 10 upper-deck windows were fitted on each side, compared to just three on the -100 and first -200Bs. The first 747 to have the internally extended upper deck was line number 147, which was handed over to Qantas in July 1971. Although externally identical to the earlier 747s, the -200B's upper hump was extended inside by another 6 feet to create an upper cabin 25 feet in length. This could seat 16 for takeoff and landing, double the original complement. The Qantas aircraft was also the first to incorporate a lower-deck galley, which was reached by an internal elevator system. Theoretically, this made the Qantas aircraft the world's first triple-deck jetliner and freed up more main-deck space for passenger accommodation. Unfortunately, the lower-deck galley also reduced cargo capacity and resulted in the slightly unfortunate nickname of "deli-belly."

With the availability of the JT9D-7AW engine, which was capable of 46,950 pounds of thrust without water injection or 48,750 pounds with, the -200B was uprated to a maximum takeoff weight of 785,000 pounds. The first to take this option was El Al of Israel, which accepted line number 212, actually the 200th 747 to be built, on April 18, 1973. Pratt & Whitney was catching up on the thrust demand, but its monopoly was about to end.

KLM again made history with the -200 series when it became the first commercial operator to use GE CF6-50 engines on its 747s. The milestone goes

The cavernous mouth of a Nippon Cargo Airlines 747-281F (SCD) yawns wide, ready to receive a cargo of horse pallets at Tokyo's Narita Airport. This was the last -200F made by Boeing. It was also the very last in the line of the -200 series. Its delivery marked the end of a successful, 21-year-long production run, and the line then switched to making -400Fs.

largely unnoticed in today's multi-option market, but in the early 1970s a choice of engines was unusual on any airliner. Boeing had offered the 707 with Rolls-Royce Conway engines as an incentive to BOAC, which bought it along with Lufthansa and Air India, but this was the exception rather than the rule. With the short-lived exception of the 707-420 experiment, every other commercial Boeing jetliner up until the 747-200 had been the monopoly of P&W.

Several factors were behind the decision to offer a choice of engines. General Electric had been developing the CF6 commercial turbofan since 1967, using technology derived from its 41,100-pound-thrust TF-39 Galaxy engine. The resulting CF6-50 engine was adopted by McDonnell Douglas for the DC-10 and offered the right power for the 747. At the same time P&W had been stretched to the limit keeping pace with the growth of the 747 and had just developed the 45,000-pound-thrust JT9D-7A, which was adopted as the standard powerplant on the -200 series. More thrust was still needed and P&W was working on a water-injected version, the 48,750-pound-thrust JT9D-7AW, when GE and Boeing announced an agreement to offer the CF6 on the 747.

"We knew we could get a more powerful engine from GE, which suited the airlines because they always wanted more range," said Sutter. "Credit goes to T. A. Wilson; he really pushed us into developing the aircraft with GE engines." Wilson's dogged determination to get GE on the 747 was particularly noteworthy at a time when Boeing was struggling to climb out of a financial black hole. The prospect of spending money (estimated at $46 million at go-ahead) on what some considered an unnecessary certification effort seemed to be bordering on the suicidal at the time. Boeing not only faced a global economic recession and enormous expenditure on the Everett assembly site, but also the $1-billion-plus development price of the 747 itself and cost overruns on the 737. The delays to the delivery of the first batch of aircraft, originally scheduled for late 1969, had cost it at least $80 million in unpaid income from September 1969 onward, and the effects were still being felt. On August 1, 1972, Boeing bit the bullet and announced an agreement with GE that would "broaden the market potential" of the aircraft.

The first 747 was re-engined with the 51,000-pound-thrust CF6-50D and flew on June 26, 1973. Boeing briefly considered renaming the GE powered -200B, the -300 to differentiate it from the P&W models, but later dropped the notion. The test-flight program went smoothly, apart from one incident in which the entire engine cowling detached from one powerplant in flight.

Boeing and GE profited from the move, but P&W saw a sudden drop in sales. In some cases, P&W customers even changed to the competing engine when re-ordering 747s, or in the case of the USAF, re-engined their aircraft. The USAF became the first customer for the CF6 on the 747, when it selected the aircraft-engine combination for the airborne command post role in mid-1974 (see Chapter 8). The aircraft were designated E-4s, and the first two were handed over with P&W JT9D-7W engines. The third E-4, line number 232, was actually the first production 747 fitted with GE engines and was handed over to the USAF on October 15, 1974. The first two P&W-powered E-4s were re-engined with the CF6-50Es (known to the USAF as F103-GE-100 engines) in 1976. KLM meanwhile received its initial aircraft, a -200B Combi (a 747 variant discussed later in this chapter), line number 271, a year later in October 1975. The -50Es were capable of 52,500 pounds of thrust, which enabled the Combi's maximum takeoff weight to grow to 800,000 pounds.

Earlier that same year Rolls-Royce engines finally were fitted to the 747 when British Airways (BA) ordered four 747-200s on June 17, 1975, adding to its existing fleet of P&W-powered 747-100s. It had been a long struggle for Rolls to get aboard the big Boeing, mostly because it had to persuade the

From 1993 onward, airlines began inspecting and modifying the fuse pins and the engine mid-spar fittings, and also strengthening the upper link and diagonal braces, after a number of in-flight separations and two crashes. The cost was estimated at about $1 million per aircraft, with a downtime of up to 42 days. Here, the engine struts from a Polar Air Cargo 747-122F (SCD) receive treatment from U.K.-based FLS of Stansted. Note the difference in length and contours between the two outboard engine struts (farthest from the camera) and the inboard struts.

Belgian flag carrier Sabena used its two 747-129s on the two busiest trunk routes to New York and Kinshasa, capital of what was then the Belgian Congo. When Belgium gave independence to the new nation of Zaire, traffic dropped on the route, and the 747 was suddenly too big for the airline's remaining routes. Boeing hit upon the idea of cutting a side cargo door in the fuselage and making the aircraft into what were to become Combis. This aircraft, pictured here before its delivery in an all-passenger configuration in December 1970, returned to Boeing for conversion in April 1974. *Boeing*

British government that the investment would be worthwhile. The engine company depended on the government to fund half of the development of the more powerful -524 version of the RB.211 engine that had been developed originally for the Lockheed L-1011 TriStar. The engine program had been fraught with difficulty and eventually forced Rolls into bankruptcy. The British government stepped in and rescued the engine maker, but as its major creditor, effectively controlled the company's every move.

Rolls-Royce made the first run of the prototype RB.211-524 in October 1973 but required development aid to produce a production-quality engine for the TriStar and 747. The company hoped to have the -524 certificated by mid-1976, but the British government delayed its funding decision, costing the engine maker almost one valuable year. Eventually, in mid-1975, the government agreed to provide launch aid for the 50,000-pound-thrust engine and at the same time agreed in principle to support further development to

53,000 pounds of thrust. The British government's share, about half the estimated £45 million, was to be recovered by a levy on sales.

The first Rolls-powered 747, line number 292, made its maiden flight on September 3, 1976. Boeing test pilot Paul Bennett described the 111-minute flight as "very routine," which was an immense relief to the British engine maker. The RB.211-524 was noticeably quieter on the flight deck and had a lower idle thrust level on the ground. It also had the best cruise-

The side cargo door of this Air Canada 747-233B Combi can be seen in the port side of the rear fuselage as it touches down at Vancouver International, British Columbia. Note the local structural strengthening extending fore and aft at the base of the door and the inclined sill near the apex of the fuselage above the door; the sill prevents rainwater from running into the opening.

speed fuel consumption of any 747, but the engine was distinctly heavier per ship set than its rivals because of its triple-spool layout. Both GE and P&W engines were two-spool designs, a distinction that continues with their successors to this day. Despite the RB.211's heavier weight, the fuel economy of the Rolls engine meant the aircraft could fly longer routes. Importantly for BA, it offered about 700 nautical miles more range than the airline's original P&W-powered fleet of 747-136s carrying the same load, and could fly up to 15,000 pounds more payload from hot and high airfields like Nairobi, Kenya, to London.

On November 1, 1976, the Rolls-powered test aircraft established a new world record for maximum mass lifted to 2,000 meters (6,562 feet), when it took off from Lemoore Naval Air Station, California, at a weight of 840,500 pounds to complete noise flyover tests at 820,000

pounds. The aircraft reached the required altitude in 6 minutes, 33 seconds, and the record was later recognized officially by the Federation Aeronautique Internationale (FAI). The Rolls-powered 747, designated the 747-236, was certificated in May 1977, and the first airline-ready -236, line number 302, was handed over to BA on June 16. The 747 then became the first aircraft to be offered with all of the big-fan engines.

Pratt & Whitney fought back with a series of ever-more-powerful engines, ranging from the 50,000-pounds-wet-thrust JT9D-7F/7FW, which became available in 1975, to the 54,000-pound-thrust JT9D-7R4G2, the "R" reportedly standing for "Rosati," the P&W engineer who had seen the engine through to success from its nightmarish start. The first -200B to fly with the -7FW engine (rated at 48,000 pounds dry and 50,000 pounds wet), was line number 260 for Qantas. The aircraft had a max-

imum takeoff weight of 809,000 pounds and was equipped with optional 800-gallon extended-range fuel tanks for the Australian airline's long over-water routes. Total fuel capacity was increased to 53,160 gallon; the weight of this fuel load, more than 355,000 pounds, was greater than the maximum takeoff weight of a 707.

A later redesign of the engine, the 53,000-pound-thrust JT9D-70A, featured a long-chord fan cowling and shared a common nacelle with the JT9D on the DC-10-40 and Airbus A300. Despite the advantages of the shared cowling for operators with mixed fleets of Boeing and Douglas or Airbus jetliners, many operators preferred the shorter-chord cowling on the JT9D -7Q engine, which powered a Northwest 747 on May 23, 1979, when it achieved a new takeoff-weight record of 851,000 pounds. The -7Q-powered 747 was certificated by the

Two Swissair 747-357s bask in the bright fall sunshine at Zurich. The original SUD design emerged from Boeing's product development group with a 200-inch upper-deck extension, but this was further extended by another 80 inches after wind-tunnel tests showed a longer stretch would give better cruise-drag results.

FAA in September 1979, by which time 19 airlines had ordered 71 Boeing 747s powered by the JT9D-7Q engines. Singapore International Airlines (SIA) was so impressed by the increased performance it rechristened its aircraft "Super Bs."

The following year Boeing offered an optional increase in takeoff weight to 833,000 pounds with some changes to the engine pylons and uprated powerplants. Cargolux took a P&W-powered freighter uprated to the new weight in October 1980, though the first airline to opt for the higher weight aircraft was Qantas. Powered by 53,000-pound-thrust RB.211-524D4 engines, the Qantas aircraft could carry a maximum load of 436 passengers and 25,350 pounds of cargo over 6,275 miles compared with its earlier P&W-powered -200Bs, which carried the same payload over 5,295 miles. All three engine makers continued to offer higher powered engines for

the -200. Pratt & Whitney's efforts culminated with the 54,000-pound-thrust JT9D-7R4G and 56,000-pound-thrust JT9D -7R4H, while GE introduced its new CF6-80 series, which included the 54,000-pound-thrust CF6-80B and 56,700-pound-thrust CF6-80C281. Rolls-Royce eventually offered an RB.211-524 engine rated at 53,000 pounds of thrust for the "classic" 747s.

Freighters, Convertibles, and Combis

Although the 747 was built to be a cargo carrier from the very beginning, it was not until 1971 that the first freighter was built, and even then it was a -200 version, and not the -100. The -100 was offered in all-cargo and passenger/cargo convertible configurations, and orders were placed for both types. However, no 747-100s were actually built from scratch with the capability to carry cargo on the main deck, and orders for early freighters

were either canceled or converted to all-passenger aircraft before delivery. Some early aircraft were, however, later converted to cargo carriers by inserting a side loading door (see Chapter 8).

To begin with, Boeing confidently expected that up to half of the first 400 aircraft sold would be freighters. The predicted supersonic revolution never took place, however, so 747s kept on flying as passenger jets rather than being converted to freighters. In addition, the cargo market itself did not grow as quickly as forecast, with both yields and loads lower than hoped. The worldwide economic recession of the early 1970s destroyed any hopes of early growth. Last, due to insufficient power from the early engines and the growth of the aircraft's empty weight, the first 747s did not have sufficient power margin to operate efficiently with an upward-hinged nose door, one of the main features of the original freighter concept.

Boeing reprofiled the upper deck to incorporate the stretch by working aft from about where the emergency exit door on the standard upper deck was located. The extra 280 inches was inserted from the third window back on the upper deck to the fourth window aft of the new upper-deck door. The longer upper deck was faired into the fuselage much further aft, above the main-deck exit over the wing, rather than just behind the wing leading edge. Some of these production joins are faintly visible on this aircraft, *Big Boss*, belonging to French carrier UTA.

With the availability of the higher thrust JT9D engines, however, Boeing could at least lay the foundations for the -200F freighter, which was ordered into production by Lufthansa, the flag carrier of West Germany. The first 747-200F, line number 168, had a strengthened main-deck floor, cargo-handling and fire-detection systems, the upward-swinging nose door, and no passenger fittings. By the beginning of April 1971, the unusual nose, cockpit, and lower forward fuselage had arrived at Everett from Wichita and were fitted together for lengthy recycling tests to prove the huge hinge mechanism.

The first -200F was rolled out on October 14, 1971, and flew six weeks later. The aircraft was certificated by the FAA on March 7, 1972, after a speedy test program, and two days later was handed over to Lufthansa. The big freighter was put into service between Frankfurt and New York the following month, a few weeks ahead of schedule. The aircraft could carry 17,000 cubic feet of cargo, three times

that of the 707. Lufthansa demonstrated its capacity by loading in 73 Volkswagen cars.

Despite its capacity, the Lufthansa freighter remained alone in service for two years. At first, Boeing began to worry that the $54.2 million development cost of the -200F had been money wasted, but the -200F became a steady seller, and a total of 73 were delivered before production changed to the -400F in 1991. Sales were boosted by the $15 million development of an optional side door that could take 10-foot-high loads (as opposed to an 8-foot limit through the nose because of the flight-deck floor). The first to have the 11-foot-by-10-foot side door was line number 242 for Seaboard World. It was originally delivered with a maximum weight capability of 785,000 pounds, but with the later availability of more powerful P&W JT9D-70A engines, number 242 was returned to Everett for conversion and was redelivered with a maximum takeoff weight of 820,000 pounds. The last -200F, which was also

the very last -200 made, was delivered to Nippon Cargo on November 19, 1991, marking the end of a production run of 21 years.

The -200F was also the first version of the 747 to exhibit a previously unsuspected problem with engine mountings that eventually required inspections of almost 950 747s then in service. The drama began in December 1991 when a China Airlines -200F mysteriously crashed into the Taiwanese mountains. When investigators reached the scene, they discovered that the right wing inboard engine was missing from the debris. The search was expanded to cover the Formosa Straits, over which the 747 had flown prior to the accident. In July 1992, teams using sophisticated underwater equipment found the missing engine on the seabed. When the wreckage was raised, no trace could be found of the assembly that mounted the engine to the wing.

Three months later, an Israeli-operated 747-200F lost both starboard engines shortly after takeoff from Amsterdam and crashed into an apartment block while its pilot was attempting to return it to the airfield, killing the crew of four and more than 60 people on the ground. Following the accident in the Netherlands it took another seven months of scouring the seabed of the Formosa Straits before the missing attachment of the Taiwanese 747 was found. By then, however, Boeing already knew what it was up against. Worldwide inspections of the assembly, particularly engine-mounting "fuse" pins, had revealed widespread corrosion in first-generation pins and even some damage to a newer design pin that had been subsequently introduced on younger 747s. A major redesign of the engine mountings was undertaken, along with a change in engine-mounting philosophy.

In June 1993 the company released details of the modification, which involved installing two extra engine mountings. Made from corrosion-resistant steel, instead of carbon steel, they provided redundancy for the four existing mountings and prevented an engine falling off in flight, should any of the attachments fail. The new attachments also represented a change in thinking on 747 design. Originally, Boeing wanted 747 engines to break off cleanly under serious airborne stress—now it wanted them to stay on.

The 747 dated from a transition period in design philosophy. Until the late 1960s, all Boeing designs adopted the piston-era concept, which was that it was often safer to lose a severely damaged engine or an imbalanced propeller than have it cause damage to the wing. The 707, 720, 727, and first-generation 737 series all shared this feature, and safe in-flight engine separations did occur. Later models with higher bypass engines have been designed with fail-safe attachments that kept the engine on the wing, even if the powerplant failed. Even so, the engines on the later models were still designed to break off in the event of a ground impact to minimize the chances of rupturing the fuel tanks. The 747, by chance, stood at the crossroads of this design change. At the time of the revision, Boeing said, "The fuse pins were originally designed to hold the engine on the wing, even during an engine seizure. The fusing, or breaking, point was at the higher load that the seizure would impose on it. If anything happens on the ground, the engine is supposed to fuse and that still holds with the new design."

Before the redesign, 747 engines were connected to the wing in four places: an upper link to the front spar, a rear diagonal brace to an under-wing fitting, and two mid-spar mounts attached beneath the wing. The new mountings consisted of two more steel attachments set between the mid-spar fitting. Each of the attachments comprised two 9.5-inch stainless-steel bars bolted in the fitting. Larger mid-spar fittings, along with a stronger diagonal brace and upper link used on new-production 747-400s, were also fitted to earlier models as part of the redesign.

The new problem seemed to be growing when, in March 1993, an Evergreen International Airlines 747-100F lost an engine shortly after take-off from Anchorage International. The huge engine fell into the parking lot of a shopping mall, injuring no one, luckily. Suspicion immediately fell on the fuse pins, but an inquiry later blamed severe turbulence for exceeding the strength of the entire engine pylon, or strut. This 747F landed safely.

Boeing and the airlines faced the huge task of inspecting and modifying 948 of the 747s, at an estimated cost of $1 million per aircraft, which was shared between Boeing and the airlines. The manufacturer figured that between 35 and 42 days of downtime per aircraft would be required and that all modifications should be completed by 1998. Each aircraft had to have all four pylons removed, wing root and ribs inspected and repaired, and the modified pylons re-attached. Large 747 operators such as SIA, with more than 50 in its fleet, opened dedicated modification lines at their bases, in this case Changi International Airport, and offered the facility to other airlines. Singapore even bought a complete 747 wing from Boeing for $100,000 to help train its workforce.

While dedicated freighters provided one option, Boeing was anxious to provide operators with the cargo potential of the 747, without necessarily making them lose the chance of using the aircraft for passengers. The company's first solution was a convertible 747-200C passenger/freighter, which could be used as an all-passenger aircraft in summer months when cargo traffic was low and as a freighter during the winter when this trend was normally reversed. The -100C had been a flop, with no takers other than World Airways, which had deferred its order, but this was understandable in view of early performance limitations. Even so, Boeing voted to go ahead with the $14.6 million 747-200C development effort, and the first aircraft, line number 209, was rolled out at Everett on February 28, 1973. The aircraft made its maiden flight a month later. In April it was certificated by the FAA and delivered to the launch customer, which was none other than char-ter airline World Airways, on April 27. Despite the novelty of the idea, sales were relatively disappointing with only 13 sold at a rate of roughly one a year between 1973 and 1988.

True success on the other hand was found with the 747-200M, or Combi as it was better known. "That was another terrific idea developed by the engineers for me to save [the sale of] two airplanes at Sabena," said Joe Sutter. "When Sabena lost the Congo and only had the North Atlantic left, the 747s were too big for them, although they still needed the freight capacity. I went to Sabena and showed them sketches for putting a cargo door in the side, and putting freight in the back and passengers up front. We put together a contract in that room and brought their airplanes to Everett [for conversion]. We were only building one 747 a month at the time. The Combi took off like wildfire."

Assembly of the first Combi, line number 250, began in 1974. It was rolled out at the end of October and made its maiden flight on November 18. Air Canada took delivery of the first -200 Combi on March 7, 1975, and used it the following winter to replace a stretched DC-8 on the London-Toronto route, allowing an almost daily service. By March 1976, Combi utilization was well ahead of standard passenger aircraft, despite fears that cargo loading would cause delays. Sabena was reporting 11.1 hours per day, Air Canada about 11 hours and KLM 9.5 hours, compared with the average 747 fleet level of the day of 8.8 hours. In all, some 78 Series 200 Combis were delivered between 1975 and 1988, not counting several other conversions.

Airlines liked the Combi because, with six main-deck cargo positions, it offered about the same passenger capacity as a wide-body trijet (DC-10 or L1011) and the cargo capacity of a 707 or DC-8 freighter. "The 747 Combi was one of the smartest buys we ever made," said Sabena. In a classic example of Parkinson's Law in action, its two Combis gradually built up cargo service from Brussels to New York from the equivalent of two 707 freighters per

In February 1997, KLM became the first airline to commit to an extensive cockpit upgrade of its 747 Classics. The $53 million modernization included the installation of seven Smiths Industries active matrix liquid crystal display screens in each aircraft; digital fuel monitoring systems; a condition monitoring, flight management system with satellite and inertial navigation; and the introduction of the ACARS airline communications, addressing, and reporting system.

week to the equivalent of two 707 freighters a day. Sabena's Combis were arranged so that one zone in the cabin could be converted within 1.5 hours from a six-pallet cargo area to a 116-seat passenger section. All seats were mounted on pallets (like cargo containers) and could be loaded by means of the existing cargo roller system. Lavatories and galleys were left fixed in position. The airline frequently converted the aircraft using this layout for its busy weekend flights from Belgium to the European sun-spot destinations of Majorca in the Balearic Islands and Tenerife in the Canary Islands.

Combi operations continued safely and successfully until disaster struck in November 1987, when a South African Airways (SAA) -200B Combi crashed into the Indian Ocean en route to the island of Mauritius. The last transmissions from the crew,

who perished along with more than 150 passengers, said that smoke was in the cockpit. Many months later, after a painstaking deep-sea salvage operation, the investigation concluded that a fire had developed on a freight pallet in the main deck area and quickly burned out of control. The board of inquiry found that the smoke-detector systems and fire-fighting equipment were inadequate. The board also found that the pressure lock between the cargo compartment and the main passenger section was not strong enough to prevent the smoke from spreading forward.

Big changes were implemented as a result of the findings, including the mandatory use of higher standard fire-resistant ceiling and sidewall liner panels in the cargo compartment. More powerful fire-extinguishing systems and fire-fighting equip-

ment were also required that would give the crew time to find and put out the fire. In addition, all cargo from then on was to be carried in flame-penetration-resistant containers with built-in smoke detectors and fire-extinguishing systems.

Sales of the 747-200B began to wind down into the mid-1980s as airlines switched their attention to the 747-300 and later the 747-400. Before giving way, the -200 family had a profound impact on the destiny of the 747. Boeing delivered 393 of the 747-200Bs, making it the most popular version of the big jetliner, up until the emergence of the 747-400.

Stretched Upper Deck and the 747-300

Throughout the first decade of 747 operations, airlines had continued to clamor for extra payload and range. Even though -200B versions with progressively higher weight had become available, as engine power allowed, the airlines still asked for more range and passenger capacity. Boeing believed it could meet the range demand with a version designated the 747SP (see Chapter 5) and, in parallel, studied a selection of possible stretches to increase passenger capacity. After years of deliberation, Boeing announced the go-ahead of the most modest of these stretches on June 11, 1980, one that would enter service as the 747-300. Boeing's solution to the capacity question was a stretched upper deck (SUD), which simply extended the hump further aft by 23 feet, 4 inches. The new SUD would seat about 44 more than the standard -200B in typical circumstances. This provided room ultimately for up to 91 passengers in the upper deck in an all-economy layout, a far cry from the exclusive, club-like upper deck of the original 747, with its seating for just eight.

Changes were also made to the main cabin, creating the largest capacity passenger aircraft in history. A grand total of 660 could be carried by placing five pairs of wider Type A exits on the main deck, which would accommodate 550. The upper deck was also given two larger exits and extra windows. The familiar mid-stairway of the -200Bs and later -100s, which replaced the original circular stairway of the first -100s, was superseded by a new straight stairway that led upward to the aft section of the upper deck. In practice, no airline ever used the full seating potential of the 747-300, though French carrier Corsair achieved a seating record in the mid-1990s by fitting out a -300 in all-economy configuration with seating for 580. Even the airline's -200Bs, such as its former KLM aircraft, were converted by Bedek-IAI, to seat 534.

The SUD, or extended upper deck (EUD), was launched with an order for four from Swissair. The aircraft was originally offered as a SUD version of the -200B, and indeed an earlier aircraft already on order for the Swiss airline was to be "delayed to incorporate the stretch," according

to the airline. By the time the first aircraft (line number 570) was rolled out, however, the SUD/EUD effort was redesignated the 747-300. This identity originally had been loosely attached to the extra-long-range 747 studies in the mid-1970s which later emerged as the 747SP.

The only real problem with the 747-300 was that the extra structure of the upper deck increased empty weight by about 10,000 pounds compared with the -200B, limiting range to 5,600 nautical miles with 452 passengers and baggage. Compensating for this, the largely unexpected bonus was that the aerodynamically refined contouring of the longer upper deck reduced drag, increasing the typical top cruise speed from Mach 0.84 to 0.85, keeping the 747 well ahead of its nearest subsonic rivals.

The first 747-300, a Combi version, was rolled out on September 15, 1982, and made its first flight on October 5. A passenger version flew for the first time on December 10, 1982, and was delivered to French airline UTA on March 1, 1983, five days before Swissair took delivery of its first 747-300 Combi. In all, some 21 Combi versions of the -300 were sold, but although offered, no freighters were delivered. Total sales of passenger versions reached a rather disappointing 60, although later potential sales were diverted to the 747-400.

Another group of 747s was built between 1984 and 1986 under the 747-200 SUD program. These aircraft were so similar to the 747-300 that even Boeing production workers could not tell them apart. The SUD was initially offered as an option for new-build -100 and -200 aircraft, but following the decision to designate the SUD/EUD initiative as the -300 series, the SUD title was applied to aircraft that were converted from -200s. KLM was the major customer for the option as part of a deal struck with Boeing in October 1983, one month after the airline received its first 747-300. In addition to agreeing to buy one more -300, the Netherlands flag-carrier also returned

all 10 of its GE -powered 747-200Bs to Boeing for conversion to SUDs.

Boeing hoped the option would not only help stimulate new sales but would also provide new work for the Everett plant, where the 747 production rate had been in decline since peaking at seven per month in 1980. By the time the -300 was being rolled out, the rate had plummeted to less than two per month. In late 1983, the order book had dried up even more, and production for the following year dropped to an all-time low of one per month.

The modification work on the 10 Dutch 747s was extensive and involved removing half of the upper fuselage as far back as the leading edge of the wing. Three new upper fuselage sections were then built on, while interior modifications were also performed. The first aircraft arrived back at Everett in late 1984. Almost three months later, in December of that year, the jetliner returned to the Netherlands as a "new" 747-200 SUD. Two more KLM -200Bs and seven -200B Combis arrived in 1985 for the same treatment, and the last of them flew back to Europe in March 1986. Boeing also modified two GE-powered -200s with upper decks for UTA of France and built two new short-range SUD versions of the high-gross-weight 747-100B (see Chapter 8) for JAL. The first aircraft, line number 636, carrying the rather complicated designation 747-100B (SR/SUD), was completed in the winter of 1986 and was delivered (and certificated) on March 24.

In all 95 747s were built with SUDs, of which 81 were -300s, 12 were -200 SUDs, and 2 were -100B (SR/SUDs). The numbers themselves, although not large by Boeing standards, were important for keeping the 747 line busy during a relatively flat period for six vital years in the early to mid-1980s. The true importance of the -300 and its other SUD contemporaries was in providing the structural foundation for the next-generation 747-400, thereby providing the launch pad for the most successful version to be built.

CHAPTER FIVE

The short, stubby-looking 747SP stands out in Boeing history for two main reasons. First, it was the first of the entire jetliner family to be shortened, rather than stretched. Second, only 45 were built, making it the smallest production run of any 747 variant and one of the most commercially limited jetliners sold by Boeing.

Ironically, the aircraft itself was to prove a technical triumph. When it entered service the 747SP had the capability of flying further, higher, and

faster than any other subsonic airliner. It consistently broke world records for altitude, speed, distance, and payload, some of which remained unbroken 20 years later. In addition, the development of the aircraft posed some unique challenges, which stretched Boeing in new directions and gave it valuable experience for future programs.

The roots of the 747SP go back to 1971, when the first generation of wide-bodied trijets were being introduced. The Lockheed L-1011 TriStar and the

The pronounced vertical tail extension and shortened fuselage gave the 176-foot, 9-inch SP a distinctively squat appearance from the side. The first SP, line number 265, flies over Washington state's Puget Sound area on an early test sortie in 1975. Following certification in February 1976, the aircraft was reregistered N530PA and renamed *Clipper Mayflower* for Pan Am, which took delivery of the aircraft in late April that year. *Boeing*

McDonnell Douglas DC-10 were selling well and fitted neatly into a niche between Boeing's stalwart 169-seat 707 and the 380-seat 747. The early trijets were soon plying across the continental United States and over similar distances elsewhere around the globe, but they rarely ventured on longer-haul routes. Realizing the sales potential of the long-range market, McDonnell Douglas quickly began development of the intercontinental DC-10-30/40 models. Both intercontinental DC-10 versions were certificated within a month of each other in 1972. while Lockheed worked on similar plans for an extended-range L-1011.

Airlines started to view the longer-range trijets with hungry anticipation. They would become the ideal way of expanding "long, thin" routes, which were the domain of 707-320s and DC-8-60s. These first-generation jetliners were getting older and needed replacing. They also operated routes that could not support aircraft as big as the 747.

Sensing an important opportunity, Boeing began searching for a solution. One possible option was a long-range version of the 7X7, a 200-plus-seat "paper" airplane study that was aimed mainly at short to medium routes. The problems were obvious. First, the market was emerging quickly, and so were the competitors. The time taken to develop an all-new design, not to mention the cost, would be hard to justify given the ready availability of the DC-10-30/40 and extended-range L-1011s. The airlines would simply not wait for Boeing to develop a long-range 7X7 while their competitors were flying the new trijets.

"People asked us if we could do anything to get into this game," said Joe Sutter. "We said let's shorten the 747 and see what we can make of it. Some of the sales and management people laughed at us, but we thought we could make it work by taking the weight out of it and giving it the right passenger/range combination." The option had logic on its side. The 747 was currently in production and a derivative, no matter how radical,

The enormous structural strength of the 747SP was amply demonstrated by this aircraft on February 5, 1985, when it dived out of control for 30,000 feet over the Pacific, reaching close to the speed of sound. The SP was at 41,000 feet when the number four engine apparently failed. The crew called for permission to descend and carry out an air-start. Suddenly, the aircraft slipped out of control and went into a spiral dive toward the ocean. The crew fought for control as pieces of the control surfaces and undercarriage were ripped off. Finally, at 11,000 feet, the crew stabilized the SP and by 9,000 feet arrested the descent by relighting the three working engines, which had flamed out in the dive. The aircraft limped into San Francisco for an emergency landing and was later repaired. It is seen here at Hong Kong seven years to the month after its brush with catastrophe.

right and below; Boeing's first serious study into shortening the 747 was the -3 concept developed in 1968. The -3 was, however, a very different beast than the SP, as it was aimed at competing against the DC-10 and L-1011 on the transcontinental routes. It was configured with a range of 2,650 nautical miles, half that of the SP, with room for 301 passengers. The 200-foot-long, 175-foot-span aircraft would have had a takeoff gross weight of 490,000 pounds, compared to 700,000 pounds offered as a maximum option on the SP. *Boeing*

would be easier and less costly to develop than a new aircraft. Not only would a shorter 747 be available in half the time of an all-new model, but its commonality would also appeal to the ever-growing number of 747-100 and -200 operators. Boeing also had the option of studying derivatives of a derivative. It could use basic elements of the current 747 and mix and match with new parts. The fuselage, for example, was basic to most design studies, but wings, engines, and tails could be changed.

The biggest challenge was how to tailor the basic design of a short-bodied 747 to produce the operational costs of a trijet like the DC-10-30/40. These costs were expressed in terms of seat-per-mile costs: how much it would cost the airline in dollars to fly one passenger one mile. At the same time, Boeing had to ensure that the aircraft-per-mile costs were lower than for the then-top-of-the-range 747 model, the -200B. Aircraft-per-mile cost is another method of calculating the overall economics of flying an airliner in revenue service and refers to the cost in dollars of flying the aircraft on a per-mile basis as a breakdown of airframe, engine, and equipment costs, crew expenses, fuel used, and so on.

Boeing's other major design goals were largely tied to achieving commonality with the basic 747. These included retaining the handling and flight characteristics of the bigger aircraft because this would cut down on crew-training expense. Operational and maintenance commonality was also high up the list

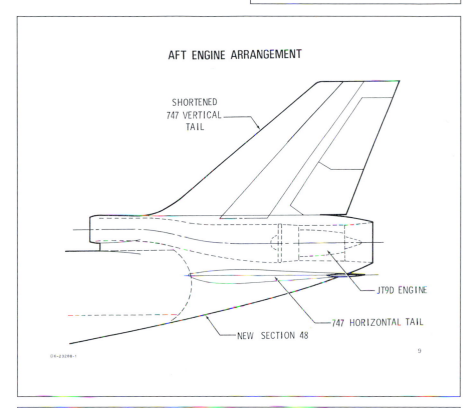

AFT ENGINE ARRANGEMENT

SHORTENED 747 VERTICAL TAIL

JT9D ENGINE

747 HORIZONTAL TAIL

NEW SECTION 48

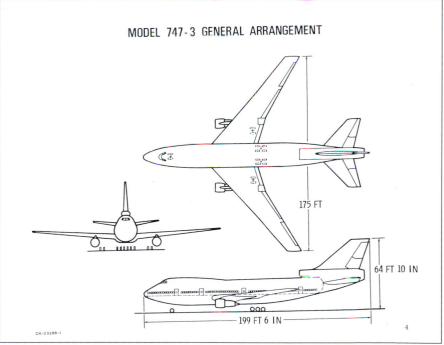

MODEL 747-3 GENERAL ARRANGEMENT

175 FT

64 FT 10 IN

199 FT 6 IN

One of two 747SP-B5s delivered to Korean Air Lines in 1980 and 1981 is pushed back for departure at Hong Kong. Asian carriers were able to make use of the SP's unprecedented range on transpolar and transpacific routes, both of which later became regular routes for the 747-400. Note the double-hinged rudder and revised fuselage contouring around the base of the fin, particularly near the dorsal and below the registration number.

because this would cut the need for unique spares and reduce the requirement for new ground equipment and staff training. Finally, and very important in its war against the trijets, the new 747 would have to exceed the takeoff, payload, range, speed, and initial cruise-altitude performance of its competitors.

Options and Decisions

One of Boeing's early design dilemmas was the number of engines to put on the 747 derivative. Some held out that to be competitive against trijets, the new 747 should also be a trijet. This was a valid point, as the weight associated with the four P&W JT9Ds, related systems, and hardware on the standard 747 added up to almost 57,000 pounds. Simple math suggested that 14,000 pounds of weight could be saved by opting for a trijet configuration. In addition to weight, the removal of an engine would have simplified operations, reduced the number of systems, and cut down fuel burn, a major concern at a time when the Arab oil embargo was still fresh in the memory of aircraft designers and airline executives alike. Statistically, and somewhat ironically, supporters of the trijet plan also pointed out that the removal of one engine meant one less powerplant to give technical problems.

Like everything in aircraft design, however, taking off one engine was not as simple as it sounded. To start with, where would the third engine go? Boeing looked at bizarre arrangements with two engines grouped together on one wing with one on the other. It then studied a more classic trijet arrangement with the number two engine buried in the root of the tail fin and the horizontal stabilizer attached to the top of the tail in a 727-like configuration. It even blew the dust off a preliminary trijet study, dubbed the 747-3, which had been hurriedly put together in 1968 in an abortive attempt to thwart the sale of DC-10s to Northwest Orient. Removing engines from the wing also meant that the wing itself would have needed a redesign to adapt to the different stress

A fine air-to-air study of the first Qantas 747SP-38, *City of Gold Coast Tweed*, shortly before its delivery in January 1981. The one-piece engine nacelles reveal this to be a Rolls-Royce RB.211-524-powered version, of which six were sold. The SP was also offered with the P&W JT9D-7 and the -3AW, as well as the GE CF6-45A or -50E2, though no operator selected the GE option. *Boeing*

and loading characteristics. An inherent advantage of a four-engine design in which the engines are slung below the wing is that the structure of the wing can be made relatively flexible and light.

The design team saw that the trijet option created as many problems as it solved. It therefore returned to the simpler philosophy of a basic short-bodied fuselage, mounted on the same wing, with four engines.

Boeing's deliberations became more urgent as Pan Am announced it had a firm requirement for an aircraft for long, thin routes. Rumors abounded that the DC-10-30/40 or -30SB was a firm favorite for the contract through early 1973. Lockheed pitched in with counter proposals with the TriStar -2LR, following a guarantee from Rolls-Royce that it would develop a more powerful version of the aircraft's RB.211 turbofan. Although unsuccessful in this sales attempt, Lockheed later sold Pan Am a fleet of the long-range TriStar 500, itself a short-bodied version of the basic L-1011 design.

Boeing was working on its own comeback, but not everyone was in full agreement on its approach. "We developed a configuration and showed it to some of our management people, but they didn't think it made much sense," recalled Sutter. Then fate took a hand, according to Sutter: "John Borge and a colleague were coming out here to work on what eventually became the 767, and Borge always wanted to know what was happening with the 747. We had about 15 minutes to show him what we called the 747SB—or short body. By this time, Row Brown and I had convinced ourselves it was a good idea, but we were about the only ones, and very few others thought more of it.

"Borge and his colleague flew back on the red-eye to New York and talked about it all night. When they arrived, they went straight to the boss of Pan Am and told him all about it. He called [Malcolm] Stamper and said, 'Are you guys serious?' I was in the hot seat because of it, but we decided to do

something about it. I spent all day with the marketing people to come up with a better name than SB…which most people were by then calling 'Sutter's Balloon!' They eventually came up with 'SP' for 'Special Performance.'"

In August 1973, Boeing made its pitch to the board and predicted that up to 214 747SPs could be sold between 1976 and 1985, producing a net increase in 747 sales of 183 aircraft. It estimated that the SP would replace only 31 anticipated basic 747 sales, and that the stubby aircraft would generate total sales revenues of $5.9 billion over the next 10 years. "Douglas is the principal competitor hurt by the 747SP program," claimed the pitch document. "They should lose 149 DC-10-30/40 sales valued at $4.8 billion." It predicted Pan Am was the leading domestic sales candidate with a requirement for 20, while JAL, El Al, and Qantas provided the best chance of foreign sales, accounting for a combined 28 aircraft.

Near-term sales potential was pegged at 48, with sales from 1976 to 1978 anywhere between 85 and 143 aircraft. The marketeers predicted that Boeing should gear up to produce a "nominal" 96 747SPs by 1978. The break-even point for the program was set at 45 aircraft, based on a unit sales price of about $27 million. Non-recurring development costs were estimated at about $193 million. When added to the $21.5 million production cost of making up to 50 aircraft, this translated into a unit cost of $25.4 million. The unit cost naturally went down with an increased production run and was forecast to be $22.3 million for a run of up to 100 SP aircraft and as low as $20.6 million for a run of up to 200.

A combination of commonality, cost, and predicted performance won Pan Am back from the brink of ordering the DC-10, and at the beginning of September 1973 Boeing announced it was going ahead "incrementally" with the short-bodied 747. Toward the end of the month, Pan Am formally announced an order for 10 747SPs, with deliveries starting in 1976. The deal was valued at

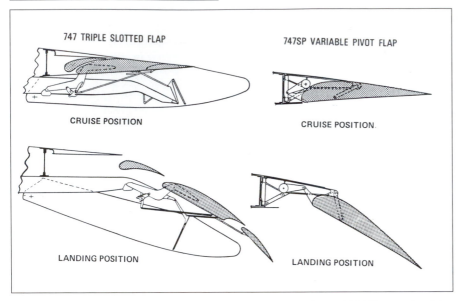

747 TRIPLE SLOTTED FLAP

CRUISE POSITION

LANDING POSITION

747SP VARIABLE PIVOT FLAP

CRUISE POSITION

LANDING POSITION

The radically simpler flap design of the SP (right) helped shave almost 12,5000 pounds off the weight of the wing set. *Boeing*

$280 million, including spares and options on a further 15 aircraft. It was Pan Am's first major commitment to a new aircraft in seven years. Not counting spares, the aircraft were sold at a cost of $27 million each, some $3 million less than the standard 747 at the time. By the time the first aircraft were handed over, three years later, actual fly-away cost was about $31 million. Once again Pan Am had launched a new Boeing jetliner.

The Final Configuration

Boeing sized the 747SP to carry 281 passengers in a typical mixed-class layout, against 385 in the standard -100s and -200Bs then being produced. The shorter cabin size meant that fuselage length was reduced by 48 feet, 4 inches to 176 feet, 9 inches, making it slightly longer than the 707-320 and around the same length as the 767-300 that was to follow a decade later.

At first glance, the 747SP looked as if Boeing had simply taken out a couple of slices of fuselage and then stuck the remaining pieces back together. The reality was far more complicated. It involved some clever engi-

neering to achieve common handling and flying qualities with the larger 747. Not only were handling qualities retained, but performance was reoptimized to new levels because weight and drag had been reduced. In all, about 42,000 pounds had been trimmed from the empty weight.

Although commonality was the key to keeping the 747SP affordable, a large proportion of the massive fuselage needed to be changed. Despite the enormous length of the standard 747 fuselage, very little was actually parallel-sided, so cutting length involved more than removing "plugs." A section of fuselage forward of the front wing spar was removed as was the roof section of the next section back. This latter piece was taken out to make room for the fairing of the raised upper deck, which now became flush with the fuselage over the mid-chord position of the wing rather than by the leading edge. The nose section (Section 41) remained unchanged, but the large wing-body fairing was replaced with a smaller, or "cropped," fillet. Additional stiffeners and soundproofing were also added to the upper lobe

section, mostly due to its proximity to the wing, and the front wing spar/fuselage frame was also modified.

Other portions of the fuselage were removed from aft of the trailing edge and forward of the rear pressure bulkhead. The center section was redesigned to save weight and an entirely new fuselage section was produced to replace the long piece removed from forward of the pressure bulkhead. The new aft section was considerably shorter, but it still had to mate up to the existing narrow tail structure. As a result, the SP aft fuselage was unusually contoured, giving the impression that it had been squeezed into the tail.

In addition, the base of the fin in the reprofiled tail section ended up 38 inches lower than on the basic 747. Together with an additional 60 inches added to the top of the fin, this resulted in the SP tail becoming 24 inches taller overall than the basic 747's tail, giving it a slightly more slender appearance. The fin height was increased to compensate for the reduced fin moment arm. Additional changes to the tail included the use of a double-hinged rudder. The entire tail section was also rotated up one degree to help counteract the predicted effect of the shorter body on directional stability. The strength of the fin torque box, which forms the structural heart of the tail, was also improved to take the higher rudder actuator loads. To help counter expected changes in pitch characteristics, the tips of the horizontal stabilizers were also extended by 60 inches. Finally, a new dorsal fin was fitted to help aerodynamic flow over the recontoured area around the base of the fin.

Weight was attacked from the beginning, with much of the effort put into the wing. The overall shape was basically a standard 747 wing planform but reduced-gauge materials were used for the spars, ribs, skin, and stringers in the wing box and center section. This was possible because the reduced takeoff weight meant the SP would operate at lower wing loadings (120 pounds per square foot compared

Some unexpected local airflow changes, including a drag-inducing shock wave, were discovered during testing. The wing-fuselage fillet was redesigned as a result with more contouring over the top of the wing. The forward section of the fillet is shown here on this 747SP-31, which was originally delivered to TWA in 1980. In 1985, it began a new life as a VIP transport for the United Arab Emirates' Dubai Air Wing.

with 140 pounds per square foot on the 747-200B). The wings were also fitted with simpler flaps, something that was readily observable to anyone watching the SP land. The complex but highly efficient triple-slotted devices of the standard 747 were replaced with single-slotted flaps with a new support structure. The entire design was geared for increased reliability and reduced weight.

Ultimately, the SP wing ended up almost 12,500 pounds lighter than the 88,537-pound wing set of the 747-100. The fuselage came second for weight reduction, losing more than 11,000 pounds and resulting in a final body weight of 59,515 pounds. The larger vertical tail on the other hand, with its more complex rudder and stronger torque box, gained almost 1,500 pounds, and the improved nose gear put on an extra 230 pounds. In the end, Boeing pared off an impressive 44,100 pounds to give the aircraft an operating empty weight of 315,000 pounds, compared to almost 360,000 pounds for the 747-100.

Testing the Special Performer

The 747SP first flew on July 4, 1975, 10 days ahead of the official target date set at the launch of the program in 1973. Jack Waddell, who had captained the first flight of the 747, was in command of the crew who left Paine Field to conduct "the most ambitious maiden flight ever undertaken," said Boeing. The flight was truly spectacular. Accompanied by the company F-86 Sabre chase plane, the crew completed a preliminary evaluation of handling and systems, airspeed calibration, and fuel consumption. After discovering that the new flap system was trouble-free, the crew performed a stall—a dramatic event for a maiden flight. They did not stop there. The SP was flown through the full speed range from stall right up to Mach 0.92. During the 3-hour-4-minute flight, the aircraft reached 30,000 feet and 630 miles per hour and performed a basic assessment of flutter up to the maximum permitted speed for all operations (Mmo).

Even more unusually, the aircraft was flown for a second test flight, lasting 52 minutes, later the same day. Boeing faced a tight test program because certification was scheduled by the end of the year, and Pan Am expected to take delivery of its first aircraft early the following year. By October, the first two aircraft were flying and had built up 160 hours between them. The first SP had by then moved down to Edwards AFB, where it was using the extraordinarily long runways at the desert base to establish landing and takeoff distances.

Already, some milestones had been passed, including stall-testing and full flutter clearance. Landing performance proved slightly better than expected, in spite of its simpler flap system, which Boeing introduced to save weight and cost. During automatic-brake-system testing, a low-weight 747SP landed into a light wind and came to a full stop in 1,600 feet, the normal landing distance of a light twin-engined aircraft. This was also remarkable given that the primary (turbine) thrust reverser had been deleted, saving more than 1,100 pounds in weight. Fan reversers were retained.

The aircraft also proved itself a high-flyer and was cleared for an in-service maximum operating altitude of 45,100 feet. Even at the slightly higher altitude of 46,000 feet, Boeing discovered that the 747SP's relatively bigger wing gave the aircraft a rate of climb of 600 feet per minute. Clinching good high-altitude performance was vital to the 747SP marketing plan. Boeing predicted that airlines would be attracted to an aircraft that could cruise in the smoother air of the higher altitudes, avoiding the congestion of the crowded lower levels and saving fuel at the same time.

It was not all good news, however, and the certification target date slipped from December 1975 into January 1976 as problems emerged. One of these concerned the discovery of an unexpected local shock wave around the cropped wing-fuselage fillet. This was later cured by reprofiling the fillet. The drag from the unusually shaped aft fuselage, on the other hand, was not as bad as once feared.

Despite a 9 percent forward shift in the shorter SP's center of gravity, plus a 30 percent reduction in tail moment arm, Boeing aimed for the same rotation and takeoff characteristics as the standard aircraft's characteristics. Rotation-rate targets were therefore about 3 degrees per second for a lightly loaded aircraft and about 1.5 degrees per second at heavy weights. Pitch attitude was generally limited to about 15 degrees, particularly if fuel loads were less than 20,000 pounds. A SAA-owned 747SP-44, leased to Air Mauritius, is pictured on climb out.

The SP's automatic landing system was more advanced than the basic 747 system when first introduced. With a sink rate of less than 3 feet per second, the system could "spot" the SP into a 1,000-foot-by-46-foot box on the runway 95 percent of the time. This 747SP-94 was delivered to Syrian Arab Airlines as *Arab Solidarity* in July 1976.

Clipper Constitution poses for the camera ship before delivery in March 1976. After almost 10 years in service with Pan Am it was sold to United. *Boeing*

The flight tests also revealed that the stabilizer trim was about one degree more nose-up than expected, but the trim stability matched predictions. The extra nose-up trim slightly reduced control column forces and small adjustments were made to the aircraft's artificial-feel system to maintain the correct amount of force. The larger horizontal tail surfaces also eliminated any prospects of Mach-tuck characteristics cropping up.

The shorter fuselage also resulted in a 50 percent reduction in pitch inertia compared with its larger sibling. Uncorrected, this meant that full use of the standard 747 spoilers and speed brakes (located on top of the wings) could potentially cause the aircraft to pitch violently. Through trial and error, the test team limited two pairs of spoilers (3,4 and 9,10) to 30 degrees rather than the usual 45 degrees for speed-brake operation. The inboard spoiler pair (6 and 7) were rigged to operate automatically when either the left or right wheels touched the runway, but the test team discovered it was not necessary to inhibit the operation of the outboard spoilers (1 and 2) in any way.

One area where the shorter length of the aircraft was expected to cause some problems was in its ability to rotate during the takeoff roll at various trim settings. The minimum unstick speed (Vmu), or lowest speed at which an aircraft can safely rotate and lift off the runway, had been a sensitive issue since the first days of jet airliners when a number of crashes involving the British de Havilland Comet 1 were caused by "over-rotation" or rotating too soon. Even some versions of the 707 had been fitted with a large dorsal fin below the tail that doubled as a stabilizer and a guard against over-rotation. Boeing's concerns with the SP related to two main factors: A 9 percent forward shift in the center of gravity caused by the shorter fuselage and the reduction in tail moment arm by 30 percent. The 747 prototype was used to measure nosewheel lift-off speeds with varying elevator settings, and as it turned out, the result showed that the SP had plenty of rotation margin. Nevertheless, a variable-trim "green band" was developed for the SP to provide good takeoff trim rotation

characteristics, while at the same time keeping a wide mis-trim margin. The system was later adopted for the -200 and subsequent 747 versions. Some handling changes were also produced on landing. Waddell recalled that "The one area where it differed from the standard airplane was on touchdown, when the nose wanted to drop a little bit quicker."

A large part of the test effort was also dedicated to proving the performance and structural adequacy of the larger rudder, which was fitted with a geared trim tab that extended to 50 percent of the rudder chord. The aircraft was tested in strong crosswind landings and with excessive side slip. Approaches were also made with one engine turned off to assess the capabilities of the rudder. To Boeing's delight, the results showed that minimum control speeds were actually slightly lower than predicted. However, not everything went to plan, and on one late test flight to evaluate performance at high "Q" (high indicated airspeed at low altitude), the lower rudder section developed sudden flutter and disintegrated. "It was probably more startling to the chase pilot, because we didn't even really notice it," said Waddell. Panel fastenings in the fin structure were made stronger as a result.

The tests also included an assessment of the SP's automatic flight-control system and automatic landing system, which contained some improvements over the same systems on the basic 747. Automatic landings were declared to be excellent, with the SP system achieving a tight touchdown "footprint." Results showed the system would land an aircraft within a box measuring just over 1,000 feet long by 46 feet wide more than 95 percent of the time. The new system also produced a sink rate of less than 3 feet per second after the autothrottle was adjusted.

As the intensive test effort wound up in late January 1976, Boeing was increasingly confident in the SP. Take-off gross weights were available ranging from 660,000 pounds to 690,000 pounds with only minor changes to wheels, tires, and brakes required. (This was later extended right up to 700,000 pounds.) Payload-range was within 0.1 percent of the original goal and cruise Mach number, at 0.85, was 0.01 Mach higher than expected. With P&W JT9D-7 engines, the aircraft's specific air range was also within 1.25 percent of estimates. When combined with the aircraft weight, which came out at about 1 percent less than expected, the result was a long-range cruise performance 0.1 percent better than expected. The company knew that even such a small advantage could make or break a sale. The long-range trijets, particularly the DC-10-30, and even Boeing's own progressively heavier 747-200Bs were direct threats to the SP. It tacitly acknowledged that the SP would be perfect for routes of 5,700 nautical miles or longer, but secretly feared that this niche would prove too small for market success.

Demonstrations and Service Entry

Boeing decided the best way to advertise the long legs of the SP was by breaking a few long-distance records. On November 12, with three months still to go before certification, the fourth 747SP flew nonstop from New York to Tokyo with 200 passengers in a flying time of 13 hours, 33 minutes, setting a record.

Passengers on the flight included Pan Am chairman William Seawell, several senior Boeing personnel, and a party of 15 from JAL, which operated DC-8-62s on the same route, with a refueling stop at Anchorage, Alaska. JAL had not ordered the aircraft but knew that Pan Am planned to use the SP on new direct services linking Tokyo with New York and Los Angeles.

The aircraft took off at a gross weight of 675,000 pounds, nearly half of which was made up of fuel. During the flight, the aircraft achieved Mach 0.86 and a height of 49,000 feet and landed at Tokyo with more than 30,000 pounds of fuel remaining after flying a distance of 6,927 miles. The flight proved some essential points for Boeing, particularly that the SP's fuel burn performance was about 27 per-

This SAA-owned 747SP-44 also operated long-range flights under lease for Air Mauritius, UTA, and Luxair before flying in the bright livery of Air Namibia. Although displaced by the 747-400 in SAA service, the aircraft proved a useful long hauler for Air Namibia for its European routes from 1991 onward.

cent better per seat than a typical long-range narrow-body.

After Tokyo, the aircraft continued on a month-long world demonstration tour covering 700,000 miles, including a 7,130-mile nonstop flight from Sydney, Australia, to Santiago, Chile. It later flew from the high-altitude airport at Mexico City directly to Belgrade, in what was then Yugoslavia, covering a distance of 7,140 miles. High-altitude takeoffs were also conducted from La Paz, Bolivia, which at 13,354 feet above sea level, is the highest large commercial airport in the world.

The 747SP was granted its type certificate by the FAA on February 4, 1976, seven months after its first flight. On March 5, the first 747SP, *Clipper Freedom*, and the fourth off the production line, was delivered to Pan Am. Services were inaugurated in April, and 12 aircraft were delivered by the end of July. On May 1, Pan Am's *Clipper Liberty Bell* made a

The SP makes an excellent corporate and VIP aircraft because of its long-range capability, relatively large payload capacity, and large floorspace area. This particular aircraft was originally delivered to Braniff Airways in 1980 and subsequently passed through the hands of both Pan Am and United before it was bought by the government of Oman in December 1992. Work began in 1996 on fitting a glass cockpit into a VIP SP, making it the first of any 747 Classic versions to receive such an upgrade.

record-breaking around-the-world flight by flying from John F. Kennedy Airport, New York, via Delhi, India, and Tokyo, Japan, back to JFK in 46 hours, 26 minutes. Soon, Pan Am was using the 747SPs for more than 13 hours a day and dispatch reliability had reached about 97 percent. The aircraft really began to come into its own on the long-distance routes. Pan Am virtually trebled passenger loads on its new daily nonstop New York to Tokyo route. Even Japanese passengers, who were traditionally loyal to their national airline, JAL, admitted swapping to Pan Am because the 747SP did not have to refuel at Anchorage.

South African Airways, the second SP customer, bought the aircraft to operate nonstop flights to London from Johannesburg's hot and high runway. Although the carrier's 747-200Bs could manage nonstop legs on less-demanding, cooler days, the 747SP was more suitable because the standard 747 was too big for the route. The third airline to buy the SP was Iran Air, which was soon enjoying 90 percent load factors on its nonstop Flight 777 between Tehran and New York. Another Middle Eastern carrier, Syrian Air, flew the SP between Damascus and London. Like SAA, Syrian preferred the SP for the route because the standard 747 was too big.

The 747SPs continued to rack up records. In October 1977, Pan Am carried 165 fare-paying passengers on a round-the-world trip in N533PA, which had been specially renamed *Clipper New Horizons*. The journey marked the airline's 50th anniversary and began and ended in San Francisco. It included a transpolar flight to London, a flight across Africa to Cape Town, and a transpolar flight across Antarctica to Auckland, New Zealand, before the return leg to the United States. The 26,706-mile flight took 56 hours, 7 minutes, breaking the previous record by 8 hours, 20 minutes, set 12 years earlier by a modified 707.

Pan Am's fortunes began to wane by the mid-1980s, and the 747SP fleet was sold to United Air Lines in 1986. Two years after the takeover of Pan Am's SP fleet by United, United flew the 747SP *Friendship One* (originally Pan Am's *Clipper Fleetwing*) from Boeing Field, Seattle, on a round-the-world flight to raise money for a children's charity. Each of the 100 passengers paid $5,000 for the journey, which was accomplished in 36 hours, 54 minutes, with refueling stops in Athens and Taipei.

In spite of the aircraft's obvious long-range capabilities Boeing's earlier fears began to materialize, and the SP market niche closed as quickly as it had opened. Passenger loads on some long-range routes grew to fill the longer range versions of the 747-200B that were subsequently developed. Others were operated more efficiently by the later trijets or an emerging new breed of long-range twinjets. The last few sales came in the 1980s, with the 44th 747SP going to the Iraqi government as a state transport, and the last in 1987 to the United Arab Emirates as a VIP aircraft.

By the late 1990s the aircraft was enjoying something of a renaissance, with more than a quarter of the surviving fleet in use as luxury VIP or business jets. United gradually retired its fleet to the desert for storage in Las Vegas. The first batch of aircraft, including nearly all the early record breakers, were later flown to Ardmore, Oklahoma, for disposal and were expected to meet their fate at the hands of the cutter's torch by the end of 1997.

One former United aircraft, N145UA, was also selected to become the world's largest flying astronomical observatory. In December 1996 NASA awarded a $484-million contract to the Universities Space Research Association (USRA) and a team including United and Raytheon E-Systems to design, assemble, test, and operate the Stratospheric Observatory For Infrared Astronomy (SOFIA). The 747SP provided the best platform because of its high-altitude cruise capability, long-range endurance, and excellent payload capacity.

The SOFIA is expected to begin flights in 2001 with United managing the flight operations for USRA, a consortium of more than 80 U.S. universities set up to manage scientific research programs. The aircraft is to due to be modified by Raytheon, while the infrared (IR) telescope, measuring more than 8.2 feet in diameter, is to be developed and built by MAN of Germany. DARA, the German space agency, will provide 20 percent of the funds, with NASA providing the rest.

Flying at higher than 41,000 feet, the SOFIA will be above 99 percent of the interfering water vapor that blocks out most IR radiation from space, and will have a view of the universe unmatched by ground-based telescopes. SOFIA's telescope, located in the aft part of Section 46, was designed to study the IR radiation given off by planets, stars, the center of Earth's galaxy, and even distant galaxies. A moveable fuselage panel, located on the left side above the window belt and forward of the vertical fin, will slide open in flight to allow the telescope to begin observations.

Pan Am's SP fleet enjoyed a brief, but busy, career with United, which used the aircraft primarily on long-haul transpacific routes from the U.S. West Coast. Here N142UA, formerly Pan Am's *Clipper Constitution* (shown elsewhere in this chapter in its Pan Am livery), approaches Los Angeles International at the end of one such flight. Typical accommodation in UAL service included first-class seating for 18, business-class seating for 62, and economy-class seating for up to 164.

CHAPTER SIX

Boeing made one of its best and most important decisions early in 1985 when it elected to go ahead with a new version of the 747 designated the -400. On October 22, 1985, Northwest ordered 10, allowing Boeing to formally launch the -400 program. At a stroke, the order also ensured the 747's longevity for upward of another 20 years. The new version could carry more people farther and would completely revitalize sales of the big jetliner family, sustaining 747 production at Everett well into the twenty-first century.

The -400 was also important because it taught Boeing some valuable, if painful, lessons on how not to develop a major derivative. The Next Generation 737 family, the 777, and other subsequent derivative efforts such as the 767-400 all benefited from the hard-won experience of the 747-400.

In many ways, the development of the -400 was virtually inevitable. As early as 1981 the company was being forced to reconsider its 747 strategy because of a variety of market forces. The world was changing

THE REBORN 747-400

A United 747-422 rotates at Los Angeles International in front of the airport's newly completed control tower in December 1996. Deliveries of the first -400s to carriers such as United were delayed because, according to the airline, Boeing had underscoped the program. Lessons learned in the -400 development program by both Boeing and United were later used to good effect in the 777 program.

and soon Boeing would have to react. A year earlier it had announced the -300 with a stretched upper deck, but even before its rollout in 1982, the company knew that something more radical was needed to ensure the insuperable dominance of the 747. Other factors also came into play. Production had tumbled from seven per month in 1979 and 1980 (equaling the frantic post-introduction year of 1970) to half that by late 1981. By 1984, production had dipped to an all-time low of one per month.

Outside forces were also at work. McDonnell Douglas was working on a much larger and radically modernized derivative of the long-range DC-10-30/40 series. The MD-11, as it became known, was finally announced at the 1985 Paris Air Show, four months before the -400 received its official go-ahead. Airbus Industrie, a well-known advocate of high technology, was also close to defining a new pair of very advanced long-range, high-capacity aircraft, and within two years of the 747-400 launch, Airbus came out with the A330 and A340. Although none of these projects posed a direct threat to the 747, they served as a timely reminder that the competition never stood still.

The 747 even faced pressure to change from within Boeing. The advent of the two new twins, the 757 and 767, had suddenly left the 747 a generation behind in terms of avionics, materials, and systems. The 747 still used electro-mechanical instruments on the flight deck, very like the original 747 of 1968. Yet the high-tech 767 was rolling off an adjacent production line with cathode-ray tube (CRT) displays, making its big brother seem like an anachronism. The 747 was simply being overtaken by a rising tide of technology.

A Question of Balance

Based on airline reaction to the -300 and growing pressure to modernize, Boeing drew up a hit list of five major development objectives for the "advanced series 300" as it was still called in 1984. First, the aircraft would feature upgraded technology. Second, the interior would be enhanced. Third,

The 747-400's two-crew flight deck and six-tube glass cockpit display system had 365 lights, gauges, and switches—or roughly a third as many as the flight deck of the three-crew Classics. Here an ANA 747-481 nears the end of its long journey from Japan and turns southeast over London at 7,000 feet and 220 knots to intercept the localizer of Heathrow's Runway 27L.

This view of a -400 simulator clearly shows the two duplicated 8-inch-by-8-inch displays in front of each pilot. The left screen, or primary flight display, shows the horizon, attitude, airspeed, altitude, vertical speed, and heading. The right screen, or navigation display, shows a map and superimposed color-weather-radar image. On the main panel between the pilots are two more screens. These are displays for the engine indication and crew alerting system (EICAS), showing engine data, gear and flap positions, fuel status, and other systems status.

Lightweight composite winglets increased long-range capability by 3 percent. Their application followed pioneering development work by Dr. Richard T. Whitcomb, a research engineer at the NASA Langley Research Center who won America's prestigious Collier Trophy for developing the "area rule" concept for supersonic fighter design. Boeing decided to adopt the design following wind-tunnel work and flight tests conducted on a modified KC-135A at NASA Dryden between 1979 and 1980 that confirmed winglets' drag-reduction benefits. Airbus also adopted the technology, as did McDonnell Douglas for the MD-11.

the range would be increased by 1,000 nautical miles. Fourth, fuel burn would be reduced by as much as 37 percent over that of the first -100s. Last, operating costs would be reduced by 10 percent. These were ambitious targets and, as Joe Sutter remarked in 1986, "No mean feat for a third-generation derivative based on an airframe designed nearly 20 years ago."

To achieve the longer range, the -400, as it became by 1985, would be given more fuel capacity and aerodynamic improvements. Advanced engines would contribute to the range and cost targets by burning less fuel and improving performance. Lighter materials would be used to reduce aircraft weight, allowing more payload or fuel to be carried. A new, more powerful APU in the tail would help improve reliability and support the heavier power requirements of the jetliner. The inside would be gutted and replaced with an all-new interior to meet new fire standards and use advances in cabin technology. Last, it intended that the three-person flight

crew would be upgraded for "minimum change" rather than be all-new.

After its initial decision to minimally upgrade the flight deck, Boeing reassessed the situation. Cathode-ray tube instrument displays and other advanced technology for the flight deck were available and in production. The labor-saving opportunities were endless, giving the option of a two-crew cockpit for the first time on the 747. But a new looking cockpit meant a new training syllabus. It also meant getting rid of the flight engineer, a sensitive issue with some airlines that had caused problems during the introduction of the 767. One version of the 767 even had to be built with a flight-engineer station to appease Air New Zealand's pilot union.

Like all derivative developments, it came down to a question of balancing new features against the cost and marketing benefits of commonality. Boeing decided to ask the airlines what they preferred—until then a strange, if not alien concept. A consultative group was formed and included BA, Cathay Pacific, KLM, Lufthansa, Northwest, Qantas, and SIA. Most were in favor of a "glass" or digital cockpit, having tasted this technology with the A310, 757, and 767. Cathay Pacific, however, originally stuck out for retention of the original electromechanical instruments, referred to as "steam" or "clockwork" within the industry. Boeing then responded with a 757-based flight deck, keeping the same autopilot in an attempt to keep to its minimum-change philosophy.

Ultimately, an all-new digital cockpit layout was adopted, and it proved so popular with flight crews that often the only question asked was, "How on earth did we manage before?" In all, about 400 pilots and engineers and 200 non-flying staff visited a simulator that was used to define the finished flight deck. The revised display was a lot less cluttered than those on earlier 747s. Simpler systems, automation, and the removal of the flight engineer's panel drastically cut down on the number of switches, gauges, and dials. The -400 cockpit has

365 lights, gauges, and switches, compared with 971 on previous 747s.

To reassure carriers such as Cathay Pacific that the two-crew design would work safely, a set of automated and streamlined procedures was developed. For normal procedures, the -400 checklist had 34 line items compared to 107 for the -200 or -300. Emergency procedures were even more rigorously honed down. For example, to deal with an engine fire, the -400 crew needed to check off 4 line items, compared to 15 on the earlier aircraft. A cargo fire needed only 2 actions, compared to 16 on the older types. A rapid cabin depressurization and emergency descent required only 3 actions, compared to 20 before.

All primary flight, engine, and systems information were designed to be displayed on six identical Collins-made CRTs measuring 8 inches square. In the event of a system failure, an automatic switching system was developed to make sure that the crew would always be able to see basic flight information such as airspeed, altitude, and heading. Three electronic interface units (EIU) provided data concentration of analog signals from aircraft systems and digital data from the communications and navigation sensors. Any one of the three EIUs could support independent formats simultaneously on all six displays. This meant the aircraft could be "dispatched," or allowed to take off on a flight even with a failed EIU—an important factor to more traditional airlines whose engineers were sometimes skeptical of the high-tech claims made by Boeing.

Four main displays were designed for the crew. The electronic attitude director indicator (EADI) or primary flight display (PFD) showed the aircraft's airspeed, vertical speed, heading, and altitude in a TV-version of the classic "T" format that has been standard for most aircraft since the days of Lindbergh. Airspeed was displayed in a vertical tape on the left with barometric (pressure) altitude and vertical speed on the right. Aircraft heading was shown on a box on a compass arc at the bottom of the screen. The navi-

Carbon brakes were part of a massive redesign effort put into the 747-400's undercarriage. Carbon brakes cooled much more quickly than the standard steel brakes, which required up to 2 hours of cooling time. If brake energy per brake exceeded 10 million foot pounds, the brake-temperature indicator in the Classic flight deck entered the amber band. If energy entered the red band and exceeded 30 million foot pounds (for example, due to severe braking or a rejected takeoff), brakes would often catch fire and fuse plugs would melt, deflating tires and leaving the aircraft stranded. If temperatures were still high after takeoff, crews were advised to extend the undercarriage in flight to cool the brakes.

gation display (ND), or electronic horizontal situation indicator (EHSI), which showed where the 747 was in space, was normally placed alongside the compass screen. The ND featured a map mode with a maximum range of 640 nautical miles to give the crew an early picture of navigation aids on an approaching coastline after a long over-water flight. Navigation waypoints could be combined on the screen with the four-color picture from the weather radar to show if the crew needed to route around bad weather along their projected flight path. The aircraft was represented by a triangle and a dashed line indicated where the predicted position would be if conditions remained constant. The triangle looked forward to part of a compass arc or could be moved into the center of the TV screen and surrounded by a complete compass rose so the pilot could "look behind" during tight

maneuvering in the terminal area of a busy airport. Should all the flight and map screens fail, the -400 was also fitted with basic stand-by electro-mechanical airspeed, altitude, vertical speed, and compass instruments.

More Flight-Deck Changes

In the center of the display panel and on the pedestal immediately in front of the throttles, Boeing placed another two CRTs, which showed engine and systems data. The engine indication and crew alerting system (EICAS) had been pioneered on the 757 and 767 and was slightly refined for this second-generation Boeing application. Primary engine data such as fan speed, thrust, and jet temperatures and pressures were displayed on the upper screen in either round-dial or tape format. The upper screen, because it was more eye-catching, also displayed major "aircraft-status" infor-

mation about gear and flap positions, doors, tires, and fuel states.

The lower screen showed more engine data such as compressor speeds, oil pressures, and temperatures, as well as "synoptics" of the hydraulic, electrical, and fuel system. Using the display like a manual, the crew could select an electronic "page" to show the desired system. Circuit breakers and other remnants from the flight engineer's panel were located overhead.

An important new tool to improve reliability was the Collins-made central maintenance computer (CMC). This was plugged into the aircraft's digital data bus, an electronic digital highway resembling the body's nervous system. Like a doctor doing the rounds, the CMC constantly checked the health of about 70 individual systems. If a fault was found, the individual unit would be identified and data transmitted by radio to the ground, saving hours of laborious troubleshooting by engineers and the delays this invariably caused. Faults were flagged up on a screen in plain English with a simple description of what was wrong, for example: "ILS antenna inop [in-operative]."

The system was aimed at speeding up fault fixing on the ground, though when the plane was above 10,000 feet the information was available for use by the crews themselves. Boeing considered that below this height there were too many distractions, and the company was anxious not to overload the crew with too much information.

The 747-400 cockpit was also designed with a more sophisticated flight management computer (FMC). The Honeywell-made FMC could perform calculations five times faster than the previous computers, which were often described as being not much better than slow-witted calculators. The FMC works out the optimum altitude, speed, and routing for a flight, given the relevant inputs from the crew. An important feature of the -400 FMC was its ability to perform "4D" navigation. This is the calculation of whether or nor the aircraft could reach a certain altitude by a certain navigational way-

Advanced aluminum alloys were used extensively on the upper and lower skins of the extended wing torsion box, which is the gray-colored section clearly visible on this overhead view of an Asiana 747-48E Combi, parked on the pre-delivery ramp at Everett. The new materials, which were based on the alloys developed for the 757 and 767, saved about 6,000 pounds in weight.

span. The winglets were canted outward at 29 degrees and were swept back at 60 degrees for maximum efficiency at the high cruise speeds where most of the flying would be done. Even so, Boeing took the opportunity to slightly increase span at the same time with a 6-foot wing-tip extension. This took the unladen span up to 211 feet, 5 inches, compared with the 195 feet, 8 inches of the first 747s. Due to the flexible wing structure and the outward-canted winglets, the span actually grew by almost 2 feet to 213 feet when the -400 was fully fueled!

The winglets were also lightly constructed of graphite (carbon-fiber) composite front and rear spars covered with a skin made up of a carbon-fiber and epoxy honeycomb sandwich to minimize weight. The winglet itself produced a 3 percent increase in range on long-distance flights through drag reduction. It also helped improve the aircraft's takeoff characteristics and enabled it to attain higher cruising altitudes. An extra leading-edge flap (making 11 each side, not counting three sections of Krueger flap) was fitted to the wing extension, further aiding takeoff and landing performance. The large composite fairing covering the join between the wing and the fuselage was also recontoured to cut drag. The careful shaping of the new fairing owed much to advances in aerodynamic analysis in the 1980s.

Changes were also made to the "tail feathers," including a big new fuel tank between the front and rear spars of the horizontal stabilizer. The tank could hold 3,300 gallons, or more than half the total fuel capacity of the 737, and was worth about 350 nautical miles of extra range. Higher up, the deflection of the huge rudder was increased 6 degrees to plus/minus 30 degrees to improve ground handling. The extra play of the rudder meant the minimum speed at which the rudder could be used to control the aircraft on the runway was decreased by 10 knots. The heavy balance weights running the length of the upper rudder and the dual tandem actuators were removed and replaced by three actuators with triple

point. This was an increasingly crucial calculation on busy international routes by the late 1980s.

The new autopilot flight director system (AFDS) was a Collins-built derivative of the 757/767 autopilot. The FCS-700A had a new feature called "altitude intervention" that allowed the crew to change height without recalculating the flight plan following an unexpected instruction from air traffic control. The AFDS also controlled the auto-land capability of

the big jetliner and was cleared to bring the -400 in for automatic landings with a decision height of 0 feet and a forward view along the runway of less than 655 feet.

Stretching the Range

The 747-400 was made instantly recognizable by the addition of 6-foot winglets on each wing tip. The novel devices were the best solution to reducing drag and providing additional wing area without dramatically increasing the

1. Sideways-hinging radome, housing weather radar, localizer, and glideslope aerials
2. Front pressure bulkhead
3. Two-crew flightdeck plus two observers seats
4. Crew rest bunks
5. Toilets (two)
6. Passenger entry door 42x76 in (plug type, containing escape chutes, total 12)
7. Upper deck, business class shown, 52 seats at 38-in pitch, or 69 seats at 34-in pitch economy class (max)
8. Cabin attendant's folding seat
9. New contoured ceiling and sidewall panels
10. Galley unit
11. Coat stowage
12. First-class section, 34 fully reclining seats at 62-in pitch
13. Bar unit
14. Galley units (total eight)
15. Center-line toilets (total ten)
16. Sidewall toilets (two shown, total five), vacuum-flush odorless system
17. Economy cabin, 302 seats at 33-in pitch (life vests under seats)
18. Waste tanks (two each side, 85 US gal), single-point service panel below aircraft
19. Outer overhead stowage bins (10.9 ft³ per 60 in long)
20. Center overhead stowage bins (5.7 ft³ per 40 in long), reduced-angle opening
21. Life raft and escape rope stowage over each door
22. Overhead cabin-crew rest area (four bunks and four seats), one of three versions, access via stairs
23. Stairs to upper deck
24. Forward containerized belly hold, capacity 2,800 ft³
25. Cargo floor ball transfer panel (powered floor optional)
26. Forward and rear cargo hold Freon-gas fire extinguisher bottles
27. Water tanks
28. Rear containerized freight hold (2,340 ft³)
29. Aft bulk cargo hold (845 ft³)
30. Bulk cargo hold door (44x47 in inward opening)
31. Cargo hold doors (104x68 in), electrically powered
32. Rear pressure dome
33. Two-spar multi-rib/stringer fin torsion box
34. Removable light-alloy leading edge and fiberglass tip (provision for HF aerials)
35. Two-piece rudder, dual hydraulic actuators lower half, triple hydraulic actuators upper half
36. Continuous two-spar tailplane torsion box
37. Multi-rib and stringer, split-skin tailplane panels, Thiokol-sealed for tankage
38. Long-range fuel tank (3,300 US gal)
39. Surge and vent tank
40. Hydraulically actuated tailplane drive unit (electrically driven autopilot trim charge drive)
41. Two-piece elevator (hydraulically activated)
42. Pratt & Whitney Canada PW901A auxiliary power unit (APU)
43. APU air inlet
44. APU exhaust, ejector cooled
45. APU housed in titanium fireproof compartment
46. Freon gas bottle fire extinguisher
47. Cooling-air inlet for accessories
48. APU air delivery duct
49. Wing torsion box, two spars continuous root to tip, with center spar from root to outer pylon
50. Four-panel wing skins (top and bottom), rear panel continuous
51. Extruded channel-section stringers (Thiokol-sealed for tankage)
52. Multi-plate web/riveted stiffened ribs
53. Wing extension, 6 ft
54. 6-ft high winglet, carbon fiber front and rear spar covered with carbon fiber epoxy honeycomb sandwich skin panels
55. Aluminum leading edge
56. Detachable fiberglass laminate tip
57. Recontoured wing/fuselage fairing
58. Krüger flap, three sections, forms underside of wing when retracted (pneumatically actuated)
59. Leading-edge flap, 11 sections each side (pneumatically actuated, electrically actuated standby)
60. Inner high-speed aileron (hydraulically actuated)
61. Outer low-speed aileron (hydraulically actuated)
62. Triple-slotted Fowler-type flaps
63. Flap tracks and carriages (hydraulically actuated torque-tube drive via angled gearboxes and ball screwjacks)
64. Spoiler/speedbrake panels (hydraulically actuated)
65. Elevator and rudder cables run from the control columns to the rear quadrants and feel units via pulleys
66. Main flap, aluminum honeycomb skin panels, light-alloy ribs and spars; leading slat similar; with fiberglass honeycomb leading edge; trailing flap has fiberglass trailing edge
67. Wing/fuselage mainframes, built-up forged and machined light alloy
68. Wing main undercarriage support beam (titanium)
69. Fiberglass flap track shroud
70. Engine support pylon hung from strengthened chordwise ribs
71. Front and rear engine attachment lugs, interchangeable with the three engine alternatives
72. Pylon/wing upper attachment link
73. Diagonal brace/thrust strut attached at the rear end to the center and rear wing spars
74. Engine-driven hydraulic pump; air-driven pump with electric standby supplies four separate and independent hydraulic systems (one per engine)
75. System reservoir (32–37 1/2 gal/min. 3,000 lb delivery)
76. Air tapped from engine 8th and 15th stages, to air conditioning packs
77. Pre-cooler and air exhaust
78. Engine fire bottles (Freon gas)
79. Hot-air duct to engine intake anti-icing
80. Hot-air delivery duct to leading-edge de-icing spray tube; from outboard of inner pylon to the tip
81. Main distribution manifold
82. Ram-air "in" to air-conditioning packs (three beneath center section)
83. Plenum chamber for conditioned air delivery
84. Riser ducts to overhead cabin distribution ducts

33° INBD
32° OUTBD
FLAPS
53° INBD
52° OUTBD
(LANDING)

Alternative engines

GENERAL ELECTRIC CF6-80C2

ROLLS-ROYCE RB211-524G

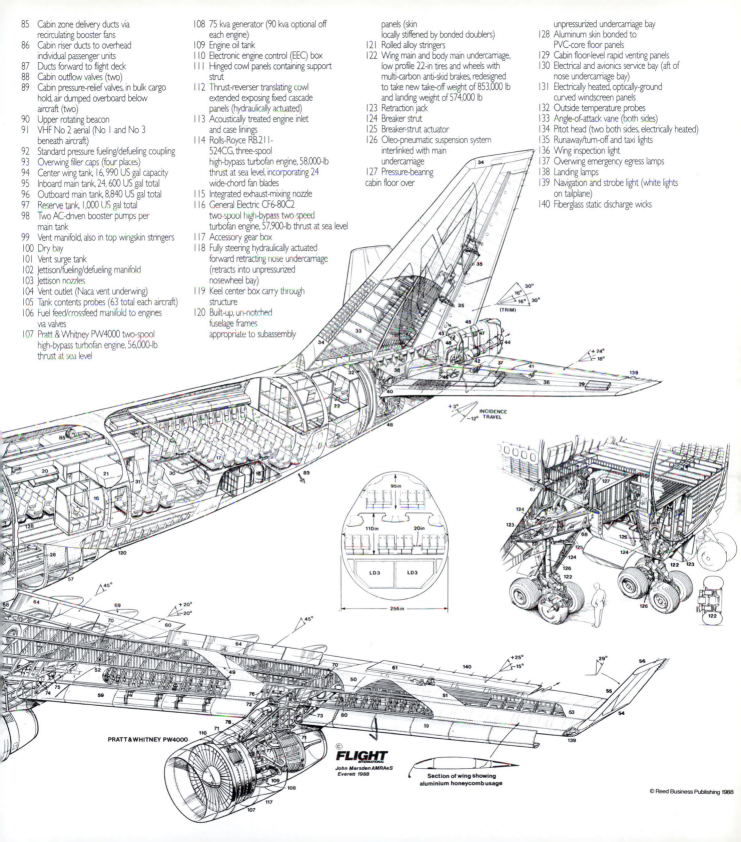

85 Cabin zone delivery ducts via recirculating booster fans
86 Cabin riser ducts to overhead individual passenger units
87 Ducts forward to flight deck
88 Cabin outflow valves (two)
89 Cabin pressure-relief valves, in bulk cargo hold, air dumped overboard below aircraft (two)
90 Upper rotating beacon
91 VHF No 2 aerial (No 1 and No 3 beneath aircraft)
92 Standard pressure fueling/defueling coupling
93 Overwing filler caps (four places)
94 Center wing tank, 16,990 US gal capacity
95 Inboard main tank, 24,600 US gal total
96 Outboard main tank, 8,840 US gal total
97 Reserve tank, 1,000 US gal total
98 Two AC-driven booster pumps per main tank
99 Vent manifold, also in top wingskin stringers
100 Dry bay
101 Vent surge tank
102 Jettison/fueling/defueling manifold
103 Jettison nozzles
104 Vent outlet (Naca vent underwing)
105 Tank contents probes (63 total each aircraft)
106 Fuel feed/crossfeed manifold to engines via valves
107 Pratt & Whitney PW4000 two-spool high-bypass turbofan engine, 56,000-lb thrust at sea level

108 75 kva generator (90 kva optional off each engine)
109 Engine oil tank
110 Electronic engine control (EEC) box
111 Hinged cowl panels containing support strut
112 Thrust-reverser translating cowl extended exposing fixed cascade panels (hydraulically actuated)
113 Acoustically treated engine inlet and case linings
114 Rolls-Royce RB.211-524CG, three-spool high-bypass turbofan engine, 58,000-lb thrust at sea level, incorporating 24 wide-chord fan blades
115 Integrated exhaust-mixing nozzle
116 General Electric CF6-80C2 two-spool high-bypass two-speed turbofan engine, 57,900-lb thrust at sea level
117 Accessory gear box
118 Fully steering hydraulically actuated forward retracting nose undercarriage (retracts into unpressurized nosewheel bay)
119 Keel center box carry through structure
120 Built-up, un-notched fuselage frames appropriate to subassembly

panels (skin locally stiffened by bonded doublers)
121 Rolled alloy stringers
122 Wing main and body main undercarriage, low profile 22-in tires and wheels with multi-carbon anti-skid brakes, redesigned to take new take-off weight of 853,000 lb and landing weight of 574,000 lb
123 Retraction jack
124 Breaker strut
125 Breaker-strut actuator
126 Oleo-pneumatic suspension system interlinked with main undercarriage
127 Pressure-bearing cabin floor over

unpressurized undercarriage bay
128 Aluminum skin bonded to PVC-core floor panels
129 Cabin floor-level rapid venting panels
130 Electrical and avionics service bay (aft of nose undercarriage bay)
131 Electrically heated, optically-ground curved windscreen panels
132 Outside temperature probes
133 Angle-of-attack vane (both sides)
134 Pitot head (two both sides, electrically heated)
135 Runaway/turn-off and taxi lights
136 Wing inspection light
137 Overwing emergency egress lamps
138 Landing lamps
139 Navigation and strobe light (white lights on tailplane)
140 Fiberglass static discharge wicks

(TRIM)

INCIDENCE TRAVEL

PRATT & WHITNEY PW4000

© FLIGHT INTERNATIONAL
John Marsden AMRAeS
Everett 1988

Section of wing showing aluminium honeycomb usage

© Reed Business Publishing 1988

First of the breed. This Northwest aircraft was the first 747-400 to fly and carried the Boeing test registration N401PW to denote its P&W PW4056 powerplants. Now registered N661US, the aircraft plies Northwest's long-range routes around the Pacific rim and is pictured on final approach to New York's JFK International at the end of one such flight. It first flew on April 29, 1988, and was finally delivered to the airline in December 1989.

Air France was one of many carriers to choose GE's CF6-80C2B1F engine, which produces 58,000 pounds of thrust. Others adopted the more powerful 60,800-pound-thrust CF6-80C2B1F1, while GE began to contemplate a simpler system of engine classification. The French carrier took delivery of this 747-428 Combi in February 1992.

control valves. The lower rudder's tandem actuators were also replaced by two actuators with dual control valves. The new arrangement was lighter, more efficient, and more effective.

Another weight saving of 1,800 precious pounds was made by a drastic redesign of the wheels, tires, and brakes. The massive five-truck, 18-wheel undercarriage architecture remained unchanged, but the diameter of the wheels was increased 2 inches to 22 inches to house new carbon brakes. The new brakes would wear better and last for double the number of landings of a traditionally fitted steel brake set. The tires were lower profile so that the same overall diameter of 49 inches could be maintained. Boeing expected the change would enable the -400 to stop in shorter distances, operate at higher gross weights, and make a faster turnaround time between flights because the BFGoodrich carbon brakes would cool more quickly than would steel brakes. The new wheels were the 16th version of the 747 wheel, each one strengthening up previous crack-prone weak spots found in service. For the first time, a cockpit tire-pressure indication system was also offered. This enabled the crew to check if the pressure of each tire was above or below safe limits.

A further saving of almost 6,000 pounds was achieved by using advanced aluminum alloys (2000 and 7000 series) for the upper and lower skins of the wing torsion box. These alloys were lighter and stronger versions of the original alloys used on the 747 series. These alloys had been developed for the 757 and 767. In other areas, particularly the nose section (Section 41), the weight was slightly increased because entire areas of the structure were strengthened with thicker frames, skins, and doublers. The structure was also given additional treatments to fight corrosion, an area that Boeing acknowledged needed improvement in the 747. This included more wet-sealing of fasteners, more painting using special epoxy material, and a waterproof membrane or dampcourse.

California sunshine glints off the fan blades of a Rolls-Royce RB.211-524G-powered Qantas 747-438 as it reverses thrust at Los Angeles at the end of its long flight from Sydney, Australia. The -524G was the first wide-body engine from any manufacturer to make use of wide-chord-fan-blade technology, Rolls-Royce having first developed it successfully for the -535E4 engine used on the 757. The fan consists of 24 hollow titanium blades, compared with 38 on a comparable turbofan of conventional design. Qantas, which took delivery of *City of Perth* in April 1990, was the first -400 operator to adopt a 5,000-pound upgrade kit, which took maximum takeoff weight to 875,000 pounds.

Boeing's plan was to package these improvements, together with more efficient engines, to reduce fuel consumption per passenger mile by 7 percent, compared with the -300. Compared with the first -100 models, the new 747-400 could carry 40 more passengers an additional 2,500 nautical miles.

Powerplants

Just as it did with avionics and structures, Boeing was able to take advantage of some big improvements in engine technology in designing the 747-400. Much of this was owed to the fast pace of twinjet development, which had accelerated the demand for highly reliable, fuel efficient, and powerful turbofans. As a result, the engines for the -400 were virtually interchangeable with those of the 767.

As with any new aircraft from the early 1980s onward, low noise was a major design consideration. The 747-400 would have to meet stringent Stage III noise requirements. In the end, the new engines reduced the takeoff noise area by more than 40 percent compared with the 747-300.

First off the mark was P&W with the PW4056 engine, which was ordered by launch customer Northwest. The engine was a third-generation turbofan

derived from the JT9D family and was originally known as the PW4256. New technology included single crystal turbine blades and a full authority digital engine control (FADEC), which was the engine's equivalent of the aircraft's FMS. The PW4000 series had a 7 percent lower fuel consumption than the JT9D, and much of its additional power was derived from the increased work of the high-pressure spool. The high-pressure compressor's pressure ratio was increased by about 10 percent and the high-pressure rotor itself operated at 27 percent higher speed.

General Electric was next in line, following an order from KLM, with the latest model of its burgeoning CF6 engine series. The 58,000-pound-thrust CF6-80C2B1F, like others in the -80C2 family, differed from previous CF6 engines in having a four-stage (rather than three-stage) low-pressure compressor (or booster) matched to the fan. The airflow through the core was upped to 340 pounds per second, compared to 276 pounds per second for earlier engines and the 14-stage high-pressure compressor produced an overall pressure ratio of 30.4:1. One of the two stages of high-pressure turbine was also made of a new-technology material that was directionally solidified, allowing

the alloy to withstand much higher temperatures. The low-pressure turbine was fitted with an extra (fifth) stage to match the enlarged low-pressure compressor. Like the P&W engine, the GE engine was also FADEC equipped.

Rolls-Royce offered the latest version of its RB.211-524 family, which Cathay Pacific ordered in June 1986. Apart from its unusual three-shaft arrangement, the -524 also differed from the competition in having a fan made up of wide-chord blades. These were wider than those in the other engines, with a total of 24 hollow titanium blades per set, compared to 38 in both U.S. engines. The wide-chord blades were bigger versions of the ones developed for the -535E4 engine used on the 757. Rolls offered two versions of the engine for the 747-400, the 58,000-pound-thrust RB.211-524G (which entered service in 1989) and the 60,000-pound-thrust RB.211-524H (which flew in service on both the 767-300 and 747-400 the following year).

Engines from all three manufacturers reduced the average amount of fuel burned on a typical flight by between 5 and 10 percent, compared with their previous, 1983 versions. Some careful aerodynamic research had also gone into the design of their nacelles and the struts (or pylons) that connected them to the wing, and all were more streamlined as a result.

Another new but rather less obvious feature of the 747-400 was the improved APU in the tail. Garrett (AlliedSignal) had provided all of the APUs for the 747 series until the -400, but Boeing decided to put the new unit out to competition. Sensing an opportunity, Pratt & Whitney Canada (P&WC) proposed, and won, with their PW901A APU. The loss was a tremendous blow to AlliedSignal, which began a complete overhaul of its APU business as a result.

The little engine was based on P&WC's turboprop line and burned up to 40 percent less fuel than its predecessor. It could also maintain a 75 degree F cabin temperature when it was 100 degrees F outside on the ramp. It drove two generators to produce a total of 180 kilovolt-amps and could be automatically started and shut down. Boeing predicted that the new APU could save an airline $125,000 per year in fuel bills alone. Unlike some earlier troublesome units, the new APU quickly established a reliability level of 99.95 percent in the first 16 months of service.

New-Look Cabin

From the passenger and airline perspectives, the 747-400 was an all-new aircraft inside. Everything was different from the shaping and materials of the cabin walls to the lavatory system and overhead bins.

An innovation at the time was the vacuum lavatory system, which was odorless and improved corrosion prevention, but most importantly allowed the airlines to choose from up to 121 possible lavatory positions around the cabin. This was made possible by the development of a "sewer" for the 747-400. Two-inch-diameter waste pipes were run through the length of the main cabin floor, with an extension to the upper deck. Toilets could be simply plumbed into the nearest access point to the sewer, providing 6 lavatory "footprints" on the upper deck and 33 on the main deck. Waste was collected in 4 tanks at the rear of the belly, which were easily accessed from a single servicing point. To cope with the unwanted byproducts of up to 400 passengers on, for example, a 15-hour flight from Los Angeles to Sydney, two of the tanks held 85 gallons each, while the other two held 65 gallons each.

Feeding the same 400 passengers was just as much of a challenge. Boeing designed the cabin with a number of utility hookups, enabling airlines to locate galleys in up to 12 different areas, offering a total of 157 possible locations.

At the back of the cabin, hidden away from the passengers, was an optional crew rest cabin with bunks for eight and two seats, or different combinations of both. The little room was located above the ceiling of the main cabin and was reached by three steps and a small vertical ladder. The problem

Externally identical to the 747-300, the short-ranged 747-400D lacks the distinctive winglets of the long-range -400s. The D was primarily developed for the Japanese domestic market, but Boeing hoped the growing Chinese and Indian markets would eventually generate extra sales. This -481D of ANA is configured to carry 27 business-class and 542 economy-class passengers.

of crew rest on long overseas routes had already been recognized on the 747-300, which had been offered with a crew rest module, or "Portakabin," at the rear of the cabin. The Portakabin rested on the main-deck level at the cost of 20 passenger seats, whereas the attic-like location of the -400 crew rest area meant no loss of revenue-generating seats. For a long time, this huge area above the main-deck ceiling had remained unused; this was the first module to make use of the space. Another crew rest area, with two more bunks, was located on the upper deck, behind the flight deck, for the use by the pilots.

The cabin itself was made to look even wider by a clever redesign of the paneling and overhead stowage bins. This was quite a feat given that the bins themselves were considerably bigger than previous versions. In all, Boeing estimated that the -400 had the biggest overhead stowage volume per passenger of any wide-body, with up to 2.8 cubic feet per passenger. Its nearest competitor on this score was the Airbus A300/A310 with 2.67 cubic feet.

An important safety feature of the new cabin was literally built into the walls. The plastic paneling was fire-resistant material (able to withstand a heat release of 65kW/m sq) that set a new safety standard that every manufacturer was supposed to meet in new aircraft by late 1990. Epoxy/glass was replaced by phenolic glass or carbon

composite for partitions, doors, closets, galleys, lavatory walls, and major surfaces. To reduce the amount of smoke and toxicity in case of fire, polycarbonates were replaced by a new thermoplastic composites. Ceilings were made from improved polyester and phenolic sheet molding materials instead of standard polyester.

Flight and Frustration

Engineering design of the 747-400 continued through 1986, and 90 percent of the structures were released to manufacture by the end of February 1987. Parts slowly began to come together at Everett, and major assembly began by September 1987. Finally, on January 26, 1988, the first 747-400 was rolled out at Everett on the same day as the new 737-400 emerged at the Renton factory—the first double rollout for Boeing.

The wider span of the new 747 gave the impression that the entire aircraft was somehow bigger, even though it was really the same length and height as the very first aircraft that had rolled out 20 years before. Its gleaming, polished-aluminum finish, complete with neat red, white, and blue cheatline, gave the -400 a purposeful look. The winglets reminded everyone that the new jet possessed the very latest in technology. In short, Boeing was pleased with its latest creation.

More importantly, the airlines were also pleased with the -400 and had already ordered more than a 100 by the time of the rollout. Singapore Airlines, KLM, Lufthansa, Cathay Pacific, and BA booked 49 of the -400s between them in 1986. The next year saw another 58 sales as even larger orders poured in from United and Air France. Everything until then had gone smoothly, and sales were off to an incredible start. Optimism was high for an equally successful test flight and development phase. Unfortunately, everyone was disappointed.

Problems began almost immediately. To begin with, Boeing had planned a tightly packed schedule that called for the first P&W-powered -400 to begin flight tests in March. The second test aircraft, with GE engines, was due to fly in April and be followed, two months later, by the first Rolls-powered aircraft. Certification and deliveries were to begin around December 1988 and follow, in rapid succession, until the March 1989 time frame, when the first Rolls-powered aircraft would be delivered to complete the test and certification phase. Boeing knew it was ambitious to certificate and deliver three different engine-and-airframe combinations in almost as many months, but the orders were pouring in, and it had to get a move on.

Frustration grew as the giant was prepared for its first flight. Nagging problems cropped up on many of the new systems that were designed to reduce crew workload. One of these was the electrical system, which had much more automation than previous systems, including automatic start-up, load transferring, and load shedding. Problems refused to go away and were compounded by late delivery of parts from some suppliers. The planned first flight date in March 1988 slipped. By late April, all systems were go, and on April 29 the first -400 took off from Everett, powered by PW4056 engines. Unfortunately, the six-week delay of the first flight was only a hint of the problems to come. The first GE-powered -400 was also running late and, having rolled out in May, joined the test program four weeks late, on June 27. The -

400 effort was given a boost the same day when the first aircraft set a new world record by taking off at the incredible gross weight of 892,450 pounds—almost six times the maximum weight of the 707 "Dash 80" prototype.

Two months later, the first Rolls-Royce-powered aircraft, in the colors of Cathay Pacific, joined the test effort. The test aircraft flew virtually around-the-clock to make up for lost time. The test fleet was averaging 65 hours of flying per month by September, with both of the first two aircraft setting test-flying records of more than 90 hours per month early in the effort. Boeing's resources were truly stretched to the limit, and inevitably something was going to give. Finally, on October 11, Boeing announced "limited delivery delays." Out of 161 aircraft on order by 21 customers at the time, 20 would be delivered an average of one month late. Dean Thornton, president of BCAG, announced, "We intend to obtain FAA certification of the 747-400 in December, to deliver the first two aircraft that month, and to be back on our original schedule by mid-1989."

As it turned out, even this was slightly optimistic. A series of software problems bugged the -400's sophisticated electronics, adding to the already huge workload. According to Boeing, this was one of the main reasons for the delay. Other reasons included the vast number of configuration differences specified by customers, a mistake that Boeing never repeated. Configuration changes include all the options available to an airline and could range from the size and location of galleys to the color shades of warning decals inside the cabin. Changing position of the lavatory block, for example, required up to 7,000 hours of engineering work. "That is a very small amount, compared to the whole job of building the airplane, but if you get 20 customers coming along who all want the lavatory positions changed on their airplanes, that's when you get problems" according to one frustrated Boeing engineer.

In order to attract such a flood of orders, Boeing had also promised ear-

Cargolux took delivery of the first 747-400F freighter in November 1993 after launch-customer Air France deferred its orders. The -400F retains the short upper deck, 120-inch-by-134-inch side door, and 136-inch-by-98-inch nose door of the -200F, but is otherwise structurally identical to the passenger version of the 747-400. The -400F can carry up to 44,000 pounds more payload than earlier freighters over a 5,000-nautical-mile range. This aircraft was one of four ordered by Asiana. Overall orders for -400Fs slowly began building in the mid-1990s and had topped 21 by early 1997.

lier deliveries. This meant having to ramp up the production rate much faster than originally planned, from two per month to five per month. The upturn in 747 orders coincided with similar upturns for the 737, 757, and 767 lines. More, and sometimes inexperienced, workers were hired, and quality suffered as a result. Work had to be repeated in order to get it right, resulting in more delay. "It really brought out some glaring weaknesses in production when you had people up front putting in stuff while people down the back would be tearing stuff out," said one disgruntled airline technical manager from the time. "The -400 turned into a great airplane, but boy did it suffer from quality control to start with!"

The PW4056-powered -400 was finally certificated on January 9, 1989, but was not delivered to Northwest until January 26, after more software and other electronic changes were made to satisfy the FAA. The aircraft entered service on February 9, plying rather ignominiously between Phoenix and Minneapolis to let the crews get used to the new Boeing. The 747-400 finally got to stretch its legs overseas when SIA began a daily non-stop Singapore to London -400 service on May 30. Northwest's first international services with the type began on June 1, 1989, between New York and Tokyo.

As deliveries at last began to roll, Boeing began to relax, thinking the worst was past. Unfortunately, it was in for one more unpleasant surprise when in May, with just one week to go before delivery of the first GE-powered -400 to KLM, the European airworthiness authorities said the aircraft failed its specifications for tolerance to structural damage. Boeing was flabbergasted. The FAA agreed with Boeing that the aircraft was a derivative design but the JAR (European Joint Airworthiness Requirements committee) insisted the -400 was a new aircraft and must therefore meet the latest regulations. The area of dispute was the upper-deck floor, under which ran the control cables and wiring from the cockpit. The JAR maintained the floor did not meet the latest specifications for resistance to collapse in the event of a sudden major cabin decompression. Boeing stressed that the -400 upper-deck design was identical to the -300's and, because it had not placed any more demands on the -400's structure than on the -300's, the -400 should not have to meet different standards.

The JAR said it had challenged Boeing on the floor issue 15 months pre-

Boeing celebrated the rollout of the 1,000th 747 on September 10, 1993. Many of the original "Incredibles" were in the crowd, as were Joe Sutter and Jack Waddell. The 747 became only the fifth commercial jetliner, after the 707, 727, 737, and McDonnell Douglas MD-80 to have sold more than 1,000 units—quite a feat for a model that was expected to wither on the vine after about 400 sales. The aircraft flew 19 days later and was delivered to SIA in October. Singapore Airlines was the world's largest operator of -400s by early 1997, with 40 in service, narrowly ahead of BA with 34 and JAL with 32. *Boeing*

viously, but by delivery time it emerged that the manufacturer had followed FAA guidelines and not those of the JAR. The JAR defended its stance by saying a best-selling aircraft like the -400 would still be in service 30 years later. It therefore felt unhappy about still applying the original rules to a design that was already 20 years old at that point. The specific point about resistance to structural damage followed a 1980 JAR resolution, identical to those adopted by the FAA, which recognized the growing threat of terrorism and mandated that all new designs be able to survive bomb damage. Under the rule, all wide-body jets must be able to sustain a 20-square-foot hole blown in the side of the fuselage without sustaining floor damage that would cause critical problems to the controls. The size of the hole is related to the cross-sectional area of the aircraft. Although the main deck of the 747-400 met the criteria, the upper deck did not. It was built to the old standard, able to sustain a sudden blowout producing a 12.5-square-foot hole.

As the days passed and an embarrassing showdown became imminent, a compromise was reached. The delivery to KLM was allowed to go ahead on May 18, with the aircraft flying under a

temporary 90-day JAR type certificate. In return, Boeing agreed to modify the upper-deck floor by strengthening the beams and separating the control runs within two years. It made retrofit kits for aircraft already built and made changes to the assembly line at Everett. Lufthansa took its first -400 five days later under the same conditions. Finally, on June 8, Cathay Pacific received its first Rolls-Royce-powered -400, the day before the UK's CAA issued its type certificate for the aircraft. Despite the huge problems, many of them completely unforeseen, Boeing worked to get all three variants certificated and into service within four months of each other—a remarkable recovery.

Derivatives and Upgrades

The 747-400 soon began evolving into a "family within a family." The first derivative was a Combi version. The aircraft was virtually identical to the all-passenger model except for a huge main-deck cargo door measuring 120 inches by 134 inches on the left (port) side of the fuselage. The two rear "zones," or areas of the main deck, were fitted with a strengthened floor and cargo-handling equipment.

The first -400 Combi, (the 735st

747) was completed in early June 1989 and flew at the end of that month. It was handed over to KLM on September 1 and was the first of almost 50 Combis to be produced by the end of 1996. One of the biggest operators, EVA Airways of Taiwan, took two in April and May of 1996—becoming the first airline to receive consecutively made Combis. In EVA service, the aircraft had seating for 268 and space for 7 pallets. Alternative layouts on offer included seating for 290 plus 6 pallets or 220 and 12. Boeing offered up to 13 pallet configurations, realizing the broad sales potential of the giant jetliner in freight-heavy sectors such as Southeast Asia.

One month after the delivery of the first Combi, Boeing announced plans to develop a short-range version designated the 747-400D (for Domestic). With an all-economy seating configuration, the aircraft would eventually hold 568 passengers—the highest number on any commercial aircraft developed.

Like the 747SR versions before it (see Chapter 8), the -400D was developed primarily for the crowded Japanese domestic market where intra-island air traffic was so busy that even the huge 747s were easily filled to capacity. Boeing hoped the version would one day attract the interest of operators in the equally crowded lands of China, India, and possibly even on trunk routes within the United States.

The -400D was basically a standard -400 with an improved structure. On the outside, the only visible difference was the wing, which did not have the 6-foot tip extension or the winglets. (The winglets were designed to be useful over long distances and were not needed for the short-haul routes of the -400D. They could be installed later, in around four weeks, if the operator needed the aircraft for long-range missions—an option later exercised by both carriers.) On first inspection, the -400D appeared to be a 747-300. The tail tank was not used, and maximum takeoff weight was reduced by more than a quarter to about 600,000 pounds. The first -400D, the 844th 747 built, flew in March 1991 and was delivered to JAL the following October. By

1997 some 20 -400Ds had been delivered to JAL and All Nippon Airways (ANA).

Design of the inevitable freighter derivative was already under way in 1989, and by October, just as the D version was being announced, the basic outline of the 747-400F was frozen. The aircraft that emerged from the design studies was a unique combination of old and new. It had the original -200F short upper deck, together with the two-crew flight deck, strengthened fuselage, extended wing tips, winglets, and wing-to-body fairing of the -400. In addition, the stronger wing and locally strengthened fuselage of the Combi was further developed for the freighter. Inside, Boeing hollowed out the area behind the upper deck to create space for two additional 10-foot-high freight pallets, making room for a total of 23. Cunning packaging also provided room for an extra pallet in the nose and two additional LD-1/LD-3 containers in the lower forward hold in some combinations, as well as two more in the rear lower hold. In all, the -400F had 774 cubic feet more main-deck volume and up to 420 cubic feet more lower-hold volume than the -200F. Some of the extra space was created by developing a new folding ladder to connect the cockpit to the main deck to replace a fixed ladder.

The extra payload and range capability of the -400 brought a whole new meaning to the phrase "high-capacity freighter." It could carry 124 tons of cargo over more than 4,000 nautical miles. It could also lift up to 26 tons more than the -200F or, alternatively, fly up to 1,200 nautical miles further. In response to cargo carriers' wishes, the maximum takeoff weight was further increased by 5,000 pounds, to 875,000 pounds, and maximum landing weight was increased to 652,000 pounds. Boeing also provided a crew rest area with two bunks and added air conditioning for the lower holds.

The 747-400F program was officially launched on September 13, 1989, when Air France ordered five of the freighters. With the future of the -400F secured, Boeing decided not to offer the -200F any more. Major assembly of the -400F kicked off in late October 1992,

and the first -400F, the 968th 747 built, was rolled out at Everett on February 25, 1993. For Air France, the intervening four-and-a-half years between launch and rollout had been tough, so tough in fact that it canceled its order. The first flight went ahead as planned on May 4, 1993, and a Luxembourg-based specialist freighter operator, Cargolux, became the first -400F owner when it took delivery the following November.

The recession of the early 1990s hampered growth in the cargo business, and -400F sales were slow as a result. By mid-1997, only 21 orders had been placed. Boeing was not disheartened and predicted the long-term outlook was much brighter. It forecast that the world cargo industry would grow by more than 6 percent every year through 2010 and predicted that nearly 600 new large-capacity freighters (over 50 tons payload) would be needed by 2014. Unfortunately, a bid to boost the -400F by supplying it to the USAF as the C-33 transport was unsuccessful. In early 1996, the Defense Department confirmed its decision to buy up to 120 McDonnell Douglas C-17s instead (see Chapter 8).

With or without freighters, and despite its inauspicious start, the -400 turned out to be a major success. By 1997, orders had topped 550 and showed no signs of tailing off. With the expected launch of the -500X/-600X stretched derivatives in 1996, the production of -400s was expected to be phased out about 2003. However, when the -500X and -600X programs were dropped in January 1997, it breathed new life into the -400, which received additional orders as a result. Boeing also began to "blow the dust" off its earlier -400 derivative studies, all of which had been abandoned as a result of the decision to go with the all-new wing as the basis for the stretch. With airline demand for bigger versions still alive, and the threat of the rival Airbus A3XX growing, it became more certain that at least some of these studies might see the light of day. They ranged in scope from modification kits that reduced drag to wing plugs and modest fuselage stretches, though not on the scale conceived for the -500X/600X.

CHAPTER SEVEN

In order to build the world's biggest commercial airliner, Boeing had to create one of the world's largest final assembly complexes, at Everett, about 35 miles north of Seattle. The area offered some major advantages. It was adjacent to Snohomish County's Paine Field, which boasted a 9,900-foot runway, and it was within commuting distance of the skilled Seattle-Everett labor pool. It also offered good access to the north-south I-5 freeway, the Great Northern railroad, and Puget Sound's nearby harbor facilities.

The search for a new factory site had not been easy. It began in late 1964 when Boeing was still in the throes of the C-5A competition, and more than a year before the 747 was even formally considered. Boeing was confident of winning the military airlifter prize but needed somewhere new to build it. The existing site at Renton, where the 707, 727, 737, and much-later 757 were built, was too small. Boeing Field was also congested with its limited space allocated to testing, military work, and

In the early hours of the morning, the Section 41/42 subassembly is lowered by overhead crane into position in front of the over-wing Section 44 and wing sections. Shortly afterward, the aft fuselage Section 46, along with the tail-end Section 48 are joined on behind the over-wing section. The fuselage sections are joined to the center section through multi-bolt flange joints and fish plates between the stringers. *Boeing*

the development of the later-be canceled supersonic 2707 project. Boeing scoured the United States looking at more than 50 sites in areas as far away as Georgia, Colorado, and Southern California before homing in on local areas.

The search continued despite the loss of the C-5A competition in 1965. By the time of the decision, Boeing's focus was already switching to a commercial jet of roughly equal proportions, so it still had a compelling need for a new site. In June 1966, three months after the go-ahead of the 747 program, the company finally selected Everett. Boeing quickly took up options on a 773-acre wooded site at the northeast corner of the area and the immense task of clearing trees, leveling ground, and raising the huge factory began. Boeing promised to deliver the first aircraft to Pan Am just two-and-a-half years later, and it knew the timetable was so tight that the initial airframes would start to come together as the factory was still being completed around them.

One of the first priorities was to get rail service to the low plateau on which the factory would be built. A spur was hacked through the forest from the Great Northern (later Burlington Northern) railroad that snaked around the coastline to the west. Like everything else about the endeavor, even the construction of the three miles of track was a major feat of engineering. More than 1.25 million cubic yards of dirt were moved to make the track bed, which climbed from 20 feet above sea level to the western edge of the Everett site at 540 feet. The resulting 5.6 percent grade made it the second steepest standard-gauge track in the whole country. The front end of a locomotive going upgrade was 3 feet higher than its rear wheels. By late 1966, the railroad was ready for use, and the first trains crawled up the hill loaded with steel girders and other parts for building construction. Some 34,000 tons of structural steel were brought up by train during the initial phase.

As the 747 was being built virtually at the same time as the factory, the first

Fuselage panels for the 747 await their 1,000-mile train journey to Everett. For more than 30 years, identical parts for more than 1,100 747s have passed through this loading area at Northrop Grumman's Hawthorne site in Los Angeles, awaiting transport to Washington State.

The 747-400 is the only aircraft in the world with this distinctive double-deck row of windows, as clearly depicted in these Section 42 subassemblies being built at Hawthorne. Note the upper-deck exit in both panels.

buildings to be erected were low-bay manufacturing sites and a primary and subassembly area. One of the two low-bay sites, building 40.53, adjoined the 300-foot-by-300-foot area for the mock-up that was vital to the early trouble-shooting during the construction of the first aircraft. The three main 300-foot-by-1,000-foot assembly bays that formed the heart of the production line were the next parts of the factory to begin emerging from the apparent mayhem of the massive construction site. In November 1966, large roof structural beams were lowered into place to span building 40.21, the first of the major final assembly lines.

The first "Incredibles" began to occupy the final assembly building in the early summer of 1967. Construction of the main assembly area was finished a couple of months later and the site was occupied by December 1967. The clean, seal, and paint area, building 40.51, was also occupied just before December with construction of the 400-foot-by-400-foot building completed by April 1968. The huge 60,000-square-foot paint hangar was located on the other side of the 526 Highway to Muk-ilteo, which bisected the site. The hangar was in use by August 1968, though not actually completed until early the following year. This and the remaining apron area were reached by a 60-foot-wide concrete and steel overpass that bridged the highway.

A system of engineered wetlands and holding ponds was created to handle the runoff from the construction site, and later to cope with storm water draining quickly from the acres of concrete ramp space. The largest holding reservoir was constructed in a large ravine that sloped down to Puget Sound. The capacity of the reservoir was 15 million gallons, enough to float the QE II ocean liner.

The main assembly building, measuring 205 million cubic feet, became the world's largest building, by volume. The accolade stuck with it throughout successive decades as more was added. By 1997, it had grown to enclose 472 million cubic feet and covered 98.3 acres. The second major growth phase came in 1980 when the Everett complex was extended by 45 percent to house the 767 assembly line. In 1993, a third expansion phase occurred when the complex was enlarged by another 50 percent to accommodate two new final assembly lines for the 777. The entire site grew to approximately 1,000 acres, including 215 acres of paved apron and parking, and 282 acres of buildings.

By January 1967, production operations for the 747 began, and trains started to carry increasing loads of subassemblies and aircraft parts. At the end of February, Boeing started designing the massive assembly tools needed to fix together the body sections, and for the body joining process itself. Work on these tools began in June 1967 and was completed by the following April. Fabrication of the equally enormous production jigs for the wing, including the body joining fixture, was started three months ahead of the body jigs but was completed almost a month later, in May 1968. Much of the subassembly tooling was provided by the various subcontractors, such as Northrop, which also produced body-section jigs. Boeing Wichita similarly produced an assembly jig for the nose section, which was designed and made in Kansas, but assembled in Everett. A "tooling load plan" was carefully drawn up to try to avoid overstretching the available manpower, as all the parts began arriving for assembly. The plan proved successful; the program tooling estimate was underrun by 2 percent.

A tooling action center was used to monitor 48,000 tools as they were made ready for each stage of the assembly process. As a result, more than 97 percent of the critical tools were available for production of the first aircraft. In all, the 747 program required the design and fabrication of 270,000 tools with 182,000 (67 percent) of these produced by suppliers, and 88,000 (33 percent) produced by Boeing. Production also included the early use of numerical controlled (NC) machines, which helped to reduce the number of physical gauges required. All interface controls between body sections were accomplished by the use

Northrop Grumman workers near completion of a fuselage section. The man wearing the hat attaches part of the secondary support structure. This is the skeletal framework that supports the ceiling panels and interior cabin lining, as well as numerous ducts and wires.

of NC-produced simulated break rings. These multi-purpose rings served as dimensional controls as well as shipping and fitting fixtures at Boeing and their suppliers.

Jet Builder

Despite its size, Everett was designed to simply put the aircraft together and do very little actual manufacturing work. Parts poured into Everett from more than 1,500 prime suppliers and at least 15,000 secondary suppliers throughout the United States, as well as from eight overseas nations. The "aluminum avalanche" was well under way by late 1967 and has continued without serious interruption ever since.

Parts arrived by road and rail. Among the largest pieces to enter by road were the 105-foot-long main spars that were fabricated, along with most of the wing, in a specially constructed plant in Auburn, 20 miles south of Seattle. It was claimed that the 260-acre site, built at a cost of $150 million, was the most modern and mechanized fabrication facility in the free world. The company's spar, skin, and profile mills, as well as facilities for metal bonding and a machine shop that cost $35 million, were all gathered in the 4 million

square feet of factory area. The Auburn Fabrication Division contained heated autoclaves to cure metal-bonded assemblies and more than 150 NC milling machines. In 1968, the largest of these, built in Germany by Froriep Spheromill, enabled the cutter to work at any angle in a single set position.

Wing skins were produced at Auburn out of huge billets of aluminum supplied by Alcoa, some of the billets measuring more than 100 feet long, 5 feet wide, and more than 1 inch thick. The slab of metal was gradually cut down into a tapered and shaped panel, which was delivered to Everett, along with spars and stringers, on a massive, specially built truck with a 128-foot wheelbase. The trucks, which remain in use to the present day, were so long that a second driver guided the rear axle from a cab positioned in front of the rear wheels.

Once inside the Everett complex, the wing-skin panels were loaded into jigs, where Drivematic riveters joined the spars and stringers to the skin. In early versions, roughly 52,000 rivets were installed in each complete wing set by the $3 million NC machines. The riveting machines were automatically programmed to drill, ream, countersink, install, squeeze, and shave off

Once the fuselage subassemblies have been formed, the fitting of insulation, ducts, wiring bundles, windows, and cable runs begins. Note the covered pulley wheel for a control cable in the ceiling of this double-deck forward-fuselage section.

After their train journey north, the fuselage panels are put together to form major subassemblies. The double-deck sections pictured elsewhere in this chapter are joined to a crown (or roof) panel, and all three are positioned on top of a belly section formed from more panels. The whole piece becomes known as Section 42, which forms the part of the forward fuselage between the nose (Section 41) and the over-wing area (Section 44).

the head of each rivet at about the rate of six per minute. The left and right wing boxes were built up separately, from the machined panels, spars, ribs, and stringers in assembly jigs located in the subassembly bay in the main building. Each ended up being 120 feet long, 26 feet wide, and 7 feet thick at the root. The 28,000-pound units were then cleaned, sealed, and painted to form huge fuel tanks capable of taking up to 51,000 gallons. The wing boxes were moved, and the leading-edge and trailing-edge structures added, providing the platforms for the flaps and ailerons, which were attached later.

The wings were lifted to the final assembly line, where they were joined to the center section to form the complete wing assembly. At this stage, the four engine struts were added to the leading edge. The first fuselage subassembly, the over-wing Section 44, was then lowered into position on the wing centerbox and bolted into position. With the entire wing assembly taking shape, the leading-edge flaps, Krueger flaps, spoilers, and low- and high-speed ailerons were then attached to the structure.

From this moment on, the aircraft rapidly began to take shape as the larger fuselage subassemblies were moved into place. Most of the heavy lifting traditionally took place in the middle of the night when the factory was at its quietest. Following the positioning of the wing and center-body, the nose (Section 41/42) was lifted into place by overhead cranes that could lift up to 34 tons. Section 41/42, along with other large subassemblies, came to the final join process with the flight-deck equipment already installed and the lavatories and galleys already fitted. In the early years of production, all the internal fixtures were added after major body join, rather than being pre-stuffed into the subassemblies. By about 2 A.M. the huge nose section had normally been lowered into place ahead of the center section. The aft subassembly, made up of the rearmost Section 48 and the bulky aft fuselage Section 46, was then carefully maneuvered into position behind the center section.

The horizontal stabilizer was then slotted into place in Section 48 about 6 A.M., just as the day shift was clocking on. Three hours later, the main trailing-edge flaps were attached to the trailing edge to complete the wing assembly. The large "canoe" fairings were then slotted over the flap actuation mechanism and tracks. By 10 A.M. the tail cone was fitted over the space allocated for the APU. Throughout the rest of the day the vertical fin and rudder were fitted, then painted with the customer livery for correct balancing. The nose gear and four main landing-gear trucks were installed next, so the aircraft could begin moving down the assembly line on its own wheels. The large composite wing-to-body and dorsal fairings were also added at this late stage.

The aircraft was then trundled to the fitting out area where the complex business of attaching, testing, and checking all the systems took place. The cabin pressurization system was also added, though it was not tested until later in the process. The under-floor cargo holds were also fitted, along with the cargo handling systems. Galleys and toilets, although already installed, were then plumbed in and connected to the aircraft systems. Walls, ceiling panels, and usually seats and other "buyer fur-

An unusual rear view of the Section 41 cross-section shows this part of the aircraft to be, in effect, a triple-decker, if the lower cargo hold is included. The large box-like structure visible in the lower deck is the housing for the nose leg.

nished equipment" items such as in-flight entertainment systems were also installed to complete the initial internal fitting out. The engines, being the single most expensive parts of the aircraft, were added toward the final part of the assembly process to keep inventory costs down. The weather radar and protective radome was also fitted at a late stage, as were the landing-gear doors.

After pressurization tests, the aircraft was then towed across the bridge in its green protective vinyl primer to one of the three paint hangars. The vinyl was removed and the bare aluminum skin was cleaned before an anticorrosive layer was added to protect the alloy against a range of temperatures from -40 degrees F at cruising altitude to a maximum of 140 degrees F on the ground. The customer livery was applied in a special flexible paint that contracted and expanded with every pressurization cycle of the fuselage. On average, it took up to 300 gallons of paint to cover a 747, which added 1,200 pounds to the overall weight of the aircraft. The aircraft stayed in the temperature-controlled hangar for up to three days to allow time for the paint to cure. The original Pan Am livery was painted on using only 76

Boeing's Wichita division is responsible for the entire Section 41 nose section, which includes the cockpit, or cab. Once completed, Section 41 is mated to Section 42 before passing to final body join as one large subassembly.

gallons—68 of which were for the white upper surfaces, 7 for the blue, and 1 for black. The stripes on the U.S. flag on the tail required 1 pint of red paint.

About 25 days after rollout from the factory, the aircraft was ready for delivery, pending successful pre-flight tests and a four-hour-long Boeing checklist. The aircraft was then flown for the first time on its "B-1" flight, during which Boeing crew

A ship set of mighty wings resembles that of an enormous model-aircraft kit as they near completion. Trailing- and leading-edge sections are added to the Boeing-made torque box before the whole assembly is moved to the final wing-join area.

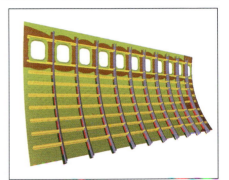

Back to the future. Boeing and Northrop Grumman decided to make a two-pronged digital attack on the 747 fuselage in efforts to improve quality, cut costs, and reduce assembly time. This CATIA drawing is one of the first fuselage panels to be digitized in a process that was expected to be completed by 1998. *Boeing*

Digital Improvement

The 747 production line absorbed gradual changes as new technology became available, but few major changes were introduced, even with the advent of the -400 series. Discreet improvements included the introduction of photogrametric equipment in 1990, which improved the way pieces were fitted together by measuring in three dimensions to an accuracy of 0.0003 inch.

Big changes were heralded by the introduction of the 777 assembly line, which brought radical advances in technology from 1993 onward. Most were introduced during a $1.5 billion expansion of the site that involved pouring 275,000 cubic yards of concrete (enough to make 44 miles of a four-lane freeway) and erecting 85,000 tons of steel, or virtually double the amount needed to build the Empire State Building. Yet the most fundamental changes, and those which would later affect the 747, were invisible to the naked eye and took place in the computerized world of cyberspace.

Boeing's big experiment with computerized design and construction really began with the 777. Some small parts of earlier designs had involved some primitive two-dimensional com-

checked out the general handling and performance of the aircraft and its systems. Assuming that no major faults were found, or following the correction of any anomalies, the customer then took the aircraft for its "C-1" check flight to ensure that everything was to their liking. By early 1997 the pass rate on B-1 flights was up to 80 percent, and about 75 percent of new 747s were being accepted by customers on the C-1 flight.

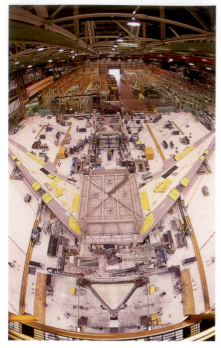

The process of assembling the actual aircraft begins with the wing-stub join. The two wings are mated to the enormous carry-through structure, which also forms the center-wing fuel tank. Note the upturned spoiler panels, made from an advanced aluminum honeycomb, still in their yellow-colored protective coverings.

With vertical and horizontal tail surfaces attached and fuselage basically complete, the aircraft has gradually become a recognizable 747. It then moves down the final assembly line on its own undercarriage while being progressively fitted out with interior systems and fittings. Sharp-eyed observers may notice that the aircraft nearest the camera has a short upper deck. This was JA8190, the last 747-281B delivered to ANA, dating the photograph to 1989.

More interior work goes on as the 747 progresses down the line. Toward the very end of the process comes the complex task of installing and checking the sophisticated avionics and flight-deck instrumentation. Here, an avionics engineer checks the various modes of the EICAS (engine indication and crew alerting system), and VHF radio.

puter-aided design but nothing like on the scale attempted with the 777. The company had done some research that showed that a huge portion of the manufacturing costs could be saved if parts fitted together better the first time. This meant expensive rework was avoided. The better it fitted together, the less reliance would be placed on huge, expensive jigs, which wore out over time and began introducing errors into the structure. In short, it meant Boeing could move toward a more flexible, snap-together type of assembly process.

Boeing used the IBM/Dassault digital design system called CATIA (computer-aided three-dimensional interactive applications) to design the 777, which became the company's first 100 percent "paperless" jetliner. All parts of the aircraft were designed straight on the computer screen as solid three-dimensional images, and the digital information about the piece was stored in the

memory. Adjacent parts were fitted together in the computer's digital brain, which instantly recognized if the fit was not perfect and if some parts, such as ducts and wires, interfered with each other. The various subcontractors making the parts for the aircraft were also linked directly into the database, which ensured a first-time fit, no matter what corner of the globe the part originated.

It was this last element of CATIA that appealed to the 747 assembly team. Their aircraft was already designed, but if computerized images of each part could be created and issued to the relevant contractors, then every 747 in the future would fit together much better. This would reduce costs, improve quality, and cut the time to complete assembly, which had add-on affects such as speeding up the flow of inventory. In addition, Boeing had already committed to drastically cutting the cycle time needed to make all its aircraft, from the time it

A brand new 747-4B5F, with side cargo door, stands in the sunshine for the first time, only a few hours after being rolled off the Everett line. Fuel is pumped into the aircraft's tanks as part of checks for leaks and other faults. The 747 will then visit the paint hangar, where its livery will be applied. This aircraft is HL7497, bound for Asiana Airlines of South Korea.

Nearing the end of the line, a 747-422 for United (the airline's 26th) receives undivided attention. Note the ballast blocks hanging from the inboard engine struts to simulate the structural weight of the missing powerplants. The real thing will be fitted within hours. Space is tight on the line, particularly since the wingspan increased with the -400, as witnessed by the proximity of the fuselage to the winglet of the adjoining aircraft. As a result, the winglets are some of the last major structural parts to be fitted.

received an order to delivery. This was part of an initiative to reduce its vulnerability to dramatic swings in the airline's profit-and-loss roller coaster. The increased flexibility of the new manufacturing system was in keeping with this goal, which BCAG President Ron Woodard termed "the six-month airplane." The size of the 747 meant the best it could realistically aim for was 10 or 11 months.

"We're basically digitizing the 747 fuselage using CATIA, and are scanning everything in from the inner and outer mold lines," said Edward Renouard, Everett site vice president of 747/767 programs. "We think we can really improve the quality and reduce the variability using the power of CATIA." The first of 28 panels that made up the main fuselage sections was digitized in September 1996, and the company hoped to complete the process by late 1998.

Northrop Grumman, as fuselage supplier, had a big part to play in the process and developed its own initiative, called accurate fuselage assembly (AFA). While Northrop Grumman began digitizing its assembly processes to make much more accurate panels, Boeing's CATIA-based design change addressed the aging tooling at Everett. The Boeing initiative was called FAIT, or fuselage assembly integration team. "The goal is to have AFA and hardware come in at the same time as we finish FAIT," said Jack Jones, the director of the Everett 747/767 Fuselage Responsibility Center. "The first FAIT tool for Section 44 should be coming on-line in the first quarter of 1998." Section 42 tooling was expected to follow in mid-1998 with Section 46 coming on-line by the end of the year. "Quality was the driver for this whole process," added Jones. "It has been 30 years since most of these parts were designed and there have been a lot of technical advances since then. When

we got into it we saw several opportunities to improve the design, as well as to reduce cycle time and cost."

The digital initiative was complemented by a move to "lean manufacturing" techniques pioneered by Japanese car giant Toyota. This was basically a more flexible "pulse" system that enabled Boeing to be more responsive to the changing market conditions. Parts were brought into the factory on a just-in-time basis, which again helped to reduce costly inventory. The company also "cleaned up its bill of materials" and streamlined the more complex parts of the assembly process such as the wing-body join. "By 1998 we should be getting a lot of benefit and by 2000 it will be a really nimble process," said Renouard. One of the big indicators of how successful all the changes had been was in the time taken from the definition of the interior configuration by a customer to the actual moment of delivery. By 1997, this had already been shortened from 18 months to 10.5 months, and further reductions were planned.

CHAPTER EIGHT

Boeing was soon working on new 747 variants to join the baseline -100 and -200B, and by 1972 was offering the 747SR, or short range. "We thought, why don't we put a lot of seats into the aircraft and redefine it?" recalled Joe Sutter. "We put a lot of fatigue resistance into the wing and of course the aircraft had the flexibility to do that. At the time we were studying the SR, other Boeing people were studying the stretched 727 for the same Japanese domestic market. Anyway, we proposed it, and the sales department did not want to do it, but JAL did."

Japanese domestic traffic over the late 1960s had grown at the staggering rate of more than 20 percent per year, and the new wide-body transports were the only real answer to the increasing problems of congestion that threatened to strangle the system. Indeed, Boeing's sales campaign to the Japanese included the fact that two 747s, seating up to 1,074, took up only 450 feet of airport terminal frontage, whereas six 727-200s seating 1,068 would have required 800 feet. Boeing also aimed for a planned turnaround time of just 35 minutes.

SPECIAL ROLES, MODS, AND CONVERSIONS

The bulbous nose-mounted laser turret of the AL-1A is prominent in this artist's impression of the aircraft destroying multiple ballistic missiles. The Airborne Laser was likened in importance to the discovery of gunpowder and the Manhattan project. The USAF planned to have a force of up to seven AL-1As operational in 2008. *Boeing*

Average domestic load factors in Japan had reached 85 percent by 1970, and the total number of passengers carried during the year reached 4.6 million. A fleet of 727s and DC-8-61s sustained most of the major trunk routes, but JAL's domestic competitor, ANA, had already taken the wide-body initiative and ordered a batch of six Lockheed L-1011 TriStars. Japan Air Lines responded by placing orders for four 747SRs on October 30, 1972, in a deal worth $44 million. In the end, JAL ordered 16 SR derivatives, while ANA later took 17 SRs based on the -100B airframe.

Boeing carefully tailored the aircraft so that it could operate with a maximum landing weight of 505,000 pounds, which enabled it to fly the 270-nautical-mile Tokyo to Osaka route as a round trip, without refueling. At the same time, the basic gross weight of up to 735,000 pounds was still theoretically available so the aircraft could fly longer international routes. In practice, the standard domestic, all-economy maximum takeoff weight was to be 520,000 pounds, but it could be easily increased to 600,000 pounds, which brought other places, such as Hong Kong, within range. In later service, the initial aircraft, designated 747SR-100, ended up in day-to-day service with a maximum takeoff weight of 571,000 pounds.

The 747SR-100 was essentially a stronger standard -100. Strengthened areas included the fin attachment, crown splices over the center body, undercarriage support, stabilizer root, fin root, wing lower surface, wing/body splice, in-spar ribs, spoilers, ailerons, and trailing-edge flap supports. The middle and rear spars were also improved, as were the leading edge and nacelle support structures. The idea was to give the airframe an economic lifetime of 52,000 flights during 20 years of operations, compared to the standard long-range aircraft's lifetime expectancy of 24,600 flights over the same period. The aircraft was originally configured to carry 498, including 16 in

Boeing's 747SR demonstrator poses for a picture in the fall of 1972, a picture that could never be repeated today. It is highly unlikely that the words "Super Airbus" will ever again appear on the sides of a Boeing demonstrator aircraft, and the outline of nearby Mt. St. Helens has altered drastically since it erupted in May 1980 and lost 1,300 feet of elevation in the process. *Boeing*

the upper lounge, but by the later years in service had been extended to seat between 523 and 528 in a two-class layout.

Boeing also examined possible stretch SRs, which would have a stretched upper deck with capacity for 98 and a main deck load of 547 for a total passenger complement of 645. Another stretch plan envisaged two plugs, one forward and one aft of the wing, extending the length by 240 inches in both sections. The extra length would increase top-deck capacity to 122 and main-deck capacity to 627—a total capacity of 749 passengers. The 747-300SRs bought by JAL later carried up to 563 (see below), though the record for the most people carried on one 747 was held for some time by a Qantas 747-238B, (City of Melbourne). On December 29, 1974, it evacuated 674 passengers (306 adults, 328 children, and 40 infants) from Darwin to Sydney, following the devastating Cyclone Tracy. Because the aircraft was fitted with only 369 seats, every adult had a child on his or her lap or, in some cases, on the floor between the

legs. Other seats were occupied by two children.

This record was broken in 1991 when an El Al 747 carried more than 1,200 Ethiopian Jewish settlers from Addis Ababa to Tel Aviv, Israel. The crammed aircraft, a 747-200C Combi, had been specially converted to passenger configuration with 760 seats as part of Operation Solomon, a top secret mission to airlift 14,000 Ethiopian Jews to Israel before Addis Ababa fell to rebel troops. The 747 was on the ground at Addis Ababa for only 37 minutes while the 1,200 settlers were hastily loaded. Two other standard passenger configured El Al 747s, with normal seating for 454, carried 920 passengers each. Four 767s carried 430 on their 224 seats and floor, and two 757s involved carried 360 on their 197 seats and in any available space. Eight Israeli Air Force 707s had seats removed and rubber matting laid on the cabin floor and carried an amazing 500 people each.

The first 747SR, powered by P&W JT9D-7s operating at a derated setting of 43,500 pounds of thrust, was rolled

All Nippon Airways introduced the 46,500-pound-thrust CF6-45A engine into service on its 747SR-100Bs. In service, these aircraft are referred to as 747SR-81s and carry 20 business-class passengers and up to 508 economy-class. Note the JAL 747 turning in toward the airfield as JA8139 makes a spirited departure from Tokyo's Haneda.

out on August 3, 1973, and flew for the first time at the end of that month. The initial aircraft, line number 221, was certificated on September 26 and was handed over to JAL the same day. Seven SR-100s were built over the next two years, and all entered service on JAL's limited domestic network. This was restricted to the main trunk routes between Tokyo and Sapporo, Osaka, and Fukuoka, as well as Osaka to Fukuoka, Fukuoka to Sapporo, and Sapporo to Osaka. In addition, from May 1972, it was also cleared to operate services from Tokyo, Osaka, and Fukuoka to the island of Naha. Formerly known as Okinawa, the island had been occupied by the United States since the end of World War II but was handed back to Japan that year and technically became a new domestic destination for Japanese airlines.

It was another three years before further interest was revived in an SR derivative. This time, ANA became the customer for a short-range, stronger version of the higher-gross-weight 747-100B airframe. The aircraft were developed for ANA as the 747SR-100B,

though three aircraft also produced later for JAL were curiously designated in reverse as 747-100B(SR)s. The first aircraft for ANA, line number 346, differed from previous SRs already in service by having 46,500-pound-thrust GE CF6-45A engines. It first flew on November 3, 1978, and was delivered to Japan on December 21. A total of 17 were produced for ANA, followed by three JT9D-powered versions for JAL.

Japan Air Lines later took advantage of the SUD development for the -300 model to increase total passenger capacity to 563. In 1985, JAL ordered two 747-100Bs with the stretched upper deck, designated -100B (SR/SUD). The first of these curious hybrids flew on February 26, 1986, and was certificated on March 24 and delivered to JAL the same day. The next year, JAL also took delivery of the first of four SR derivatives of the 747-300. Designated 747-300 (SR), the first aircraft, line number 692, flew on November 24, 1987, and was delivered to the airline on December 10. Like its predecessors, the -300 (SR) models were powered by P&W JT9Ds, but the

higher weight version was fitted with the more powerful 54,000-pound-thrust JT9D-7R4G2 engines.

Tragically, the third 747SR delivered to JAL, JA8119, made its terrible mark on history by crashing into a mountain northwest of Tokyo on August 12, 1985, killing 516 passengers and crew—the largest number ever killed in one aircraft. The 747 had earlier suffered a hard landing and damaged the aft section beneath the tail. The rear pressure bulkhead was inadequately repaired, and on a later flight between Tokyo and Osaka the bulkhead failed. Pressurized cabin air vented through the fractured bulkhead repair and blew away a large part of the upper vertical tail, critically damaging the multiple hydraulic systems. The crew disengaged the autopilot and managed to regain some control of the crippled aircraft by juggling the engine power and control surfaces on the wings. Unfortunately, after the aircraft had been slowly turned around in an attempt to crash land at Haneda, more hydraulic fluid was lost and the remaining flight controls became ineffective. The aircraft lost height and the crew was unable to maneuver around 5,000-foot-high Mt. Ogura, which it struck at a speed of approximately 125 miles per hour.

One of only two 747s of its type in the world, this hybrid aircraft is a higher-gross-weight 747-100B combined with SR strengthening and a -300/SUD long upper deck. In recognition of its mixed-up heritage, the aircraft is designated a 747-146B (SR/SUD). Seating is provided for 25 business-class and 538 economy-passengers.

Another 747 joins the growing band of converted freighters. This -200B, built in 1978 and formerly Thai Airways International's *Visuthakasatriy* (HS-TGA), is seen undergoing special freighter conversion at Boeing Wichita's modification center. Much of the rear of the left-side fuselage panel is replaced with a new section containing a door measuring 134 inches wide by 120 inches tall, which opens level with the strengthened main-deck floor. Note the removal of the tail fins so the 747s can fit inside the hangar, which was originally built for B-47s.

Air Force One delivers President Bill Clinton to Albuquerque, New Mexico, during his successful 1996 re-election campaign. Note the lump on the nose of the VC-25A, which marks the location of the air-to-air refueling receptacle. The aircraft is festooned with communications antennae, including one mounted on the horizontal stabilizer. It is also fitted with comprehensive threat warning receivers and is protected from heat-seeking missiles by a countermeasures package visible at the aft end of each engine strut.

The first SR was later bought back by Boeing and sold to NASA in 1988, while the second aircraft was returned to Everett in the same year, where it was used for structural testing to evaluate the long-term fatigue properties of the airframe.

Despite the accident, the SR remained popular and had become a vital part of the Japanese transport infrastructure. Boeing kept the concept going with the -400 family when plans were announced in October 1989 to produce the 747-400D Domestic (see Chapter 6). As with the SR series before, the -400D was ordered by both JAL and ANA, and required major structural reinforcement to adapt to the high cycle operations. The first -400D, line number 844, flew on March 15, 1991, and was handed over to JAL on October 10. By early 1997 some 20 747-400Ds had been delivered to JAL and ANA.

Special Freighters and CRAF

Boeing had predicted that up to half the first 747s would be sold as cargo aircraft. However, in the first three years, virtually no interest had been shown in a freighter version, apart from Lufthansa, which had introduced a single new-build 747-200F into service in 1972. Boeing's original expectations had been based on assumptions that the cargo market would quickly expand and that a fast-growing fleet of supersonic airliners would force the conversion of the 747s into cargo-haulers.

The supersonic fleets never came, at least not on the scale expected by Boeing, and the air-cargo market saw only modest growth. A new stimulus for the cargo version of the aircraft came in 1973 and 1974 when oil prices rocketed because of an oil embargo, and a world economic recession soon followed. Passenger loads dwindled on some 747 trunk routes, particularly across the North Atlantic, and some 747-100 passenger aircraft began appearing on the secondhand market.

Boeing saw its first opportunity to offer conversions at its Wichita site in Kansas. This partially helped to compensate for the dramatic fall in pro-

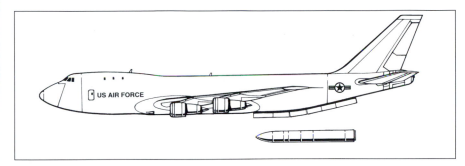

One of several missile-carrying MC747 study concepts involved dropping a ballistic missile through enormous bomb bay doors cut into the base of Section 46. The missile would have been released at 0.72 Mach and 30,000 feet and was supposed to tilt base down as it fell below the 747, and ignite when clear of the aircraft. The ICBM was then expected to pass through the 747's flight path about 5,000 feet ahead of the aircraft. Thirty seconds after launch, the missile would have been 20,000 feet in front and 7,000 feet above the 747. Boeing believed this launch method would increase the missile's range by up to 15 percent, compared to an equivalent ground-launched missile. The range could be stretched by up to 25 percent by launching in a climb. *Gareth Burgess*

duction rates, which had tumbled from a peak of seven per month in early 1971 to only two per month a year later. The aircraft were designated 747-100SF, or Special Freighters, because they had not been originally built as cargo aircraft with either a nose or side freight door, and therefore required special modification. The conversion involved ripping out and rebuilding the interior with a strengthened main-cargo-deck floor and cargo handling system. A 120-inch-by-134-inch side cargo door was cut into the left side between the trailing edge of the wing and the tail.

The first of 24 conversions began in 1974 on a former American Airlines aircraft for the cargo carrier Flying Tigers. The work also increased the maximum takeoff weight to 755,000 pounds. All-cargo conversions were also undertaken for American, Pan Am, and the Imperial Iranian Air Force, as it was called before the 1979 Islamic revolution. Two additional Combi aircraft were also converted for Sabena in early 1974 and these were fitted with a strengthened aft-deck floor to carry up to six freight pallets.

By the late 1980s, the freight market again began to show signs of faster growth, and Boeing Wichita's Modifi-

cation Responsibility Center decided to launch a new conversion program in August 1989. The program was extended to cover -200s and offered a wider range of higher takeoff weight growth options. By 1995, it had been further extended to include the -300 versions. At first, only freight conversions of the -300 Combi were offered, but by 1997, Boeing had also developed a full passenger-to-freight conversion package. Boeing offered the basic -100/200SF conversion for almost $20 million, with an extra charge of $900,000 to take the maximum takeoff weight up to 750,000 pounds. The converted -300SF, which started with a baseline takeoff weight of 775,000 pounds for most versions, was offered with a payload capability of up to 245,000 pounds.

In April 1997 Boeing announced the first freighter conversion of a 747-200 SUD when it clinched a $42 million contract from KLM for the modification of two aircraft. The work involved shortening the upper-deck floor, enabling 20 full-height 10-foot pallet positions, plus 10 shorter pallet positions (one more than the standard -200F). The two aircraft were due to be returned to KLM in March and May 1998.

Wichita also performed the first aftermarket cargo conversions of the 747-400 in 1994, when it modified two Taiwan-owned, EVA Air aircraft from passenger to Combi configuration. By 1997 Boeing Wichita had modified more than 70 747s into freighters.

By the early 1990s, competition in the conversion market was growing increasingly fierce, with several companies offering -100 and -200 modifications. First off the mark was the GATX/Airlog partnership, which obtained a supplementary type certificate (STC) in May 1988 to convert 747-100 passenger aircraft to freighters. Along with Airlog, the holder of the original STC, GATX later extended this to include the 747-200. The first five -100 conversions were carried out by Pemco Aeroplex at Dothan, Alabama. The first -200 was converted in 1994 for the partnership by Chrysler Airborne Technologies at Waco, Texas. The former Qantas aircraft was delivered to American International Airways after certification was received in October 1994. The following year, Mobile Aerospace won an order to convert two former Kuwait Airways 747-200 Combis to full freighters for cargo airline Connie Kalitta/American International Airways, using the GATX/Airlog modification kit. The conversion also used a cargo handling system supplied by AAR Advanced Structures.

Business was good for the group, as operators lined up for conversions. In 1992, it signed a deal with BA to offer the airline's original fleet of 15 747-136 Classics for resale as ripe for conversion to freighters. In 1995 the FAA issued an airworthiness directive affecting all the 19 aircraft converted using the GATX/Airlog STC. The agency found the longitudinal floor beams between fuselage stations 1265 and 1480 had not been upgraded to withstand the higher "running loads" that would be experienced in service as a freighter. The problem mostly affected the area over the keel beam in the midsection of the fuselage above the undercarriage area. As a result, all affected aircraft could only operate with a reduced payload (120,107 pounds down from 220,195 pounds) until modifications could be made.

Other companies competing with Boeing included Hong Kong Aero Engineering Company (HAECO), which completed its first 747-200SF for SAA in 1995. Later that year, it won a contract from Atlas Air to convert up to 10 747-200 Combis to full freighters. Another aggressive competitor was the Bedek Aviation Division of Israel Aircraft Industries (IAI), which completed its first conversion, a 747-200 Combi for Lufthansa, in August 1990 and won subsequent work from Air France, among others. IAI was the only other company, apart from Boeing itself, that possessed a finite structural analysis computer model of the 747. GATX/Airlog was later in negotiation with IAI, its direct competitor, when it had to use the model in order to develop modifications to its conversion kit that would be acceptable to the FAA.

In response to all this competition, Boeing Wichita increased the pressure by developing a new process to cut conversion downtime by up to 10 days. The new method, revealed in 1995, involved using prebuilt floor assemblies, which meant that beams could be replaced up to six at a time instead of one by one.

Wichita was also heavily involved in a program called the Civil Reserve Air Fleet (CRAF) conversion. This covered the conversion of 19 Pan Am aircraft, at a cost of up to $20 million per aircraft, to provide the USAF with a readily available fleet of reserve aircraft that were capable of carrying cargo in times of national emergency or when its standard airlift capacity was stretched with multiple commitments. The conversion covered 14 747-100s and four 747-200Bs, and was similar to the standard SF package but did not include a powered cargo system. The aircraft were designated C-19As. The strengthening and new door added 13,000 pounds to the empty weight of the aircraft. As a result of the weight increase, the USAF paid compensation to Pan Am during commercial passenger operations. However, a clause in

The space shuttle prototype *Enterprise* lifts off NASA's first 747, N905NA, during one of two free flights of the *Enterprise* without the streamlined tail cone over the engines. The atmospheric glide and landing tests conducted in 1977 at NASA's Dryden Flight Research Facility at Edwards AFB, California, paved the way for the first mission into space with *Columbia* in April 1981. The NASA 747 still wore part of the livery of American Airlines, which had owned it for nearly four years before selling it to the NASA. *NASA*

the conversion contract prevented the aircraft from being used as commercial freighters for up to 12 years after the work, unless payments were made to the USAF. The 747 part of the CRAF program, which originally began during the Korean War in 1952, ran from 1985 to December 1989. Wichita subsequently reconverted five of the CRAF aircraft into full freighters.

Military 747s

Boeing realized the vast military potential of the 747 from the start, yet the aircraft was used in surprisingly few but vital roles. The first military versions, designated E-4As, were announced by the USAF's Electronic Systems Division on February 23, 1973. Boeing was awarded a $59 million fixed-price contract for two 747-200Bs to be adapted to E-4A airborne command posts. Within five months, a second contract, valued at $27.7 million, was issued for a third aircraft. In December 1973, a fourth aircraft was contracted for, at the higher price of $39 million. This covered the installation of more advanced engines and equipment, and the aircraft was designated the E-4B.

The E-4s were bought to replace the 707-based EC-135 airborne command posts of the National Military Command System and Strategic Air Command. At least one aircraft was constantly on the alert and airborne 24 hours a day in case of a nuclear attack from the Soviet Union. In the event of a sudden strike, the aircraft's job was to provide a critical communications link between the U.S. National Command Authority (NCA) and retaliatory forces such as the USAF's bomber and missile bases and the U.S. Navy's nuclear submarines. The first E-4s were also equipped with wiring to add the so-called "Looking Glass" capability. This would enable the E-4 staff to launch intercontinental ballistic missiles if ground centers were knocked out, but these "black box" systems were never actually fitted.

The first three E-4s were fitted by E-Systems (later part of Raytheon) with the avionics equipment taken out of the EC-135s. The first E-4A made its maiden flight on June 13, 1973. After fitting out, it was delivered to Andrews AFB, near Washington D.C., in December 1974. The second and third followed in May and September 1975 and were initially operated as National Emergency Airborne Command Posts (NEACPs). The third E-4 was also the first production 747 (line number 232) to be powered by GE CF6 engines. The first two E-4s were later re-engined with the CF6 and all were subsequently upgraded to the more powerful CF6-50E2 standard. These engines had improved fuel economy, allowing longer patrol times, and higher takeoff thrust in hot ambient temperatures. This meant that more runways would be accessible in times of emergency. With the new engines, the aircraft's takeoff run for an eight-hour mission was an impressively short 5,000 feet, opening up a huge number of potential operating bases.

The first E-4B was fitted with a 1,200-kilovolt-amp electrical system, compared with the 240-kilovolt-amp systems on the standard 747s of the day. The system was driven by two 150-kilovolt-amp generators mounted on each engine. This enormous power supply supported the advanced avionics, which included 13 external communications systems operating through a vast array of 46 different antennae. These ranged in size from a small super-high-frequency (SHF) satellite antenna mounted in the largest of several fairings on the fuselage roof aft of the upper deck, to a trailing wire for dual very low-frequency (VLF) and low-frequency (LF) communications that was up to 5 miles long when fully deployed. The VLF was particularly valuable to the aircraft because VLF was hard to jam and was designed to ensure communications even through the distorted atmospheric conditions caused by a nuclear attack. The aircraft's high-speed, secure-record communications equipment was also able to tie into commercial telephone and radio networks. If needed, this would have enabled the senior officer on the E-4B to issue radio broadcasts to the nation while in midair.

Up to 94 crew members could be carried by the aircraft on three decks. The upper deck contained the flight deck and a 330-square-foot flight-crew rest area, while the 185-foot-long main deck was divided into compartments for an NCA area, briefing and conference rooms, a battle staff work area for

up to 30 crew members, communications and technical control centers, and a crew rest area. The forward and rear lobes housed electronic equipment, a maintenance workshop, and a small station in the tail for the VLF antenna winch operator.

The first E-4B with the complete systems, including nuclear thermal shielding, entered service with the USAF in January 1980. The first converted E-4B was delivered three years later, followed by the last two in 1984 and 1985. The main operating base for the E-4 fleet is now Offut AFB, Nebraska, under the control of Air Combat Command.

The 747 was also selected as the President's personal transport. Designated as a VC-25A, the aircraft carried the call sign of Air Force One when the President was aboard. It was operated by the 89th Military Airlift Wing at Andrews AFB. The two VC-25As replaced the aging VC-137Cs (Boeing 707-320Cs), which first entered the presidential fleet on October 12, 1962. Powered by four 56,750-pound-thrust GE CF6-80C2B1s, the VC-25As were capable of an unrefueled range of more than 6,900 miles. For self-sufficiency, they were also equipped with a second Garrett GTCP331-200 APU in the tail and self-contained airstairs in the lower lobe.

The onboard equipment included secure voice terminals and cyptographic systems for writing and deciphering classified messages. In late 1996 these systems were augmented with a Ball Aerospace satellite communications system with up to 12 channels of secure voice and circuit-mode data. The Airlink system enabled Air Force One to use the Inmarsat global aeronautical communications network for worldwide communications. A "gateway" converted signals between the analog secure telephone unit (STU-III), and a digital satellite data unit provided by Collins. Worldwide secure service was provided by three specially equipped COMSAT-supported stations. These were in Southbury, Connecticut; Santa

Special attachments to carry the space shuttle are visible on the fuselage of NASA's second shuttle carrier, a former JAL 747SR-46 that NASA bought from Boeing in 1988. The aircraft is seen at Marana, Arizona, where it is maintained by Evergreen.

One of the first batch of 747s, line number 25, which was originally delivered to Pan Am in March 1970, began a new life in 1992 as an engine test bed for GE. The aircraft replaced the company's venerable 707 test bed and has been used to test the CFM56-7 engine for the Next Generation 737 as well as the growth CF34-8C1 for the Canadair CRJ Series 700. Its primary mission, however, was to test the massive GE90 turbofan for the 777. The 747 was the only aircraft large enough to handle the job.

Paula, California; and Eik, in Norway. The navigation system, which was originally dependent on Litton ring-laser-gyro inertial navigation systems, was also updated with global positioning system receivers.

The VC-25A interior was modified to create 4,000 square feet of floor space. This provided room for an executive suite that included a presidential office, stateroom, and washroom. Two galleys, each capable of providing food for up to 50 people, and an emergency medical facility were also built in. The aircraft also had work and rest areas for the presidential staff, news media, and USAF crews. The first VC-25A rolled out in September 1989 and both were delivered to the USAF in 1990.

The 747 was heavily pushed several times by Boeing as both a tanker and transporter for the USAF. Boeing said the 747 could off-load approximately 230,000 pounds of fuel after both a B-52 and the tanker had flown 4,000 nautical miles. This gave the B-52 about 2,600 nautical miles more range than if it had been refueled by a KC-135. At the height of Cold War tensions, the 747 tanker also could provide a fast response in the event of a nuclear attack. Painting a bleak scenario of the unexpected first-strike attack the United States most feared from the Soviet Union, Boeing estimated that a 747 with the APU running could begin its takeoff run "within 70 seconds after the klaxon. The aircraft is off the runway in 120 seconds. Within 180 to 300 seconds (depending on the warhead) the aircraft is far enough away to escape a burst over the base."

Simulated air-to-air tanking trials were conducted with the first 747 modified with a flying boom mounted beneath the tail. Dry hookups were completed successfully with a B-52, Lockheed SR-71, McDonnell Douglas F-4, and General Dynamics F-111—all representative of the different types in the USAF inventory. The work was funded by the USAF, but none of the 747 tankers was ever ordered by the U.S. military. Ultimately, the Shah of Iran bought a fleet of 12 former-airline 747s for the Imperial Iranian Air Force and, having converted 10 to freighters, added tanking capability to at least two, becoming the only customer for the specialized aircraft.

One of the more outlandish military 747 proposals was the missile-carrying MC747. In 1972 concept studies,

The original 747 development aircraft, RA001, continued to work hard for Boeing long after the original flight-test program was concluded in 1969. Apart from 747 development work, it was used in 1972 to demonstrate air-to-air refueling capability to the USAF with a mock-up flying boom. Throughout the remainder of the 1970s and into the early 1980s, it tested engines for the 747, 757, and 767 programs until in October 1983 it was flown to Las Vegas, Nevada, for three years in storage. In August 1986 it came out of mothballs and flew to Wichita, Kansas, for use as a mock-up for the development of the VC-25A. *City of Everett*, as it was christened, was donated to Seattle's Museum of Flight in 1990 but was leased back by Boeing, for a very nominal fee, in 1992 to provide an engine test bed for the 777 effort.

the 747-200F derivative was seen as an airborne launch platform for four Minuteman ICBMs. The missiles were to be dropped out of huge bomb bay doors located in the base of the aft Section 46. The missiles would either be dropped out facing backward, in which case the 747 would launch facing away from the target, or would fall out facing backward but rotate up and over the 747 to fly toward the target. A third method was a forward-facing missile that dropped below the 747, ignited, and crossed the aircraft's flight path about 5,000 feet ahead of the aircraft.

Later carrier configurations included up to seven 57,000-pound missiles with bomb bays forward and aft, and two enormous 200,000-pound missiles that were to be dropped out of a bomb bay more than 65 feet long. Another version carried up to 43 air-launched cruise missiles (ALCMs). The missiles would be loaded onto carriage racks through the nose door and shuttled aft to be launched from side-arm launchers through plug

doors. Alternative ALCM proposals used the lower lobes for rotary launchers or stack racks, as on the B-52.

The 747 Ocean Surveillance System was another scheme that got nowhere. Proposed as a combined early-warning and command-and-control platform, the key element of the design was a giant L-band phased-array radar, with an antenna arranged along the roof of the aircraft. The antenna was built to fit flush with the forward hump and measured 140 feet by 6 feet. It ran parallel with the fuselage roof, back to the tail fin. The narrow radar beam could be steered through a 120-degree azimuth sector on either side of the aircraft and to elevation angles from directly overhead to 30 degrees down. Boeing estimated that by flying at 30,000 feet in a circular search pattern, the aircraft would be able to scan a 200-square-nautical-mile area of water every second.

Boeing did not give up easily, particularly with the 747 transporter idea for the USAF. In the late 1970s

On 17 May, 1997, the UK Defence Evaluation and Research Agency deliberately blew up an ex-Air France 747-100 to test new container linings which could help prevent a repeat of the 1988 Lockerbie disaster. Three "bombs" placed in modified cargo bays or strengthened containers were successfully exploded without causing critical damage. The fourth, placed in a standard design container, resulted in the chilling image seen here. Note how the fuselage, which was pressurized to 9 pounds-per-square-inch to simulate the differential pressure at 35,000 feet, is bursting open under the combined blast-shock and cabin pressurization.

The global economic recession of the early 1990s forced many wide-bodies, and early 747s in particular, into desert storage with an uncertain future. While some airframes were parted out for spares, others escaped the cutter's torch and returned to service as the economy recovered. Resembling model aircraft, 6 of up to 30 stored 747s are pictured under a baking sun at Marana, Arizona.

and early 1980s it again floated the idea of selling off-the-shelf 747Fs as a "near term augmentation of the current airlift force." The C-5A had suffered from wing cracking, and in 1978 Lockheed had been contracted to develop new wings that would increase service life to 30,000 hours. More than 70 C-5As were rewinged by 1987. Boeing still hoped to sell a few 747s to the USAF but its old

nemesis, Lockheed, once again foiled its plan by winning approval in 1982 for the manufacture of 50 new aircraft that were designated C-5Bs.

To encourage more interest in its proposal, Boeing even developed a special nose jack design that allowed the 747 to kneel to unload tanks and trucks through the nose door. The retractable jack allowed the door sill height to be lowered by 6 feet, to 10 feet off the ground. The jack was stowed up inside the nose cone during flight and could be lowered to the ground for unloading. The nose landing gear was then retracted, and the front of the aircraft was lowered slowly on the jack until the loading ramp formed an angle of 13 degrees with the ground. The concept was demonstrated at Everett in 1980 when a Flying Tigers 747-200F was taxied into a specially dug trench to simulate the lower sill height.

In 1994, Boeing tried once again to sell the idea to the USAF, this time with its bid for the Pentagon's non-developmental airlift alternative (NDAA) project. The competition was spawned because of cost-overruns on the McDonnell Douglas C-17 Globemaster III program. Eleven companies submitted proposals for an off-the-shelf airlifter to supplement the final number of C-17s purchased. Boeing's bid, with teammate P&W, was declared the winner in 1995. Boeing proposed a PW4056-powered version of the 747-400F, with an increased maximum takeoff weight of 920,000 pounds and a 7,800-nautical-mile range.

It supported its proposal, designated C-33A, with data from the 1992 Gulf War, which showed that the largest proportion of supplies brought in by air during Operation Desert Shield and Desert Storm had arrived by 747. During and after the conflict, the 747 fleet flew 3,700 missions, carrying 644,000 troops and 220,000 tons of equipment. The Defense Acquisition Board, which had the final say on the C-17 decision, looked as if it might approve the purchase of some C-33As, but some Boeing employees suspected that their efforts were simply being used by the Defense Department as a

stalking horse to scare McDonnell Douglas into urgent action. Whether this was true or not will probably never be known, but the decision went in favor of the C-17, and once again, the 747 was left out in the cold.

While the Gulf War did little to promote the actual sale of 747 freighters to the USAF, it pushed the use of the aircraft as a platform for its first active combat role. The Gulf War illustrated the difficulty of intercepting theater ballistic missiles such as the Russian-built Scud, which Iraq used to attack targets in Israel and Saudi Arabia. Two years after the war, a Boeing-led team was one of two selected to study methods of knocking out such missiles in midair using an airborne laser. In November 1996 the Boeing, TRW, and Lockheed Martin team was declared the winners of a $1.1 billion program definition and risk-reduction contract. This involved building a prototype YAL-1A aircraft based on the 747-400F freighter and testing a giant airborne laser (ABL) mounted on a turret in the nose.

Jerry King, who was the president of Boeing Defense and Space Group at the time said: "The members of Team ABL agree with Secretary of the Air Force Sheila Widnall's statement that the Airborne Laser program is as revolutionary as the invention of gunpowder or the Manhattan Project [the secret code name for the atomic-bomb project]." The six-and-a-half-year contract covered the mounting and test firing of the laser in the first aircraft, which was expected to be delivered to Wichita for modification in early 1999. The timetable called for it to demonstrate its lethality by destroying a theater ballistic missile by late 2002.

The TRW-made chemical oxygen-iodine laser (COIL) was expected to have a range of between 180 and 360 miles, which would allow the 747 to cruise at altitudes above 40,000 feet well away from enemy territory, yet still hit missiles within seconds of being launched. The optics and detectors, made by Lockheed Martin, were designed to pick up the launch and

After a brief blaze of glory as a movie star in *Executive Decision*, this 747 sat in storage at Mojave, California, facing an uncertain future. The black marks on the left wing are all that remain of its make-up, which was added to simulate an engine fire.

guide the laser toward the missile as it entered its boost phase during the first 30 to 140 seconds of flight. The COIL would then fire a burst of energy for approximately 5 seconds at the casing around the missile's midsection, where the propellant tanks are normally situated. Laser tests predicted that the missile would then explode, and the debris would rain back down on the territory of the hostile nation if the missile were destroyed quickly enough. The prospect of this was also an added deterrent against using missiles with chemical, biological, or nuclear warheads.

The TRW laser had shown high efficiency during earlier tests, demonstrating several hundred kilowatts of output for more than 5 seconds. In laser terms, high efficiency is a comparison of the potential energy of the reactants to actual laser-beam power. The sheer lifting capacity of the 747 also meant that enough oxygen and iodine could be carried on each mission to enable up to 30 bursts of 5 seconds to be fired. In 1997 prices, the cost in chemicals of each burst was estimated at just over $1,000, compared to more than $1 million per shot for some alternative antimissile missiles that had been put forward for the role.

Pending the outcome of successful trials, Boeing hoped to win a $4.5-billion follow-on contract to produce another six aircraft. The first three were planned to be operational by 2006, with the full fleet of seven up and running by 2008. The USAF believed this would be the minimum needed to enable at least one AL-1 to be airborne around-the-clock during a crisis. During overseas deployments, at least two aircraft would remain stationed at home to protect the continental United States. It was expected that the AL-1 might also be able to use its laser for destroying cruise missiles and even satellites in low earth orbit. Boeing also believed it could use the laser to destroy other aircraft, providing some measure of self-defense if needed.

Weird and Wonderful

Perhaps the most unusual role for the 747 has been as a ferry platform for the U.S. Space Shuttle orbiters from their occasional landing place at Edwards AFB, California, to the launch site at Florida's Kennedy Space Center. Before carrying the orbiters, however, the 747 began its association with the shuttle when it was used to launch the spacecraft at high altitude for initial handling and landing trials.

A three-phase flight-test program began at NASA's Dryden Flight Research Facility at Edwards AFB, California, on February 18, 1977, when the first unmanned-captive test of the shuttle-747 combination took place without any crew inside the orbiter *Enterprise* (named, by popular vote, after the fictional USS *Enterprise* of the TV show "Star Trek"). A second captive-active phase tested the combination with two crew aboard the shuttle. Finally, a third rather more risky free-flight phase began on August 13, 1977, in which the shuttle was released off the 747's back and allowed to glide back for a landing on the dry lake bed at Edwards.

Gordon Fullerton, who piloted the shuttle during part of the approach and landing test (ALT) program, said reaction to the piggyback, midair launch plans was somewhat mixed: "When we described our plans at a test pilots' meeting, a guy at the back of the hall got to the microphone and said, 'You can't be serious. It's the dumbest thing I ever heard of!'" The plan entailed the risk of a potentially catastrophic collision between the shuttle and the tail of the 747 as the two separated. To help the 747 crew escape in the event of a major collision, an emergency exit system similar to that used during initial 747 flight trials was developed (see Chapter 3). In this case, a chute-type slide was installed behind the flight deck that exited below the nose section. The exit was armed with an explosive charge to blow out an escape panel through which the crew, wearing parachutes, would fall. A

The end of the line for one time-ravaged 747. Still wearing its Saudia livery, this early -257B had flown for Swissair for more than a decade before beginning a nomadic career involving no less than 19 changes of ownership or operator. Ending its days at Ardmore, Oklahoma, in 1994, the aircraft had been placed on jacks after its valuable undercarriage had been sold for about $1 million. Shortly afterward, a violent storm blew the hulk from its stand and left it as pictured.

knotted rope was tied to the escape chute to help the crew crawl across the cockpit floor in case the aircraft was spinning out of control. The quadruplex hydraulic system was also fitted with new close-off valves that would prevent all pressure from being lost throughout the system if the fin was severed or badly damaged.

The tests went well and separation was clean. This was largely due to a suggestion from veteran test pilot Chuck Yeager, the first to fly faster than the speed of sound, who proposed that the shuttle be mounted on the back of the 747 with a positive angle-of-attack. The resulting airflow caused the orbiter to spring easily away from the big Boeing with no hint of sluggishness. Fullerton described the release procedure: "We'd climb as high as we could, up to about 25,000 feet. Then at 200 knots we'd push the nose over and go to full

power. As the speed built up to 240 knots, we reached separation condition; then the carrier pilot could pull the engines back to idle and deploy the speed brakes. So when the orbiter separated at just above 22,000 feet it rose up with about three-quarters of a g in it."

The first four of the five planned ALT sorties went well. On the last, progress had been so rapid that the two shuttle pilots Fullerton and Fred Haise (a crew member of Apollo 13), attempted a spot landing on the main runway at Edwards, rather than on the dry lake bed. The crew were flying the orbiter without its low-drag tail fairing for the first time, and they came in slightly too fast. Attempting to bleed airspeed off with the speed brakes and still make the touchdown point, the orbiter touched down with one wheel, then the other. Haise over-controlled the shuttle, trying to recover, and entered a pilot-induced oscillation in roll and pitch. The shuttle bounced from side to side but eventually settled to make a safe landing.

The two NASA ferry aircraft, a former American Airlines 747-123 bought in 1974 and a former JAL 747SR-100 acquired in 1988 were fitted with large end-plate fins, which improved lateral stability when the vertical tail was blanked off by the shuttle. As a result of these and other structural changes, the ferry aircraft operated under certain restrictions. Fullerton, who later flew orbiters on several space missions, was also a ferry pilot on the NASA 747 fleet. "You are aware that the orbiter is bolted on because there is a constant 'buffet'—a sort of background rumble," said Fullerton. "There is some blanking of the normal vertical stabilizer, so a turn coordination feature was built into the yaw damper. You have to use the rudder with turns up to 10 to 12 degrees of bank."

The modified support structures protruding from the fuselage roof and the end plates also meant that top speed was reduced. "We are cleared to 0.6 Mach and 26,000 feet or about 250 knots indicated air speed," Fullerton added. "We have that restriction even without the orbiter on top." Although the aircraft's maximum takeoff weight remained at the 710,000-pound limit of early model 747s, some 235,000 pounds of this was made up by the orbiter. The spacecraft helped to provide some lift to the unwieldy looking combination thanks to its angle of attack on the fuselage roof.

One of the first Pan Am 747s, N744PA *Clipper Star of the Union*, was also converted to enjoy an unusual second life. It first flew in March 1970, but 22 years later it began a new life as a flying test bed for GE, which needed a bigger aircraft to test the huge GE90 turbofan for the 777. Appropriately registered N747GE, the aircraft normally carried the test engine under the number two position on the left (port) wing. At full power, the 100,000-pound-thrust GE90 produced almost as much power as the

aircraft's three remaining P&W JT9Ds put together. The aircraft also tested the CFM56-7 engine for the Next Generation 737-600/700 and -800 family and, in 1998, N747GE briefly became a five-engined aircraft to test the growth version of the CF34-8C1 regional jet powerplant for the Canadair CRJ Series 700.

While GE invested in its own test bed for the 777 engine development effort, P&W and Rolls-Royce used the venerable and original Boeing 747 aircraft number one, which was brought out of retirement from the Seattle Museum of Flight for the task. The P&W PW4084 engine made its first flight in November 1993, mounted on the 747's number two engine position. The Rolls-Royce Trent 800 also took to the air for the first time on the old 747 in the spring of 1995.

A succession of movie roles has also maintained the 747's high profile and made it into one of the most recognizable shapes in the sky. One of its earliest appearances was as a desk model in the office of the airport manager, played by Burt Lancaster, in the movie *Airport*. Much bigger roles, literally, were to follow. In 1975, an American Airlines 747-123 starred (with Charlton Heston) in *Airport '75*. The aircraft was one of the original batch converted by Wichita into special freighters, and by the late 1990s was still in service with United Parcel Service. Another American 747, later flown by United, starred in *Airport '77*. More recent appearances have largely been in model form and include *Die Hard II* and *Independence Day*, in which Air Force One barely outruns an alien fireball that destroys Washington, D.C. A faithful mock-up of the interior of Air Force One was also used extensively in the Clint Eastwood movie *In the Line of Fire*. Another model and, in some shots, a genuine 747, was used in the 1996 Kurt Russell movie *Executive Decision*.

Some older 747s have also been used for more serious matters. A former Air France aircraft, F-

BPVE, donated to an aviation museum in Bruntingthorpe, England, was used by British and U.S. aerospace, structures, and explosives specialists in 1997 to see how design changes and reinforced cargo containers could possibly save aircraft from the catastrophic effects of in-flight explosions like the one that destroyed Pan Am Flight 103 over Scotland in 1988. Similar explosive tests were also conducted on a 747 hulk as part of the inquiry into the July 1996 crash of a TWA 747 off Long Island, New York. Some 747s, like those stored in Arizona, have also been used for anti-terrorism training, in which special forces get aboard the aircraft and flush out the hijackers.

One bizarre plan for the 747 was to develop the aircraft into a flying crude-oil tanker. This never actually came to fruition, but the proposal was hatched in the early 1970s as part of Boeing's ambitious Prudhoe Bay Tanker Project. The recession was biting hard, and the company was desperate for new openings for its big jet. When the environmental lobby began fighting plans for a trans-Alaskan oil pipeline from Prudhoe Bay to Anchorage, it optimistically sensed a new niche market. The proposed "crude oil airlift system" would have involved up to 40 specially converted 747s, flying almost eight trips per day on average. Boeing calculated that a fleet of 747s, modified to carry up to 70,610 gallons of oil in its fuselage and inner wing tanks, could transport the equivalent of 523,760 barrels per day, more than 190 million barrels per year.

To back up its scheme, Boeing even designed a concept for insulated pavement, which would have enabled the runways and taxiways to survive the freeze and thaw effects of the permafrost at Prudhoe Bay.

There is no doubt that, given the sheer versatility of the 747 design, the aircraft will continue to be given ever more unusual and diverse roles as time goes by.

CHAPTER NINE

From day one, Boeing planned to stretch the 747. Even before the baseline aircraft was firmed up in 1966, a stretch was already on the drawing board. Boeing was so sure that a larger version would be built that convenient production "break" points were designed into the first version for this very purpose. Yet, more than 30 years later, the 747 had the unusual distinction of being the only Boeing jetliner never to grow beyond its original length. Even the twin-engined 757 joined the stretch club after 14 years

when the -300 version was launched at the 1996 Farnborough Air Show.

So, with so many plans to stretch it, and so many alternative growth versions studied, why did the 747's length stay basically unchanged for all those years? In some of the early cases, the reasons were frequently technical or cost related. Engine power, for example, permanently lagged behind expectations. The most dominant factors, however, were the ever-changing airline market and the global economics that have shaped its changing fortunes.

Explosive growth in the passenger and freight markets in the Asia-Pacific region sparked renewed interest in aircraft bigger than the 747. A Canadian Airlines -400 passes the crowded tenements of Kowloon, on departure from Hong Kong's Kai Tak.

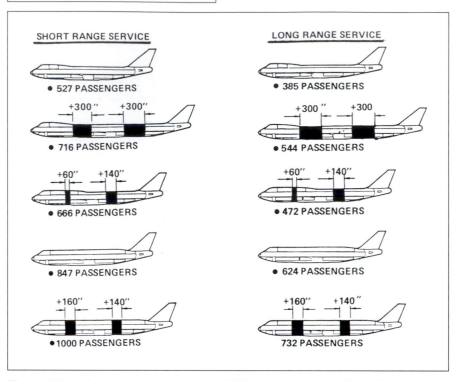

The possibilities for growing and stretching the 747 were endless, according to Boeing's active product development teams in the early 1970s. Slack demand, slow and costly engine growth, market uncertainty, and the oil crisis killed all these plans. *Boeing*

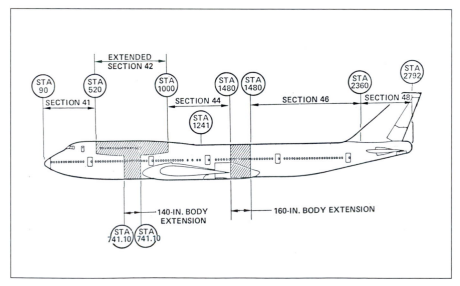

A 25-foot body extension and lengthened upper-deck study for the 747-200B came to nothing, but it planted seeds for the -300 and -400 development of later years. *Boeing*

Boeing's initial enthusiastic rush to grow the 747 was curbed by the enormous costs of developing the baseline -100 series, and the slow growth in engine power and reliability. The plan to increase the wingspan to almost 220 feet for a Phase B aircraft was soon shelved because of the spiraling program costs and technical risks (see Chapter 4). If Phase B had survived, the future course of 747 history could have been very different from 1972 onward. The bigger wing would have provided more space for fuel, establishing a platform for future fuselage growth when the demand for much-longer-range, high-capacity aircraft began to materialize. Even the capacity of the stronger wings of later versions, such as the -400F, restricted the range of planned stretches to such an extent that they were generally nonstarters.

In the early 1970s, however, the market focus was different. The priority was to develop high-capacity passenger and freight aircraft for major domestic and international trunk routes. The era of the super-long Asia-Pacific routes, which became the domain of the 747-400, was still 20 years in the future.

Boeing believed that even with the 747's basic wing, it could still serve much of the projected growth with a stretched or double-deck 747. It estimated that with only minor wing changes, either of these leviathans would still have had the "legs" for 3,000-nautical-mile routes, which would easily allow it to operate between New York and San Francisco or on busy vacation routes such as Los Angeles to Honolulu. The Japanese interest in the short-range 747 had also encouraged Boeing to explore a whole series of possible growth designs for airbus-type passenger routes.

Despite the demise of Phase B, some more significant wing changes were still being studied as early as 1972, when the company began looking for ways to kick start the seemingly stagnant cargo market into life. One option to increase payload, but not range, over that of the 747-200F was to extend the fuselage and add 53,000-pound-thrust engines that P&W had promised to develop. Payload was projected at about 275,000 pounds, versus the 200,000 pounds of the baseline model. However, Boeing realized sales would be heavily penalized by its limited range of 3,000 nautical miles. This meant that lucrative transatlantic routes such as New York to London and Paris were unattainable with winter head winds. Wing-root extensions were proposed as a solution, rather than the wing-tips extensions of Phase B. One study also mated the extended wing to a double-deck body. It looked great on paper until someone realized that it needed 65,000–75,000-pound-thrust engines, a power level unattainable at the time. The resulting aircraft would have a gross weight of more than 1 million pounds and a payload of 300,000 pounds, as well as the all-important transatlantic range. As before, none of these proposals could go anywhere without both the market interest and the available engine technology.

Boeing went back to the drawing board and, in April 1973, came up with new proposals that were more realistic over the long term. Four potential growth directions were sketched out, each of which would be adapted to either short- or long-range routes. The smallest of the growth variants entailed inserting a 60-inch plug into Section 42, ahead of the wing, and a 140-inch plug between Section 44 and 46, aft of the wing. The short-range version would have carried up to 666 passengers, while the long-range version could have taken about 470. This was one of the first design studies to examine a stretch of the upper deck, rather than a basic extension of the single-deck areas of the fuselage or an outright double-decker.

Another option was the insertion of two 300-inch plugs fore and aft of the wing root. This enormously long aircraft, more than 280 feet in length, offered seating in a short-range configuration for more than 700 and, on longer routes, seating for up to 544. Two double-deck designs were also

studied, the less ambitious of which was simply the baseline 747 with the upper deck extended aft to the tail—a concept that was to reappear many times. This offered potential capacity for more than 840 passengers on short-range routes but could also accommodate more than 620 on longer ranges. The largest of all, in terms of passenger capacity, was a stretched double-deck design with a forward plug of 160 inches and an aft extension of 140 inches between Sections 44 and 46. This monstrous aircraft offered seating for 732 on long-range routes and 1,000 on short routes.

By 1976, Boeing's product development team was more conservative. The painful impact of the 1973 oil crisis, together with more realistic estimates of future engine growth, had a sobering effect. The popularity of the 747-200B encouraged Boeing to study a 25-foot extension that would have taken overall length to about 256 feet. Interestingly, much of the study was focused on the upper deck, which was extended back over a much greater length than in previous nondouble-deck designs. Engineers homed in on the usual production break point forward of the wing, where a 140-inch plug was earmarked for insertion (at fuselage station 741.10). Instead of carrying the same plug into the upper deck, the entire hump aft of the join line with Section 41 (fuselage station 520) was stretched back to station 1000 over the wing. The hump was now faired into the fuselage almost back to station 1241, close to the wing's trailing edge. In common with earlier proposals, a 160-inch plug would also be inserted behind the wing root.

As with so many studies, the proposal died, but it had at least provided some blueprints for the first major structural extension, which soon emerged with the development of the 747-300 in 1980. The -300 was not the runaway success that Boeing had hoped for, partly because the higher capacity 747 did not offer any real range improvements and was not much of an advance over the 747-200B.

Even with winglets, wing-tip extensions, and trailing-edge aerodynamic improvements, the basic 747 airfoil had reached its limits with the -400. Boeing knew that further increases in span, either through tip or root plug insertions, would provide limited new opportunities, but real growth lay in an all-new wing design.

Worse still, the 747 suddenly appeared to be losing its technological edge to the new Airbus products, and even other Boeings. Major advances were introduced on the new Boeing twins, the 757 and 767, and airlines began to ask why none was appearing on the 747. These advances ranged from lighter carbon-composite materials and new airfoil shapes to improved systems and "glass cockpit" avionics.

Boeing itself recognized that the -300 was little more than a stopgap, and saw that more radical surgery was needed to bring the 747 back up to the state-of-the-art. Its product development team began studying yet another series of changes, some of them major. The advanced airfoil technology developed for the new twins, for example, gave rise to studies for completely rewinging the 747. Until then, most proposed wing changes had involved increasing the span either by tip extensions or root plugs. Advances in wing design meant that high cruise speed and efficiency were no longer a direct function of sweep angle. The higher-aspect-ratio wings of the new twins, although designed for lower cruise speeds than the 747, were far more efficient. This was mainly due to their aft-loaded cross-section, which meant lift was distributed more evenly across the upper surface of the wing, rather than peaking near the leading edge. Improved lift distribution delayed the onset of supersonic shock waves, which improved cruise efficiency.

Design studies reached a peak in 1984 when the first details of the new wing studies came to light. They revealed a huge span, increased from 195 feet to anywhere from 240 to 260 feet. Sweep angle at quarter chord was also reduced from more than 37 degrees to about 35 degrees. The big wing also provided the platform for a fuselage stretch, but again Boeing put off such a radical move. Its market research indicated that growth of such magnitude was not needed in 1984, but it did point to "potential introduction in the late 1990s."

The study included other advances and work continued to see how these could be rolled into the 747. First details of what was to become the 747-400 were revealed at the 1984 Farnborough Air Show (see Chapter 6). Still, the prospect of a stretched, rewinged 747 beckoned. In 1988 the product development group revealed a "potential growth study" called the 747-X. The "future block change" aircraft was outlined with a significant fuselage stretch of about 24 feet in two 12-foot plugs, a new high-aspect-ratio wing, increased gross weight to more than 1 million pounds, more efficient engines, advanced materials, and systems improvements. The familiar double-deck version again made a fleeting appearance in the Boeing brochures of the time.

The Market Stirs

Prompted by the startling pace of economic growth in Asia during the late 1980s, Boeing began low-level studies of future requirements for air-lines serving the region. These revealed the potential need for an all-new airliner capable of carrying between 600 and 800 passengers over ranges up to, and greater than, the 7,500 nautical miles of the 747-400. It was, therefore, no great surprise to Boeing when, in 1991, it was asked by United Airlines to study the development of an all-new 650-seater aimed specifically at the trans-Pacific market. British Airways later indicated interest in the study for its long-range U.K.-Asia Pacific network.

Boeing threw itself into the task and asked a select group from the major airlines to attend meetings in early 1992 to discuss its initial results. Grouped loosely under the titles of new large airplane (NLA)/N650 and 747-X, the studies looked at more than 100 alternative configurations, ranging from the original 747 stretch proposals to a giant flying wing. The length of the various study aircraft ranged from the 220-foot 747 class size all the way up to 280 feet. Wingspans similarly started at the 211-foot baseline established with the 747-400 up to 290 feet. Takeoff weights ranged from the 870,000 pounds of the -400 to 1.7 million pounds. The biggest design studies were almost twice as large as the 747-400, with up to 750 passengers in three classes. Seating arrangements included up to 12 abreast on the lower deck and 8 to 9 abreast on the upper deck.

Various issues drove the design considerations. Overall size was heavily influenced by the size and layout of the airports and the area available for maneuvering, loading, and docking at the gate. Internally, the designs were partly driven by the comfort level required in the economy sections. Maintenance was another consideration. With internal space in the double-decker fuselage at a premium, the Boeing group asked what the maintenance impact would be of putting systems such as air conditioning into new places such as the inboard wing space.

Infrastructure issues were the most pressing and included discussions on turnaround times, pavement loading,

United Airlines was involved from the start in the search for a -400 successor. One of its newer aircraft is at Everett before delivery.

taxiway width, ground fueling, and passenger embarkation. The airline group told Boeing that turnaround times were critical, and anything longer than the 747-400's time would be unacceptable to them. The challenge was huge, as a 600-passenger 747-X would have typically required the loading of 3,000 cubic feet of baggage, 75,000 gallons of fuel, and 1,800 meals for a trans-Pacific flight. All of this would have to be loaded and secure within 1 hour of the aircraft arriving at the gate.

To assess the runway and taxiway requirements, the study group also looked at 70 of the world's major air-ports and concluded that 17 runways would need strengthening with an additional 2 to 4 inches of asphalt. Most 747-X main-gear designs spread the weight across 24 main wheels mounted on four main posts, creating a pavement loading index rating in the low 70s, compared with between 60 and 70 for

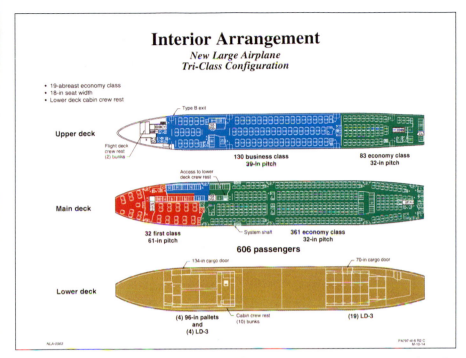

Interior Arrangement
New Large Airplane
Tri-Class Configuration

- 19-abreast economy class
- 18-in seat width
- Lower deck cabin crew rest

Upper deck

Type B exit

Flight deck crew rest (2) bunks

130 business class
39-in pitch

83 economy class
32-in pitch

Access to lower deck crew rest

Main deck

32 first class
61-in pitch

System shaft

361 economy class
32-in pitch

606 passengers

134-in cargo door

70-in cargo door

Lower deck

(4) 96-in pallets and (4) LD-3

Cabin crew rest
(10) bunks

(19) LD-3

NLA-0363

PA797-4I-6 R2 C
M-10-14

The vast interior of Boeing's NLA shows up to 19-abreast seating in economy class on the main deck, holding about the same number of passengers as a whole 747. The upper deck, configured in this arrangement, would carry about the same number of passengers as a 767. Boeing worked out that it might have taken a passenger at the rear of the upper deck almost 40 minutes to deplane if only main-deck exits were in use! The large, apparently empty spaces in the center of the lower deck were for fuel and undercarriage. *Boeing*

most "heavy" aircraft in 1992. Taxiway restrictions and inadequate separation between aircraft at adjacent gates were found to be more common problems at several airports. The group concluded that the 747-X would almost certainly need the folding-wing-tip design of the sort developed (but never selected by any customer) for the 777. The penalty for its use on the 777 was 3,500 pounds but less than 1 percent drag, whereas the impact on the much larger 747-X was expected to be much more. The sheer size of the aircraft also dictated the use of external TV cameras to allow the crew to see how close the wheels were to the edge of the runways and taxiways. This system was adopted for the 777-300.

Some novel solutions were also investigated for the loading dilemma. One suggestion was to load the aircraft as two flights, from a two-story gate via a double-deck air bridge. The lower gate would load the equivalent of a 747 while the upper would load about the same number as a typical 777. Another suggestion was an air bridge with an internal escalator up to the upper deck. Even the door sizes were re-examined, and wider doors and internal stairs were suggested. Quicker galley loading ideas included the use of specially modified LD3-sized freight containers.

Noise was also a huge issue. Using 777 technology, the 747-X could be as quiet as the 747-400. The challenge, however, was to make it even quieter. The future "Stage 3 minus" noise regulations would apply to all aircraft categories, regardless of size or speed, and would become a crucial part of Boeing's design considerations. Advanced turbofan engines were

already capable of high power and low noise, but the sheer size of the proposed aircraft meant that the airframe-generated self-noise was also expected to be a big problem.

Engine power was another major question. Thrust requirements were set by the climb, and not takeoff. For a 650-seat, 8,000-nautical-mile 747-X, takeoff thrust was calculated at about 80,000 pounds to 85,000 pounds per engine, or roughly the same as the 777 engines. However, the estimated climb thrust was 4 to 8 percent more than the power envisaged for the 777, and would have stretched into the 100,000-pounds-plus area for a planned 800-seater derivative. As history was to prove, the subsequent growth of the 777 meant that engines of this category were quickly developed, and even the larger 800-seat 747-X of 1992 would probably have had adequate thrust options by 2005 onwards.

By mid-1992, Boeing had boiled down the various proposals into three major options. Two shorter term configurations were based on stretch developments of the 747, while a third, longer term option was a brand-new NLA. The 747-400–based options offered seating for up to 480 passengers in the basic stretch, which increased length with two 12-foot plugs, fore and aft of the wing. The more elaborate stretch, with potential seating for 630 in a Japanese domestic configuration, involved a stretch of both upper and main decks and an increase in overall length of 23 feet.

Without any major wing changes, both 747 variants suffered from the now-familiar range penalty. The basic stretch, with an operating empty weight of about 438,000 pounds, would have at least 500 nautical miles less range than the 747-400, while the upper-deck stretch lost about 1,000 nautical miles and offered roughly the same maximum range capability as the -200B.

Although projected takeoff weights for both were little different from those of the -400, higher landing and operating empty weights required the use of the thicker-skinned wing then under development for the -400F.

Additional beefing up was also considered for the undercarriage, wing box, and auxiliary wing spar.

The all-new design was a blunt-nosed double-decker with four engines mounted on a high-aspect-ratio wing. It bore an outward resemblance to an aircraft called the MD-12, which McDonnell Douglas had unveiled in May 1992. The MD-12 was aimed primarily at taking the 747-400 and its immediate successors head-on with lower direct operating costs. It was to be offered in up to six different models, from a long-range, 8,000-nautical-mile 430-seater to a high-capacity 511-seater with 7,200-nautical-mile range. McDonnell Douglas hoped to launch the $5-billion project by late 1992 and begin deliveries in late 1997, but the entire effort folded when partnership talks with Taiwan Aerospace collapsed.

John Roundhill, Boeing's NLA chief project engineer, described the new design as "a short and fat" aircraft with a baseline circular cross-section. Variations on the theme included a triple-bubble cross-section, formed from three intersecting circular cross-sections, to create a spacious cabin. Boeing hoped that the circular cross-sections would help avoid the stress problems encountered with the slab-sided Section 41 of the 747. The aircraft had tri-class seating for 600, a range of 8,000 nautical miles, and at 235 feet, was just a few feet longer than the 747. It had a much larger span of 258 feet, however, requiring the use of folding wing tips to fit most airport gates. Its stretched companion, as proposed in 1992, was more than 300 feet long and had seating for more than 750 in three classes.

Most airlines favored further study of the NLA rather than the 747 options. With the airlines showing considerable interest in the MD-12, Boeing felt under mounting pressure to study something new. Further impetus came from Europe, where Airbus, which had traditionally confined itself to smaller-capacity aircraft, was showing signs of encroachment into 747 territory for the first time. In 1991 Airbus consulted

with 747 operators about requirements for a future 600-plus-seater. The resulting ultra-high-capacity aircraft (UHCA) family plan was revealed in 1992, consisting of a 600-seater created from two A340 fuselages joined together side-by-side, and a larger 800-seater with a vertical-ovoid cross-section. Several other variations were also studied around these basic themes.

NLA and VLCT

By the end of 1992, Boeing found itself confronted with the enormous risks, costs, and uncertainty of plowing ahead with its own NLA plans. Then, late in the year, it hit upon an audacious plan. Boeing believed the projected scale of the NLA program was too much for one company to take on alone. Teaming with McDonnell Douglas was out of the question, particularly since the MD-12 was apparently well defined and aimed squarely at the 747. This meant the only other global players able to tackle such a big civil project were the four major European aerospace companies: Aerospatiale, British Aerospace, Constucciones Aeronaicas C.A. of Spain (CASA), and Daimler Benz Aerospace (DASA).

These also happened to be the four major partners making up the Airbus consortium. Boeing asked, "Why not invite them to work together on feasibility studies of a very large commercial transport (VLCT)?" Airbus Industrie could not argue against the decision of its own partners, which were also individual companies in their own right, free to make independent business decisions. To the surprise of the airlines and the aerospace world in general, Boeing and the four companies issued statements on January 27, 1993, that they would be working together on a year-long VLCT study. Cynics interpreted the Boeing move as a clever gambit to drive a wedge into the Airbus team and confuse or at least delay the UHCA project. Airbus itself was deliberately excluded from the agreement, but Boeing insisted that its plan was honest and based on sound business reasoning.

The study was extended in 1994, and eventually even Airbus itself became

Turning away from all new designs, Boeing once again blew the dust off its 747 stretch studies. This time it intended to grow more than just the upper deck, which had formed the full extent of all its stretch developments to-date.

involved. Boeing meanwhile continued parallel studies of its own NLA and 747 derivatives, while Airbus remained focused on a more clearly defined UHCA, now called the A3XX. For the sake of discussion and study, the NLA and A3XX were used by their respective camps to form a theoretical common VLCT. The companies studied the possibility of forming a consortium to develop, produce, market, sell, and support a VLCT. It also studied the market requirements for a 7,000-nautical-mile to 10,000-nautical-mile range family of aircraft able to carry 550 to 800 passengers.

By late 1993, with the VLCT studies well under way, Boeing's 747-X, NLA project was coming to some conclusions. Five basic configurations were defined, four of them NLAs and one a rewinged, stretched 747. Two of the NLAs were double-deckers, one 249.8 feet long, and the other just 3 feet longer than the 747-400 at 234.7 feet. Both seated 620 in three classes and were aimed at a range of 7,850 nautical miles. The third NLA, a large single-decker, 244.4 feet in overall length, also seated about 620 in three classes. In many ways, it resembled a huge 777, with a circular fuselage and higher-aspect-ratio vertical tail. The fourth design was intriguingly similar to the 747, with a humped forward double-deck section and a single-deck aft section. Measuring 242.8 feet in length, it otherwise had nothing in common with the 747 and was described as the "747-look New Airplane." It also offered slightly more seating, with room for up to 630 in a tri-class arrangement.

The need for more range, particularly over the Pacific on routes to and from Asia, was a consistent theme among the airline advisory group. Most forecasts predicted that the economies of the Asia-Pacific region would have the most rapid growth up to 2015, so air traffic would boom as a result. Most analysts estimated that Asia's share of world traffic would grow five-fold over the first 15 years of the twenty-first century, and that by 2015, traffic on the north- and mid-Pacific routes would account for almost 25 percent and 22 percent respectively. One of the carriers looking to benefit from this includes -400 operator China Airlines, seen here departing Hong Kong.

The rewinged 747 struggled to reach the seating capacity of any of the NLA designs, and even when it was stretched to the length of 282.2 feet, it could still accommodate a maximum of about 560 in three classes. With the market seemingly focused on aircraft with more than 600 seats, things did not look good for the 747 derivative. Additionally, all the NLA designs had optional growth potential to seat more than 750. None of the NLAs exceeded the length of the rewinged 747, even when stretched to seat almost 200 more people than the 747 derivative.

Joint studies on the VLCT continued, with the Europeans led by Jurgen Thomas of DASA and the Americans led by John Hayhurst of Boeing. The groups met alternately in Europe and the United States and, by the use of cleverly erected Chinese walls, managed to discuss details without giving any serious business secrets away. Slowly, the results of the market analysis became apparent, and the news was not good. Based on their research, the group concluded that a potential market for up to 1,000 aircraft existed by 2020.

Two-and-a-half years after it had begun, the joint study was frozen at a meeting on Long Island, New York, on July 7, 1995. The next phase of the VLCT study would have looked at a common configuration and setting up a joint-venture company. Based on the small market, Boeing believed the cost of pursuing

the VLCT was simply not justified. The company estimated the nonrecurring cost would have been between $12 billion and $15 billion.

Re-enter the 747

John Hayhurst, the man at the center of Boeing's NLA, 747-X, and VLCT studies, recalled the change that came with the end of the joint studies: "The 747 gave us a different perspective on what the airlines really wanted. That caused us to re-address the issue. We worked out that there certainly was not a sufficient market for an all-new airplane with more than 600 seats. That alone caused us to look at

something smaller and a lot less costly in 1995."

Based on its 1993 conclusions, Boeing already knew the answer. All the expensive NLAs had seated more than 600. The only aircraft that was better suited to the smaller-sized market was the much less expensive rewinged 747. Suddenly the old jumbo was back in favor. The original airline working group that had helped Boeing with the outline design of the NLA moved onto the 747-X studies, and their ranks swelled to 19 airlines. "Eventually it became obvious that from cost and market considerations the 747-X was the winner. It was something we could afford to build and the airlines could afford to buy," said Duane Jackson, chief engineer of product development and operational infrastructure for what was rapidly to become the 747-500X/600X program.

The airlines then began to fall into line behind the 747 again. Virtually every operator interested in the NLA, UHCA, or VLCT was already flying 747s. The prospect of family commonality with a new generation of 747 suddenly became more appealing against the gloomy background of spiraling costs and lower yields. Another factor that played in favor of the 747 was time. Airlines such as BA and SIA declared

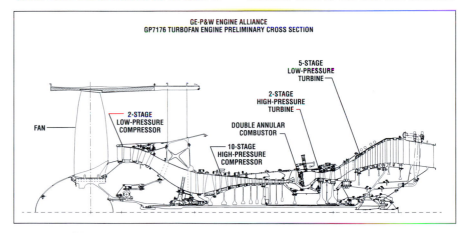

The unique GE-P&W engine alliance outlined the GP7176 turbofan for the 747-500X/600X family. GE was to take responsibility for the high-pressure side of the engine, and P&W for most of the low-pressure work, including the 110-inch-diameter fan. The GE-developed double annular combustor was a key part of the design's compliance with the latest environmental ruling. *GE/P&W*

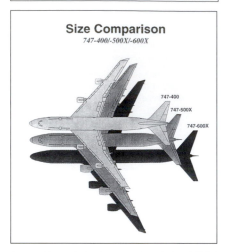

Size Comparison
747-400/-500X/-600X

747-400
747-500X
747-600X

Some idea of the huge scale of the -500X and -600X can be grasped by this simple projection. Note the subtle reduction in wing sweep angle, the large increase in wing span, and the corresponding increase in span of the horizontal stabilizer. *Boeing*

their willingness in 1995 to buy a superjumbo the instant it was available. British Airways aimed to raise the number of passengers passing through London's slot-constrained Heathrow Airport by more than 50 percent, to about 36 million, by 2010. It intended to do this while increasing the fleet by only 12 aircraft, making the requirement for a superjumbo seemingly absolute. On the other hand, SIA was already the world's largest operator of 747-400s by 1994 and could simply fill every seat it could get its hands on.

Whatever large-capacity aircraft was first to market would therefore have the advantage, even if it was a derivative of a 30-year-old design. By going down the 747 derivative path, Boeing could realistically aim at getting the first aircraft built, tested, certificated, and delivered by December 2000, at least three years ahead of the competition.

By the time of the VLCT's demise, Boeing marketers had broken down the airline requirements into two sectors. Some airlines wanted an aircraft with roughly the same capacity as the 747-400, but with more than 1,000

nautical miles of extra range. Others wanted a 747 with much more capacity than the -400, but with about the same range. In all, Boeing estimated the combined market was about 500 aircraft by 2010.

As with the VLCT market analysis, the big unknown was the effect of a growing dynamic in the long-distance arena—the extended-range twin operations (ETOPS) wide-body twin. The runaway success of the 767-200/300ER and A310 and A300-600R on long overwater flights had completely transformed the transatlantic route structure. The 747, along with all the older narrow-body jets and even the older DC-10 and L-1011 trijets, had been unseated from the world's busiest long-haul route by these new twins. In less than a decade, the 767 in particular had opened up a vast number of point-to-point routes that did away with the need for travelers to transfer at major hubs like London or New York. The new phenomenon was termed "fragmentation." Airlines were discovering that it was more economical, and profitable, to fly a medium-sized twin on direct point-to-point services than to operate a sometimes half-empty 747 on what had previously been an overbooked trunk route. Fragmentation was to have an even more dramatic effect on the long-term future of the 747.

With the specter of cost looming large, Boeing focused on keeping the new 747-X derivatives as "cheap and cheerful" as possible. The 747-500X and -600X were therefore designed to use the same basic avionics and flight-deck architecture as the -400 to ensure crew-training commonality. The systems were also largely identical, as was the flight control methodology. Physically, the major change would be the design and structure of the wing, which was heavily based on a version of the advanced 777 aft-loaded wing, but scaled up 40 percent. Other structural changes included new plugs in the fuselage, larger undercarriage, and bigger tail surfaces. At this early stage, even the powerplants were practically off-the-shelf 777 engines. In the case of

Rolls-Royce, the Trent 800 looked perfectly suited to the role.

Then things began to change. By March 1996, the airline advisory group began putting pressure on Boeing for more specific data on the aircraft's operating economics. Boeing had targeted a 10 percent reduction in seat-mile costs over the -400 as a baseline, but the airlines wanted to know if Boeing could really get there. Meanwhile, Airbus was busy touting the A3XX, adding to the pressure. As if that was not enough, the threat of even more fragmentation loomed large. Boeing's own 777 proposals, a McDonnell Douglas stretched trijet called the MD-XX, and various Airbus plans for the A340 family all added weight to the fragmentation factor.

Boeing reacted by making some major changes to the proposed configuration of both versions. The maximum takeoff weight of the larger -600X stretch was raised to 1.13 million pounds. The weight increase provided for extra fuel needed to extend the aircraft's maximum range 400 to 500 nautical miles. Some airlines, such as Cathay Pacific, had argued that the -600's original 7,200-nautical-mile range provided no advantage over the existing -400, which was payload-limited as a result of nonstop flights between Hong Kong and Los Angeles. At this stage, the -600X was designed to carry 520 passengers in a typical tri-class layout, compared to 387 in a similarly configured -400. Some airport consultants had also complained that the -600X's proposed 279-foot length would cause problems, but these arguments were over-ruled because any reduction in size would have pushed up seat-mile costs.

The larger capacity of the -600X made it the favorite to be launched into production, with a go-ahead tentatively set for mid-1996. The slightly smaller 747-500X, which was originally defined with a length of about 260 feet, was designed to carry almost 490 passengers across ranges up to 8,150 nautical miles. The -500X was earmarked for launch 6 to 12 months

With high hopes of a launch at Farnborough '96, Boeing produced an artist's rendering of the -400 and its two stretched stablemates. No one at the show could have guessed that the whole plan would be scrubbed less than four months later. *Boeing*

later, with entry into service in late 2001, or a year after the -600X.

The fluctuating weight and performance of the new derivatives created a moving target for the engine makers. All three had identified the most suitable engines for the task, which called for a takeoff-thrust target range of 77,000 to 80,000 pounds. By early 1996, however, it became clear that Rolls-Royce had taken the lead. The Trent 800, though slightly too powerful for the new 747, was the only one of the 777 engines small enough to fit easily beneath the derivative's wing. In addition, by using a more powerful derated engine, Rolls felt confident that it would easily meet the stringent noise requirements. The more powerful engine would enable the 747 to climb steeply and more quickly.

Then, on May 8, 1996, the two U.S. engine giants, GE and P&W, dropped a bombshell by announcing an agreement to jointly develop a new engine for the 747-500X/600X. Boeing had encouraged the two to get

together, and following initial conversations on neutral territory at the Singapore Air Show in February 1996, presidents Gene Murphy of GE and Karl Krapek of P&W negotiated a joint venture. Both companies had spent huge amounts of money on developing and certificating new engines for the 777 and were only too happy to share the burden of yet another new powerplant program.

Rolls-Royce reacted by tailoring a new version of the Trent engine, the T900, for the 747-X. On July 15, 1996, it signed a memorandum of understanding with Boeing covering the use of the engine on the new aircraft. The Trent 900, which was also signed up for the A3XX, had the 110-inch-diameter fan of the 777 engine, as well as common intermediate- and high-pressure compressors. It had a new five-stage low-pressure turbine and new "reduced loading" intermediate- and high-pressure turbines.

Boeing moved into the summer confident that it would be able to announce a formal launch at the Farn-

borough Air Show that September. While sales teams practically camped out at the head offices of the world's major airlines, Boeing also began scouring the world for a huge new team of structural and mechanical engineers; designers; computer-aided-design engineers; and stress, weights, loads, propulsion, and aerodynamics specialists. Boeing particularly targeted the Netherlands for its new workforce, as the famous Fokker company had just gone bankrupt. Advertisements ran throughout Europe. One Isle of Man recruiting ad was typical: "Aircraft: Next Generation Jumbo Jet. An Offer Of A Lifetime Is Awaiting You In Seattle, WA USA!"

The summer also saw more dramatic changes to the entire 747-X concept, as the airlines began demanding more advanced 777-based technology, such as fly-by-wire flight control. Despite warnings by Boeing that implementing the high-tech wish list could increase cost and delay entry-into-service, the airlines persisted. Gordon McKinzie, the resident United Airlines representative on the advisory board, said, "Boeing was really surprised when most of us told them we'd rather wait another year or two than have a 'new' airliner with 15-year-old technology in it at entry-into-service. Most want to assess how successful, or not, many of these technologies have been on the 777."

Acceding to the airlines' wishes, Boeing decided to make wide-scale use of 777 systems and technology, abruptly destroying any chances of retaining high levels of commonality and inevitably increasing the development costs. The decision was not universally popular, and some airlines, such as Lufthansa, complained that Boeing was drifting away from its original commitments. However, the response from most airlines was good, particularly since many of them were also ordering the 777. Having already adopted the 777's wing design, six-wheel wing main undercarriage, and some systems, the company then took the whole process even further to

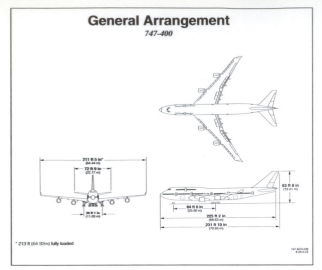

General Arrangement
747-400

211 ft 5 in*
(64.44 m)

72 ft 9 in
(22.17 m)

63 ft 8 in
(19.41 m)

36 ft 1 in
(11.00 m)

84 ft 0 in
(25.60 m)

225 ft 2 in
(68.63 m)

231 ft 10 in
(70.66 m)

* 213 ft (64.92m) fully loaded

747-6CO-039
8-26-6-LB

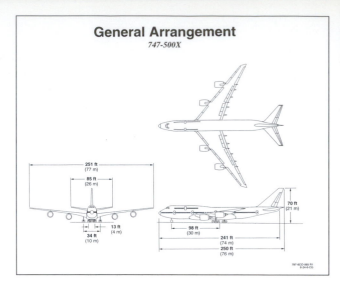

General Arrangement
747-500X

251 ft
(77 m)

85 ft
(26 m)

70 ft
(21 m)

13 ft
(4 m)

34 ft
(10 m)

98 ft
(30 m)

241 ft
(74 m)

250 ft
(76 m)

767-6CO-065 R1
8-24-6-CG

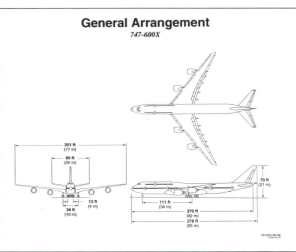

General Arrangement
747-600X

251 ft
(77 m)

85 ft
(26 m)

70 ft
(21 m)

13 ft
(4 m)

34 ft
(10 m)

111 ft
(34 m)

270 ft
(82 m)

278 ft
(85 m)

767-6CO-064 R2
8-24-6-???

include fly-by-wire, avionics, flight-deck displays, and interior architecture.

Boeing reassessed the position and felt the whole-hearted adoption of 777 technology might now actually keep the time scale on track. "The change to 777-based systems probably helped because it is the state-of-the-art and the team is mostly still here, so to take that architecture and put it in the 747 is probably an easier task than updating the 747-400," said Hayhurst in late 1996. "We made a lot of changes in systems to take advantage of 777 developments," added Jackson. "We combined that with a system architecture for four engines, and the cross-section of the 747. We've captured what is appropriate from both families."

By August more changes were made after input from the airline working group. The range of the -600X was increased and the size of the -500X was decreased. The -600X was to have a range of 7,750 nautical miles with 548 passengers in three classes, an increase of 250 nautical miles over the initial proposal. Maximum landing weight went up to 1,186,000 pounds, with maximum landing and zero fuel weights of 845,000 pounds and 790,000 pounds, respectively. The -500X shrunk by 6 feet to 249 feet, which helped increase range from 8,150 nautical miles to 8,700 nautical miles. Passenger capacity was reduced, as a result, from 487 to 462. The wing remained unchanged for both versions, with a span of 251 feet and no winglets. The huge horizontal stabilizer also remained the same, with a span of 84 feet, just 9 feet short of the wingspan of the 737-200. Overall height stayed the same, at 70 feet, as did the double-hinged, split rudder.

New changes were also announced for the landing gear. The decision to use the 777-style six-wheel bogies on the wing-mounted legs was confirmed. All four main legs were to be steerable, rather than just the inner two, as on the 747. The nose gear was to have four parallel wheels similar to the C-5's nose gear, for a grand total of 24 wheels. The approach speed was also reduced by seven knots to prevent an increase in the landing roll at maximum landing weight, compared with the -400. Other changes included the adoption of a triplex rather than quadruplex hydraulic system. Left and right systems were to be driven by the inboard engines. A center system was driven by bleed air and was designed to power the undercarriage, brakes, and flaps. A ram-air turbine was also designed for emergency backup.

As the runup to Farnborough approached, the rumors flew and tension mounted. In early September, Boeing received formal approval from its board to offer the derivatives for sale, and expectations mounted that the project would be launched at the show. Everyone was disappointed. Although it was revealed that Thai Airways International and Malaysian Airlines had signed purchase agreements for about 15 aircraft, this did not constitute a launch order. Boeing had wanted the likes of BA, Lufthansa, United, or SIA to join the eager pair of Asian carriers. None of them was prepared to sign up at Farnborough.

The only real surprise was Boeing's announcement of study plans for an even larger version, the 747-700X, which combined the new wings, engines, and systems of the -600X with an all-new 747 look-alike body. The aircraft would have been a totally new model, capable of carrying 650 passengers and, as such, was effectively a reborn NLA. The time scale was deliberately vague, and many believed the -700X was simply revealed to encourage airline faith in Boeing's commitment to a much higher capacity, new aircraft for the long-term future.

Sleeping Giant?

Wind-tunnel tests carried on into the fall as a large workforce of more than 1,000 gathered to define the giant derivatives. But while development work proceeded quickly, and results looked good, the sales teams returned to Seattle empty handed. Airlines were suddenly getting lukewarm over the 747-X, but why?

Airbus was partially to blame. Urged on by its internal partners and airlines alike, it had decided to accelerate its A3XX programs by about a year. The all-new Airbus design offered attractive operating economics on paper, which airlines could not afford to ignore. The European program diverted considerable interest away from Boeing.

Another factor was price. The airlines faced sticker shock when it was revealed that the initial price for the new 747s was going to be in the region of $200 million per aircraft. Then there was the question of filling up the giant aircraft. The fragmentation phenomenon was again at the top of the agenda. The airlines wondered whether it was right to buy 460- to 550-seat monsters for long routes that might never be properly utilized. Might the airlines be better served by some of the new-technology 300- to 350-passenger twins?

After the disappointment of Farnborough, Boeing was expected to slip the launch date to December. Instead of launching, however, Boeing President Phil Condit said at the rollout of the Next Generation 737 on December 8, 1996, that the chances of a firm go-ahead on the 747-X had been reduced to " about fifty-fifty." Industry observers were perplexed. Was Boeing playing an elaborate

bluffing game with the airlines and even Airbus? Surely it could not give up its total dominance of the immensely profitable high-capacity end of the market and leave Airbus to be heir apparent.

Boeing Commercial Airplane Group reviewed the situation in mid-January 1997 and decided to halt the 747-X program. The shocking news was made public on January 20, along with the announcement that it intended to focus on developments of the proposed 767-400ERX and 777-200X/300X long-range, high-capacity twins. "We just could not make a business case for it," said Mike Bair, vice president of product strategy and marketing. "The small size of the market meant the amount of money we'd have had to spend, with or without fragmentation, just did not make sense."

Development costs, which had originally been estimated at about $1 billion for the basic rewinged stretch derivative, had gradually climbed to an estimated $7 billion because of the jump to 777 systems and the all-new engines. The large design group was working flat out by the end of 1996 and Boeing was already reputedly spending a staggering $1 million a day. The only gem of consolation was that the aircraft itself was not the issue. "The airplane we ended up with was a good one. The airlines were pretty wellsatisfied with the product we'd defined," said Bair, who added, "We were there," with the targeted 10 percent reduction in direct operating costs versus the -400.

The decision to drop the -500X/600X was not made in isolation. Boeing was staggering under the weight of massive new commitments in a wide range of areas. In 1996, it had completed the takeover of Rockwell and had agreed to a $13.3 billion acquisition of McDonnell Douglas. Its defense sector was working hard on the F-22 fighter, had won the ABL competition (see Chapter 8), and had been down-selected for the first phase of the Joint Strike Fighter program. Work was in hand, with a variety of big new space programs such as the International Space Station and Sea Launch. In addition, its commercial

business had skyrocketed with more than 700 orders and major development projects under way. The stretch 757-300 had been launched, and work was well under way with the 777-300 as well as the best-selling Next Generation 737.

Against this background, the termination of the new 747 suddenly looked like the right decision, particularly since airline interest had become indifferent, to say the least. The shelving of the 747-X did not mean the end of the 747. Boeing said that it will continue to study "airplanes capable of carrying more passengers than today's 747." Woodard added, "This remains one of the priorities of our production development efforts. When the market develops for such an airplane, we will be ready."

Future upgrades of the -400 were therefore made more likely by the cancellation of the 747-X, and the case for an all-new NLA was also boosted in the long term. Sure enough, within two months of the 747-X cancellation, Boeing once again turned its attention to added growth weight and "simple stretch" derivatives. The initial growth version was dubbed the 747-400IGW (increased growth weight), and was expected to provide the basis for a slightly stretched version capable of accommodating 60 to 80 more passengers.

With a takeoff weight of up to 940,000 pounds, the leviathan was expected to have a range of over 8,700 miles. The stretch, on the other hand, suffered the usual range penalty of many growth models. Boeing hoped, however, that the possible availability of new 65,000 pound thrust engines could give the stretch the same range as the -400.

By mid-1997, the future direction of 747 development hinged on the continuing growth of the 777 and the expected launch of the Airbus A3XX. In the meantime, the initial decision to scrap, or at least delay, the more ambitious -500X/-600X, meant that production of the original 747 family was set to continue well into the first part of the twenty-first century. The 747s of the past, present, and future are making a record in the annals of commercial aviation that is unlikely to be beat.

Appendix I
Orders, Deliveries, and Numbers in Service

Year	Orders	Deliveries	In Service (or stored)
1966	85	0	0
1967	43	0	0
1968	22	0	0
1969	30	4*	4
1970	18	92	96
1971	7	69	167
1972	18	30	197
1973	29	30	225
1974	29	22	246
1975	20	21	266
1976	14	27	293
1977	42	20	309
1978	74	32	340
1979	74	67	407
1980	51	73	479
1981	23	53	536
1982	14	25	559
1983	26	23	578
1984	22	16	593
1985	42	24	613
1986	81	35	648
1987	66	23	670
1988	49	24	692
1989	56	45	736
1990	130	70	804
1991	38	64	867
1992	23	61	921
1993	2	56	974
1994	16	40	996
1995	39	25	1,007
1996	75	26	1,025
1997	12	45**	1,043
Totals (as of Aug. 1997)	1,270	1,142**	1,043**

*Does not include RA001 development aircraft.
** Estimate.

Appendix II
Production by Model (as of July 1997)

747 Model	Orders	Deliveries
-100	167	167
-100B	9	9
-100B (SR)*	29	29
-200B	225	225
-200C	13	13
-200F	73	73
-200M	78	78
-300	56	56
-300SR	4	4
-300M	21	21
-400	433	309
-400D	19	19
-400F	35	16
-400M	59	52
E4A	3	3
E4B	1	1
SP	45	45

*Includes 747SR-100, SR-100B, and -100B (SR/SUD).

Appendix III
Dimensions

Model 747	-100/200/300	-400	SP
Wingspan	195ft, 8in	211ft, 5in (213ft fueled)	195ft, 8in
Length (overall)	231ft, 10in	231ft, 10in	184ft, 9in
Length (fuselage)	225ft, 2in	225ft, 2in	176ft, 9in
Height (overall)	63ft, 5in	63ft, 8in	65ft, 5in
Tailplane Span	72ft, 9in	72ft, 9in	82ft, 9in
Wheeltrack	36ft, 1in	36ft, 1in	36ft, 1in
Wheelbase	84ft	84ft	67ft, 4in

Appendix IV
Performance

maximum takeoff weight (MTOW)
maximum landing weight (MLW)
operating empty weight (OEW)

Model 747

	-100	-100B	-100B SR (CF6)	-100B SR (JT9
Passengers	385	452	550 (SUD)	550 (SU
Range (nm)	4,700	5,300	1,650	1,9
MTOW (lb.)	710,000	750,000	571,000	600,0
MLW (lb.)	564,000	585,000	564,000	564,0
OEW (lb.)	358,000	378,910	362,750	359-
Payload (lb.)	168,500	166,090	112,240	125,8
Usable fuel (U.S. gal)	47,210	48,070	48,445	48,4

Model 747

	-200B	-200B Combi	-200C Convertible	-20
Freighter Passengers	452	257 (with 7 pallets)	366–452	
MTOW (lb.)	775,000–833,000	775,000–833,000	775,000–833,000	775,000–833,0
MLW (lb.)	564,000–630,000	585,000–630,000	630,000	630,0
OEW (lb.)	381,150–388,010	376,120–387,080	361,680–393,890	342,180–351,9
Payload (lb.)	145,350–150,330	153,400–158,880	196,110–228,820	238,070–247,8
Usable fuel (U.S. gal)	52,410	52,035–52,410	52,410	52,4
Range (nm)	6,350–6,900	equivalent	equivalent	equival

Model 747

	-300	-300C Combi	-SP
Passengers	400–560	289 (with 7 pallets)	331
Range (nm)	6,100–6,700	equivalent	5,000–5,950
MTOW (lb.)	775,000–833,000	775,000–833,000	630,000–700,000
MLW (lb.)	564,000–574,000	605,000–630,000	450,000
OEW (lb.)	387,750–393,180	385,430–402,700	325,660–336,870
Payload (lb.)	142,260–151,820	169,000–179,570	73,130–84,370
Usable fuel (U.S. gal)	48,070–52,410	52,035–52,410	48,780–50,360

Model 747

	-400	-400C Combi	-400D Domestic	-400F Freight
Passengers	416	266 (with 7 pallets)	568	
Range (nm)	6,000 to 7,230	equivalent	2,500–3,000	6,000–7,2
MTOW (lb.)	800,000–870,000	800,000–870,000	600,000–610,000	800,000–870,0
MLW (lb.)	574,000–630,000	605,000–630,000	574,000	652,000 – 666,0
OEW (lb.)	402,400–407,107	403,400–407,479	400,630	363,9
Payload (lb.)	138,303–138,858	137,521–161,600	134,370	4,200-nm ran 249,122 (w
Usable fuel (U.S. gal)	53,765–57,065	53,985–57,985	53,765	53,765 – 57,0

Appendix V
Major Airframe Write-offs

Date	Model	Identity	Operator	Location	Circumstance
7 Sept. 1970	-100	N752PA	Pan Am	Cairo, Egypt	terrorism
24 July 1973	-200B	JA8109	JAL	Benina International, Benghazi	terrorism (four-day hijack)
20 Nov. 1974	-100	D-ABYB	Lufthansa	Embakasi Airport	crashed on takeoff
12 June 1975	-100	N28888	Air France	Santa Cruz	Fire, after aborted takeoff
9 May 1976	-100F	5-283	Iranian AF	near Madrid, Spain	in-flight explosion (believed hit by lightning)
27 March 1976	-100	N736PA	Pan Am	Los Rodeos, Tenerife	runway collision
27 March 1976	-200B	PH-BUF	KLM	Los Rodeos, Tenerife	runway collision
1 Jan. 1978	-200B	VT-EBD	Air India	Arabian Sea	crew disorientation
18 Nov. 1980	-200B	HL7445	Korean Air	Seoul, Korea	crashed on approach
31 Aug. 1983	-200B	HL7442	Korean Air	Sea of Japan	shot down
27 Nov. 1983	-200B Combi	HK-2910X	Avianca	near Madrid, Spain	crashed on approach
16 March 1985	-300	F-GDUA	UTA	Paris, France	caught fire
23 June 1985	-200B	VT-EFO	Air India	North Atlantic	terrorism
12 Aug. 1985	SR-100	JA8119	JAL	Mt. Ogura, near Tokyo, Japan	rear pressure bulkhead failure
2 Dec. 1985	-200B Combi	F-GCBC	Air France	Galeao International, Rio de Janeiro, Brazil	Ran off runway
27 Nov. 1987	-200B Combi	ZS-SPE	South African Airways	Indian Ocean	cargo fire
21 Dec. 1988	-100 CRAF	N739PA	Pan Am	Lockerbie, Scotland	terrorism
19 Feb. 1989	-200F (SCD)	N807FT	Flying Tigers	Subang International Airport, Kuala Lumpur, Malaysia	hit high ground on approach in low visibility
2 Aug. 1990	-100	G-AWND	British Airways	Kuwait International Airport	war
29 Dec. 1991	-200F (SCD)	B-198	China Airlines	near Wanli, Taiwan	engine detached
4 Oct. 1992	-200F (SCD)	4X-AXG	El Al	Bijlmermeer, near Amsterdam, Netherlands	two engines detached
4 Nov. 1993	-400	B-165	China Airlines	Hong Kong Kai Tak	over-ran runway
20 Dec. 1995	-100	N605FF	Tower Air	JFK International, New York	aborted takeoff
17 July 1996	-100	N93119	TWA	off Long Island, New York	center fuel tank exploded; cause unknown
12 Nov. 1996	-100B	HZ-AIH	Saudi Arabian Airlines	near New Delhi, India	midair collision with IL-76
6 Aug. 1997	-300	HL7468	Korean Air	Guam, Micronesia	crashed into hill on approach